To Melind...
Brindan...
Jeannette Connell

D1483913

SPIRITUAL
CLEANSING
OF THE BLOODLINE

SPIRITUAL CLEANSING
OF THE BLOODLINE

Jeannette Connell

XULON PRESS

Xulon Press
2301 Lucien Way #415
Maitland, FL 32751
407.339.4217
www.xulonpress.com

© 2018 by Jeannette Connell

All rights reserved solely by the author. The author guarantees all contents are original and do not infringe upon the legal rights of any other person or work. No part of this book may be reproduced in any form without the permission of the author. The views expressed in this book are not necessarily those of the publisher.

Unless otherwise indicated, Scripture quotations taken from the Amplified Bible (AMP). Copyright © 1954, 1958, 1962, 1964, 1965, 1987 by The Lockman Foundation. Used by permission. All rights reserved.

Scripture quotations taken from the New American Standard Bible (NASB). Copyright © 1960, 1962, 1963, 1968, 1971, 1972, 1973, 1975, 1977, 1995 by The Lockman Foundation. Used by permission. All rights reserved.

Scripture quotations taken from the New King James Version (NKJV). Copyright © 1982 by Thomas Nelson, Inc. Used by permission. All rights reserved.

Greek and Hebrew references come from Strong's Exhaustive Concordance of the Bible 2001 by Zondervan.

Definitions come from the Dictionary.com app.

The common roots of diseases were taken from *A More Excellent Way* by Henry W. Wright. Copyright 2005, Pleasant Valley Church, Inc. The roots of bitterness were influenced by this book.

Some occult definitions, demon manifestation list, and the characteristics of demons are taken from *Healing through Deliverance* by Peter Horrobin. Copyright 2003, Chosen Books, a division of Baker House Company

The inward and outward manifestation of rejection, information was influenced by *REJECTION: Its Fruits and Its Roots* by William G. Null, M.D. Published by Impact Christian Books. The rejection roots diagram is taken from William Null's book.

The first section of the mass cleansing prayer was taken from the group deliverance prayer, appendix C from *The Handbook for Spiritual Warfare* by Dr. Ed Murphy. Copyright 2003. Published by Thomas Nelson.

Printed in the United States of America.

ISBN-13: 9781545634639

TABLE OF CONTENTS

INTRODUCTION

D URING THE WRITING OF MY FIRST BOOK, *Spiritual Cleansing: Getting to the Root,* the Lord gave me a dream that is still relevant to *Spiritual Cleansing of the Bloodline.* So, I will share it again. The dream was very simple, and it will explain the importance of dealing with root issues.

In the simple dream of revelation below, the Lord was showing me that what is seen on the surface is being fed by something much stronger and bigger within us. In *Spiritual Cleansing of the Bloodline*, I will deal with the root cause of our struggles, which most often comes through the generational iniquities in our DNA.

I dreamed I was walking through the grass and I saw spiders of all sizes hiding in the grass. I took off my shoes and began to kill them one by one. I continued for some time. Finally, out of nowhere, a giant spider appeared in front of me on the grass. I heard the voice of the Lord say, *"It is generational, and he's the male that breeds all the others."* I knew in that moment, if I could kill that one, the others would die, and the madness would stop! I knew the Lord was showing me the importance of getting to the root with Spiritual Cleansing, not just surface healing. When roots are pulled out, the fruit will cease. Then true lasting victory will come. Often, as believers, we deal with things on the surface. It is as if we are picking fruit off a tree, only to see victory short-lived. This is because over a period of time, the issues surface again, causing believers to become discouraged and feel defeated in these areas.

Through the spiritual mapping process, one can identify the real issues of bondage and target the roots of oppression, thus eliminating the fruit.

In Matthew 15:16–20 Jesus said, *"Are you still lacking in understanding also? Do you not understand that everything that goes into the mouth passes into the stomach, and is eliminated? But the things that proceed out of the mouth come from the heart, and those defile the man. For out of the heart come evil thoughts, murders, adulteries, fornications, thefts, false witness, slanders. These* are *the things which defile the man; but to eat with unwashed hands does not defile the man."* In my book on cleansing the bloodline, you will discover what really is working deeper within the heart of a man and how to stop it through the blood of our Lord and Savior, Jesus Christ.

The Spiritual Cleansing Handbook is available and designed to be used in conjunction with my books, *Spiritual Cleansing: Getting to the Root* and *Spiritual Cleansing of the Bloodline*. It will prove to be an added benefit as you use them together.

DEDICATION

I WANT TO DEDICATE THIS WRITING TO TWO special people in my life. They may not be with me in this realm, but they are alive and well in eternity. 2 Timothy 4:7 says, *"I have fought the good fight, I have finished the course, I have kept the faith."* They are still impacting my life, bringing strength and fueling passion in me to press further than before.

First, to my dad, James Adams, who transitioned to heaven in 2015.

Dad fought Alzheimer's disease and won as he was promoted to heaven. He was my first authority figure. He taught me about respect, hard work, and diligence by his example. He was a self-made man who excelled in craftsmanship and in every area of the carpentry trade. Dad always said to me, "Liz, you can do anything you set your mind to do!" He demonstrated this principle and he never allowed any of his children to use the words "I can't" when we found ourselves in difficult places. Dad had a deep burden for the lost. He had an evangelist calling and passionate love for street ministry. I still recall seeing his pockets full of tiny Bibles. He always carried these to give to strangers wherever he met them to share the message of the gospel of Jesus Christ. I am so thankful for the foundation he laid in my life of Jesus Christ and I know I will see him again someday.

To my sister, best friend, and fellow warrior, Judith Duff.

I dedicate this book to Judy who longed to see its completion. Judy was a part of the Spiritual Cleansing team and an Elder at Troy Freedom Outpost. Judy was taken to glory long before any of us wanted her to go. She passed with melanoma cancer in 2017. Judy wanted it written that she fought many things throughout life and overcame all! During our work together, Judy was healed of arthritis, migraines, a thyroid disease of thirty years called Hashimoto, and of a broken heart syndrome in which she had a heart attack with no former heart condition. This was a spiritual attack. The Lord delivered her and completely restored her heart to health, with no side effects. She would share the doctor's reports and testify of the power of God every place she went, always praying for the healing of others. Judy was an evangelist and a strong intercessor who travailed for many to be set free and healed. She had an anointing to heal and a passion for her Lord Jesus. Winning souls was her greatest joy. Today, though I miss her dearly, I continue to press on in the call of God, knowing she is alive and well with her Lord. This life is temporary, but eternity is forever. We may not always understand why things happen as they do, but God is and always will be Good and Faithful. I know I will see her again one day.

"The secret things belong to the Lord our God, but the things revealed belong to us and our sons forever, that we may observe all the words of this law." Deuteronomy 29:29

ACKNOWLEDGEMENTS

I GIVE ALL GLORY TO MY HEAVENLY FATHER for any accomplishments concerning the work of these clay hands. It was He who called me out of darkness into His marvelous light. I give all praise to the lover of my soul, my King and Lord Jesus Christ, both now and forever. I give honor to my dearest Holy Spirit, who is my power source, my comfort and shalom peace through all my labor in the kingdom. And I say, *"The Lord is my rock and my fortress and my deliverer; My God, my rock, in whom I take refuge, my shield and the horn of my salvation, my stronghold and my refuge; my savior, You save me from violence. I call upon the Lord, who is worthy to be praised, And I am saved from my enemies."* 2 Samuel 22:2–4

I want to say thank you to my best friend, soulmate, and greatest supporter in the work of the kingdom, my husband and the father of my greatest treasures, George Connell. He has been solid and unwavering in every way. He has been a source of encouragement and strength when I needed it to continue in obedience to the leading of the Lord. He has pushed me forward through the warfare and discouragement that can come in any ministry. He has never allowed me to quit or draw back, working together with me to advance the kingdom of God. I thank the Lord for the gift that he is to me. He may not always be out in front, but he is right there with me on every journey and battle that I face. Thank you, honey. I love you!

I thank God for a wonderful family of the greatest children a mother could ask for: Caleb, Zechariah, Jastine, Seth, Elijah, Isaiah, and Hannah. You inspire me to do better in life and to press past my personal limits. You are mine and your dad's greatest treasures and accomplishments. I say to you all *"You are a letter of Christ, cared for by us, written not with ink but with the Spirit of the living God, not on tablets of stone but on tablets of human hearts."* I love you and I am thankful God sent you as gifts to us. I thank you for standing strong through all the ups and downs that life has brought us. I'm very blessed and my life is full because of you!

I am thankful for my spiritual family of Troy Freedom Outpost, the Spiritual Cleansing team, and all my comrades of the kingdom. You have been a source of encouragement, support and intercession in every project, all travel and each planting of the Lord. Thank you all, *"For God is not unjust so as to forget your work and the love which you have shown toward His name, in having ministered and in still ministering to the saints." Hebrews 6:10*

ENDORSEMENTS

From the beginning to the last page this book is captivating. The details on scriptural teachings and testimonial situations as the relevance will open your eyes as you look at your own past and family history is amazing. Seeing the much-needed applications of spiritual and blood cleansing in the church is eye-opening. Her application of balance is very well visible and captivating. I highly recommend this book be given to everyone in leadership in churches around the world. Walking and living in holiness is required in seeing the awesomeness of God's presence, this requires purity. Therefore, blood cleansing is needed in your life and ministry. As the hymnal goes, "What can wash away my sins, nothing but the blood of Jesus, what can make me whole again, nothing but the blood of Jesus." Applying the Word, the blood, and the Spirit will cleanse your own bloodline from all curses. Read, process and apply the wisdom in this book written by Jeannette Connell. It will change your life! I highly endorse this book.

Mark D. White
Rapha International Ministries
Nashville, TN

Over the past five years, we started working with apostles Jeannette and George Connell from Troy, Missouri in the spiritual cleansing ministry. As leaders of the Ecclesia of the Navajo Dine' Nation, we had to go to the foundation with deliverance. We have seen tremendous breakthroughs since and have learned how to deal with generational curses in our DNA through the bloodline. We have learned to get to the root of issues like unforgiveness, witchcraft and other areas of disobedience. We have also gone to the high places, such as mountaintops where rituals were done in our nation, to pray and cleanse the land. We have seen curses broken over people's lives and our Nation. Ungodly religious covenants have been broken, and I have seen the results of obedience through the healing in the lives of those who came for cleansing. The healing power of the Blood of Christ has set our people free from many infirmities, drug addiction, peyote and alcoholism and even cancer. We have been in the Four Corners area, Utah, Colorado, Arizona, on Apache Reservation, praying over the Land, and on other native reservations and have seen great things happen. We have seen many bone miracles, arthritis healed with many short legs growing back to normal on the Navajo Nation. I would recommend that every church should have a Deliverance Ministry and have intercessors praying over communities and Nations. As a Native, I recommend that you get the Books on Spiritual Cleansing.

Apostle Pete J. Belon
Founder of Cornerstone Ministries
Navajo Dine' Nation
Representative of Heartland Apostolic Prayer Network of
Oklahoma on Dine' Nation in the Four Corners

I praise the Lord for Apostle Jeannette Connell, who is a powerful warrior for the kingdom of God. She demonstrates the power of heaven and is effectual for such a time as this. I am glad to be her brother in the kingdom of God, as we have experienced many of God's signs and wonders following her ministry. I praise God for the writing of this book. This book is in God's perfect timing. It's a book that all the five-fold ministries need in their library. God has given Apostle Jeannette a book that will cause the chains of the demonic to be destroyed in people's lives, generational curses will be destroyed as miracles and healings will come forth. Cleansing and deliverance will cause prosperity to manifest in people's lives. This is a great book that needs to be in every nation in every language. It gives you an in-depth teaching on how to get chains of darkness destroyed in people's lives.

Apostle Michael Simpson, Sr., Chicago, IL

The Ministry of Apostle Jeannette Connell and the Troy Freedom Outpost is indeed a welcome development, and long overdue answer to the cry of God's people, who have been subjected to the manipulations, bondages and captivity of the spiritual bandits that have held the flock of our Lord Jesus Christ in bondage for years. We have had the honor and privilege to have sat under the apostolic ministration of apostle Jeannette and her team at our last Meeting "EL Hakkabbod—The God of Glory," where the Lord moved mightily in the lives of the attendees and members of the Assembly. The Lord broke demonic yokes, strongholds of addiction, sexual bondages and the likes. The glory, anointing, presence and power of God descended in an unprecedented measure to conduct a Holy Ghost surgery of spiritual cleansing and deliverances, for as many that were opened to receive from the Lord. Long-time oppression, foundational bondages, curses and strange covenants were broken and there was so much liberty and freedom released into the lives of God's people, all to the glory of our Lord Jesus Christ. What a ray of hope for the Church of Christ. Now the genuine and the fake are gradually being separated and the gathering of the remnant has begun in preparation for the end-time harvest! *Spiritual Cleansing of the Bloodline* is a must for any child of God to enjoy an unhindered liberty in his or her fellowship, or their walk with God. The discovery of the mystery of *Spiritual Cleansing of the Bloodline* is one of the keys to unlocking the door to enjoying Spiritual success, liberty and freedom in this kingdom life here on earth, irrespective of your geographical, national, ethnic or racial background.

Paul Ayonote,
Assembly/Lead Pastor,
Christ Redeemers Assembly, GA

From the time I met with apostle Jeannette and her team in Kenya, my life took a different shift as well as my ministry approach because of the understanding I received when I came across the teachings of spiritual cleansing. From the teaching and books, my understanding was widened, and I began to build more interest towards spiritual cleansing. Many people that I am ministering to are now getting delivered through spiritual cleansing. I have been able to touch so many lives with this teaching, which has become a new move in Kenya. I am honored to be part of this great work the Lord has begun. Many people have invited me in their homes to do spiritual cleansing. I have come across families that I have had to minister to of incest, sexual bondages, mental illness, soul ties and many other issues. By the grace of God, we broke and released people from deep family rooted bloodline curses. Spiritual cleansing teaching has taught me to focus on the root problem of the families. This should be included in the foundational teaching of every believer.

In 2018, I will be starting a class to teach Spiritual Cleansing and I am prepared to use the book as my manual for the class. Several people that I have shared these teachings with have been transformed. May the Lord continue to bless apostle Jeannette and her team as we join our hands in teaching people about spiritual cleansing.

With much love from Kenya,
Rev Gabriel Gakio

I am thankful to the Lord Jesus for all that God is doing in these last days. He is pouring out His Spirit upon all flesh as He promises in His Word. We are thanking the Lord also for all that He has begun to do for the Navajo Nation, the Dine' people. We are seeing changes, a shifting in our government taking place. We have a president and vice president of the Navajo Nation as believers in the Lord Jesus, which is a result of prayer and intercession in our gatherings. We have been going up to the high places dismantling what the enemy had put in place through prayer and intercession, declarations and decrees. We are breaking curses over the land. These curses have devastated and plagued people for generations. We thank the Lord for apostle Jeannette Connell and the spiritual cleansing team from Troy Freedom Outpost church. They came at a strategic time to the Navajo Nation, to the Dine' people. They have brought spiritual cleansing, healing and deliverance teachings for the past five years. They have been going to different areas of the reservations praying for our people, teaching and educating our people on root issues of bondages that we have experienced for generations. Some of which are sicknesses, diseases, alcoholism, drugs, poverty, witchcraft and sorceries and different forms of abuse. For generations there has been no real change, even in our churches. We had only dealt on a surface level in the past concerning these curses. But now, thanks be to God for our sister and apostle and the Spiritual cleansing team, the root issues of generational curses are being dealt with through the cleansing prayers of deliverance sessions. Our people are experiencing real freedom. We have seen healing in arthritis and many bone miracles. I personally witnessed an elderly woman's leg, which was three inches shorter than the other, grow back out evenly! To God be the glory!

Pastor Herman Harrison
Victory Life Fellowship
Shiprock, New Mexico, Nation

I met apostle Jeannette for the first time in Mississippi. My niece from Tennessee encouraged me to come and sit under Jeannette's teaching. That was just the beginning of learning the much-needed freedom for me and others. I also sat under her mass cleansing that weekend. She started calling hurts from people in the church. She and one of the team ministered to me. The Lord healed me of a lot of church hurts that night and for that I am eternally grateful. Since then, we have had apostle Jeannette and her team come to Wisconsin and have seen a lot of wonderful things happen. Praise God! We have now begun our own spiritual cleansing ministry in Wisconsin and are excited about bringing restoration and wholeness to our region and beyond as the Lord calls.

Pastor Peggy Vesta
New Beginnings Christian Fellowship
Birchwood, WI

In this present season of increasing rebellious, idolatrous living and darkness that is even in the Church, God continues in his grace to release keys for those needing and those crying out for freedom. Many have no knowledge of and are blinded to the working of the evil one or the healing, deliverance, freedom and power available through the salvation and the finished work of Jesus Christ. I have read *Spiritual Cleansing of the Bloodline* and highly recommend this book for personal, family, church, societal, governmental and a nation's spiritual freedom. It is anointed of God and full of bondage destroying and freedom releasing revelation. Though I work in Spiritual Cleansing, reading this has taken me to another level. It gives understanding and empowers one to walk through the process of wholeness and into new areas of wholeness, if applied. I have experienced the power of Spiritual Cleansing on many levels, including in our church and personally. I have also witnessed it in the foundational work of the turning around of an idolatrous people and nation back to God. It works! It is a powerful administration of Holy Spirit. This book explains the depths of many areas of bondages and explains how to discover what curses are active but hidden in the bloodline. Revelation is released on how to get free of it and stay free and prosper in Christ.

This is a book releasing another administration of the Love of God demonstrated from the beginning, which is God, through a loving servant, to His people whom He loves.

This book on Spiritual Cleansing given by Holy Spirit to Jeannette Connell to write is one of two. The place God prepared in her heart to receive the ministry of Spiritual Cleansing was hewn out by her passionate love for God and his people and by much passionate petitioning God for her personal freedom and for the freedom of all souls. Her personal walk and personal and ministerial battles opened her spirit to receive continuing pure revelation from God for the ministry of Spiritual Cleansing. I speak this by hearing her testimony and watching her as she lives her life of ministry. Holy Spirit passion in this humble servant of the Lord was used bless the Lord by releasing a pure work of His hand that will set people free through His power and His Word. God has with great measure released life giving revelation and anointing in this work. This book is a door to obtaining the freedom prom-ised through the finished work of Jesus Christ. All Glory to God! Another tool in the hands of His people!

One of the greatest joys for me is to see His people healed and set free forever from that that has caused them physical mental and emotional disease, and God getting the Glory! As a pastor, spiritual counselor, deliverance minister and nurse, I highly and confidently recommend this book!

Respectfully submitted in Honor to God!
Bertha Weathers, Troy Freedom Outpost, MO

CHAPTER 1

SPIRITUAL CLEANSING AND MAPPING

S PIRITUAL CLEANSING IS A WORK OF inner healing and deliverance and physical healing. It involves a "cleaning out" of that which is unlike the nature of Jesus. It is a process that takes place in the soul and many times in the body through physical healing. Spiritual cleansing is an act of sanctification or consecration, being made holy. It brings inner healing to areas of our wounded soul that have been opened to pain and suffering throughout our lives. It is also expelling unwanted demonic oppression out of one's life. These demons have attached themselves to areas of one's soul that have been opened and wounded through sin. Many have legal rights through unrepented bloodline or personal sin to enter, and we will list and discuss these areas in this handbook.

Healing and deliverance is part of the finished work of Jesus Christ, and through this ministry we exercise the victory that Jesus already won for us through His death, burial, and resurrection. Jesus came to reconcile us back to the Father and to restore us to wholeness. In this cleansing process, spiritual mapping is a very effective tool to bring personal breakthrough.

Healing means to restore to health or soundness, cure, to set right, amend, to rid of sin, anxiety or the like; to become whole and sound. The Greek word for healing is *iaomai,* which means to be made whole, to be freed. Deliverance is the act or instance of delivering, or the condition of being delivered. The Greek word for saved or deliverance is *aphesis,* which means to release.

Salvation brings wholeness

In Romans 10: 8–10, it says, "But what does it say? The word is near you, in your mouth and in your heart—that is, the word of faith which we are preaching, that if you confess with your mouth Jesus as Lord, and believe in your heart that God raised Him from the dead, you will be saved; for with the heart a person believes, resulting in righteousness, and with the mouth he confesses, resulting in salvation." In verse 13, "Whosoever shall call upon the name of the Lord shall be saved" (KJV). The Greek word saved is *sozo*, which means to be in wholeness, healing, to be rescued, delivered and preserved in totality of being. The term believers use of salvation comes from this Greek word *sozo*. Jesus speaking in John 3 says, "Truly, truly, I say to you, unless one is born of water and the Spirit he cannot enter into the kingdom of God. That which is born of the flesh is flesh, and that which is born of the Spirit is spirit. Do not be amazed that I said to you, 'You must be born again.'" One must be born again by the Spirit of God to experience *sozo*. If you're reading this and you need to be sure of your salvation, the prayer of faith is simple. You can receive Jesus right now as Savior of your life and begin an amazing journey with him!

Prayer for salvation: "Dear heavenly Father, I come to you a sinner in need of the Savior Jesus Christ. I receive Your Son Jesus Christ now as my Savior. I confess, and I believe that Jesus is God's Son, that He died on a cross for me, and that He rose again. I repent of all my sin and I ask You to wash me with the blood of Jesus. I ask that You fill me now with Holy Spirit. I confess that Jesus is my Lord from now and through eternity, for evermore! In Jesus' name I pray. Amen."

Spiritual mapping

Spiritual mapping, when done thoroughly, is a process of spiritual cleansing that can assist in identifying where demons are working in the lives of people at ground level warfare, meaning personal. This is also a technique used in other levels, like discovery of demonic strongholds in the history of cities, territories, regions and even nations. The information or revelation obtained or mapped out is used to break the curses over an area which in turn causes breakthrough. Then blessings can more easily be released, received, and established in that area. For personal use, it is done through counseling or personal inquiry identifying the family history of open doors to darkness. Root issues of one's stronghold discovered through spiritual mapping will identify open doors of sin in the history of one's ethnicity and culture. It will uncover generational or personal sin, bondages, sickness and diseases, and generational struggles with demonic oppression. These revelations are keys used to bring breakthrough and freedom to one's soul and freedom to future generations. Through Christ, deliverance will bring restoration to our foundation, freeing our future generations from the assignments of Satan and his dark kingdom. Isaiah prophesied all of this in chapter 61:1–4, *"The Spirit of the Lord God is upon me, because the Lord has anointed me to bring good news to the afflicted; He has sent me to bind up the brokenhearted, to proclaim liberty to captives and freedom to prisoners; to proclaim the favorable year of the Lord and the day of vengeance of our God; to comfort all who mourn, to grant those who mourn in Zion, giving them a garland instead of ashes, the oil of gladness instead of mourning, the mantle of praise instead of a spirit of fainting. So they will be called oaks of righteousness, the planting of the Lord, that He may be glorified. Then they will **rebuild the ancient ruins, they will raise up the former devastations; and they will repair the ruined cities, the desolations of many generations**."* Jesus quotes this of Himself in Luke 4:18 as being the fulfillment of this prophecy. As believers of Jesus, we are called to be like Him and receive this promise for ourselves and the commission to restore others.

In James 5:16, it says, *"Therefore, confess your sins to one another, and pray for one another so that you may be healed. The effective prayer of a righteous man can accomplish much."* The spiritual cleansing mapping questionnaire is simple and designed to expose possible entry points of demonic oppression in one's life. It sheds light on the root or bloodline issues that had previously been hidden. Filling out the questions honestly will bring the best result. What we won't reveal could be key needed to breakthrough in areas of deep established strongholds in our life. This is a time to take off religious masks and allow the Lord to go deep within our cracked and faulty foundation and restore it to health.

Deliverance can be done personally, without a counselor/ deliverance minister. Being an experienced deliverance minister, I highly recommend one work with a prayer partner who is has some experience in deliverance, especially if this is your first time receiving cleansing/deliverance. The mapping questionnaire will still need to be completed first.

The questionnaire for mapping information is located in the back of this book and also in the *Spiritual Cleansing Handbook*. There is also self-cleansing of the bloodline information in the back of this book.

The fragmented soul

The word fragment means broken off or detached, an isolated, unfinished or incomplete part.

The word soul refers to one mind, will, and emotions. (Three-part man diagram located at the end of this chapter.)

To have a fragmented soul means that a part of our mind, will, or emotions is broken off, detached, isolated, unfinished, or incomplete. In Psalms 23:3, it says, *"He restores my soul; He guides me in the paths of righteousness for His name's sake."*

Through the fragmenting of the soul, the enemy can restrict how much love and devotion we give to the Lord. Jesus said in Matthew 22:37, *"You shall love the Lord your God with all your heart, and with all your soul, and with all your mind."* We need our mind, will and emotions restored to wholeness, so we can worship

Him fully. In spiritual cleansing and through the mapping process, one will be able to identify areas of the soul that are fragmented. Concerning healing of the whole man, Jesus not only heals the physical body, but He restores our mind, will and emotions back to wholeness. To restore means to bring back something that was taken away and put it back in place. He binds up the brokenhearted with His healing oil and calls back the pieces of their soul that was shattered or stolen through sin.

Deuteronomy 30:1–5 is a promise of restoration and gathering back of the soul. It reads, "*So it shall be when all of these things have come upon you, the blessing and the curse which I have set before you, and you call them to mind in all nations where the LORD your God has banished you, and you return to the LORD your God and obey Him with all your heart and soul according to all that I command you today, you and your sons, then the LORD your God will restore you from captivity, and have compassion on you, and will gather you again from all the peoples where the LORD your God has scattered you. If your outcasts are at the ends of the earth, from there the LORD your God will gather you, and from there He will bring you back. The LORD your God will bring you into the land which your fathers possessed, and you shall possess it; and He will prosper you and multiply you more than your fathers.*"

Trauma, abuse, witchcraft, drug addictions, sexual sin and soul ties will fragment the soul. These areas of strongholds can be called a death structure. A stronghold is a lie that has been established by Satan by false teaching or experience, which is set up as a truth in an area of our mind. A death structure is a stronghold that is fortified with lies from the enemy. It is that which the enemy sets up in the hearts of people to steal, kill and destroy us. By creating death structures, he binds us to lying thoughts, wrong actions, and dark belief systems where we destroy ourselves or live a life of death or destruction. The Lord restores us through delivering the soul from the darkness and then He lovingly heals. Deliverance and healing must be practiced together in the love of Christ for lasting results.

In Mark 7:27, Jesus says deliverance is the children's bread, meaning we can eat of the freedom and restoration He has purchased for us. Psalm 7:1–2 says, *"O Lord my God, in You I have taken refuge; Save me from all those who pursue me, and deliver me, Or he will tear my soul like a lion, dragging me away, while there is none to deliver."* Clearly, when there are no deliverers, the enemy steals the soul and keeps people in captivity. Later I will be discussing common areas where fragmentation can occur within the heart, and I will discuss soul ties and other structures more in depth.

Legal curses through sin

In Proverbs 26:2, it says, *"Like the sparrow in her wandering, like the swallow in her flying, so the causeless curse does not alight"* (AMPC). Satan is a legalist and he understands God's laws and commands. His job is to entice and tempt us to sin. It is through sin or the breaking of God's law that Satan obtains a right to attack, oppress or enter. Satan has a dominion of darkness to reign in. Because Jesus defeated Satan at Calvary, we, as children of God, now have the authority over darkness through Christ. The only entrances Satan has to us is through unrepented bloodline or generational iniquities and the door opened to him when we sin and are disobedient to God's commands. Once free, obedience to God assures protection from the oppression of the enemy in an area.

Doorways that can bring demonic oppression or curses:
- iniquity/bloodline transfer/generational curse
- rejection/abandonment
- whoredom/fornication/adultery
- witchcraft (association or participation)
- bitterness/unforgiveness/offense
- tongue iniquity
- rebellion against authority
- pride/idolatry/mammon/robbing God
- abortion
- ungodly covenants
- cursed objects in one's possession
- cursed associations
- tattoos and piercing

The definition of a curse is an appeal to a supernatural power for evil, or injury to befall someone or something; the evil or injury thus invoked; that which brings or causes evil; a scourge. A curse is recompense (a reward, payment, or compensation) in one's life or their descendants' lives because of iniquity. Through curses judgment comes. Even in judgment there is purpose. The purpose is to get one back in right alignment with the Father so again the blessing can flow. The Hebrew word for iniquity is *avown*, meaning perversity, moral evil, faulty, iniquity, mischief, or sin. This curse causes sorrow of heart and gives demonic spirits legal entry into a family to carry out their evil assignment. Perversion is turning away from what is good or morally right, to divert to a wrong end or purpose, misdirect, stubbornness, or obstinacy to what is right.

Demons work through curses and have job functions:

- to work for Satan in different levels of rankings and assignments
- to negatively affect the affairs of people, families, cities and nations
- to undermine the work of the church, causing division, splits and oppression
- to specifically oppose and attack believers with oppression, sickness and diseases
- to perform extraordinary acts through witchcraft to advance Satan's plans
- to kill, steal and destroy all of God's creation

Deuteronomy 28:15 warns of the curses that come upon the children of God through disobedience. Through cleansing we can identify these areas of curses within the bloodlines of the generations and break them. In Galatians 3:13, it says, *"Christ has redeemed us, from the curse of the law, having become a curse for us (for it is written, 'Cursed is everyone who hangs on a tree.')'"* (NKJV). As we repent, turn from sin and apply His Word and the blood of Jesus to all curses, they are broken in Jesus' name and we can receive cleansing and lasting freedom. Revelation 21 and 22 tells us that we will have to deal with curses until we live in the New Jerusalem (Rev. 21:22–27, 22:1–5).

7

Some signs that one is living under curses:
- disease and sickness
- continued poverty and lack
- broken families and broken covenants
- insanity and mental illness
- loss of children and barrenness
- no communication with God
- constant accidents
- vagabond
- cycles of bondage in bloodline

Identifying death structures

You are of your father the devil, and the desires of your father you want to do. He was a murderer from the beginning, and does not stand in the truth, because there is no truth in him. When he speaks a lie, he speaks from his own resources, for he is a liar and the father of it.

John 8:44 (NKJ)

As explained earlier a death structure is a stronghold that is fortified with lies from the enemy. It is a resource center that the enemy pulls from in our soul (mind). The word resource means that which is resorted to for aid, supply and support. Satan is the father of lies and he supports and builds his death structures in our hearts with lies. Word curses, trauma, unhealed areas of the soul, false belief systems, bitterness and unforgiveness, past failures, religion, denominational barriers, poverty, sickness, and disease — to name just a few — can be death structures that he will use to draw his lies from and speak to us. These death structures are different for everyone depending upon our life's journey, experience and what lies we have received and believed. Root issues and iniquities must be dismantled with the truth of God's word and the voice of the enemy will be silenced from within. In the chapters ahead, we will be focusing on the fragmentation of a soul through various wounds of trauma, rejection, fear, victim mentality, double-mindedness, and mental illness.

Death structures will cause us to have wrong perceptions in life and keep us from the fullness of our potential and they can be inherited through the bloodline. Jesus says in John 14:30, *"I will not speak with you much longer, for the ruler of the world (Satan) is coming. And he has no claim on Me [no power over Me nor anything that he can use against Me]"* (AMP). That is a powerful statement that should challenge us to examine our own hearts for lies that we have believed and have allowed to build in us. We have the mind of Christ through Holy Spirit within, but it's difficult to operate in it to full potential when our minds are darkened. In Matthew 6:22, Jesus said, *"The eye is the lamp of the body; so then if your eye is clear, your whole body will be full of light. But if your eye is bad, your whole body will be full of darkness. If then the light that is in you is darkness, how great is the darkness!"*

Death structures are strongholds, which the Greek word is *ochuroma,* meaning to have or to hold, a fortress or a place from which to hold something strongly. It's the word for castle, fort or a prison. Strongholds are places where demons rule with lies. The enemy's throne must be torn down and Truth established in that area. The enemy always desires to establish his rule in the hearts of men. In Isaiah 14:13–14, it reads, *"But you said in your heart, 'I will ascend to heaven; I will raise my throne above the stars of God, and I will sit on the mount of assembly in the recesses of the north. I will ascend above the heights of the clouds; I will make myself like the Most High.'"* The Hebrew word for throne is *awown,* meaning seat of honor or place of authority. Simply put is that the enemy wants to rule in places of the heart so Christ cannot.

In Ephesians 6:12, it says, *"For our struggle is not against flesh and blood, but against the rulers, against the powers, against the world forces of this darkness, against the spiritual forces of wickedness in the heavenly places."* The word wrestle in Greek is *pale*—struggling, wrestling, hand-to-hand fighting. The Greek word for against is *pros*—forward position, face-to-face encounter. This means we are in a spiritual hand-to-hand, face-to-face encounter with the spirit realm every day. This list Paul gave us is the level of darkness that operates against us. They all have a job function and we need to give people grace to be set free from darkness and its influence.

9

Here are listed the levels of darkness and their function:

- principalities—*archas*—beginning, origin, first, ruler, authority.
- powers—*exousia*—delegated authority, the right of control in a sphere or jurisdiction.
- rulers of the darkness of this world—*Kosomokrateros; kosmo*—means order or arrangement of world system; *kratos*—raw power, strength. Meaning this raw power has been put into an order or system.
- spiritual wickedness in high places—*poneros*—something that is bad, vile, malicious, vicious, impious or with no respect, malignant. Meaning their assignment is to oppress us and afflict us with all manner of bad, evil, vile things, cause us to suffer, with no regard or respect, highly injuring and threatening the life of humanity.

The three-part man diagram

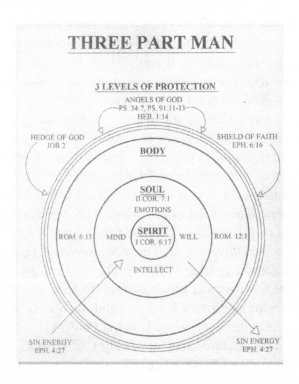

Proverbs 25:28 says, *"He who has no rule over his own spirit is like a city that is broken down and without walls."* As a spirit-led people, we must take back the authority over our own spirit, only yielding it to Holy Spirit. If one is ready to rule his own city and walk in wholeness, there are some things to prayerfully consider below.

Questions you should ask yourself before beginning the spiritual cleansing process:

- Am I willing to be consistent and faithful to my sessions?
- Am I ready to be real and honest with myself and the people helping me?
- Am I ready to work at building a deeper relationship with the Lord?
- Am I ready for the change of walking in holiness in the areas I'm seeking deliverance?

Spiritual cleansing is not:

- An overnight process.
- A quick fix.
- A one-time prayer session but spiritual cleansing is a lifestyle.

CHAPTER 2

CLEANSING OF
BLOODLINE INIQUITY

*"For as for the life of all flesh, its blood is identified
with its life. Therefore I said to the sons of Israel,
'You are not to eat the blood of any flesh, for the life
of all flesh is its blood; whoever eats it shall be cut
off.'"* Leviticus 17:14

N THIS BOOK, *SPIRITUAL CLEANSING OF THE
Bloodline*, I will be discussing generational death structures of
bloodline iniquities and other common areas of strongholds
within the lives of God's people. These generational death structures are behind the natural and spiritual sickness that many are
suffering. My prayer for all is that the information will become
revelation and bring a manifestation of healing to the whole man.
As John wrote, *"Beloved, I pray that in every way you may succeed
and prosper and be in good health [physically], just as [I know]
your soul prospers [spiritually]"* 3 John 1:2 (AMP).

It says this in the beginning verse of Leviticus 17:14, *"For as for
the life of all flesh, its blood is identified with its life."* Concerning
the bloodline, I have found in ministering cleansing, that the spiritual as well as the biological family history is recorded in the
everyone's' DNA. This earthly substance called blood keeps us

alive and is a supernatural substance full of life forms. These life forms live and thrive also because of the blood. We get our parents blood (DNA) in the womb upon conception. Whatever is in the father's and mother's history is recorded within our DNA, alive and active, good or evil. It will shape our world by influencing our person in our belief systems and in natural and spiritual inheritance. Whatever spiritual doors our ancestors opened have been opened to us, either a blessing to enjoy or a curse to deal with. While one is alive, these things can be in operation within the blood. When one dies, the spirits continue in the bloodline with the recorded curses and can transfer to the next of kin through soul ties or to the children.

Interestingly, in the book of Numbers chapter 19:11–13, it says, *"The one who touches the corpse of any person shall be unclean for seven days, That one shall purify himself from uncleanness with the water on the third day and on the seventh day, and then he will be clean; but if he does not purify himself on the third day and on the seventh day, he will not be clean. Anyone who touches a corpse, the body of a man who has died, and does not purify himself, defiles the tabernacle of the Lord; and that person shall be cut off from Israel."* Demons do not die. I have found that there can be a transfer of spirits sometimes when a person dies. It is a serious thing. The Lord warns us not to touch the dead. Demons are attached to persons, places or things. Touching unclean things could cause a transfer of spirits. One way they can transfer is by touching the dead. One should cover themselves in the blood of Jesus when going to funerals and make sure they are walking in forgiveness and generational repentance. In Proverbs 26:2, it says. *"a curse without a cause does not alight."* Most people are not knowledgeable in this area and have unforgiveness and offenses, which is a wide open door for the demons to gain access. They also have open sin doors and unrepented generational iniquities still speaking out against them in the spirit which makes demonic oppression possible. These things will be discussed in further chapters.

I recall a man dying of stomach cancer and his brother within a few weeks was experiencing the same stomach issues of his deceased brother. One might think it is coincidence. I don't believe so. Also, I recall a man passed with pneumonia and within a few weeks three people within his family all came down with a diagnosis of pneumonia, one of which was very severe. Recognizing the curse of sickness and death were trying to continue to take life, prayer warriors began to pray and came against it. No one else died in that family; all recovered. I have witnessed siblings in families coming down with the same diseases and one by one dying with the same diagnosis.

In the spirit realm within bloodlines there is much activity. In Hebrews chapter 7:9–10, it says, *"And, so to speak, through Abraham even Levi, who received tithes, paid tithes, for he was still in the loins of his father when Melchizedek met him."* Levi being inside his father's loins speaks of a spiritual account or recording credited to him as a tithe payer due to Abraham's obedience to do good, as if Levi was alive with his father at that time. In Exodus 20:5–6, it says, *"You shall not bow down yourself to them or serve them; for I the Lord your God am a jealous God, visiting the iniquity of the fathers upon the children to the third and fourth generation of those who hate Me, but showing mercy and steadfast love to a thousand generations of those who love Me and keep My commandments"* (AMPC). This iniquity is in the children's blood until curses are broken through repentance, renouncing and cleansing. What our forefathers have done, good or evil, is recorded in our spiritual DNA and we receive an inheritance from them. To stop evil inheritances from continuing down the bloodline, repentance and cleansing of generational iniquities are needed. In Romans 3:34 says, *"For all have sinned and fall short of the glory of God."* therefore, all bloodlines need to be washed through the blood of Jesus.

The DNA is defined as deoxyribonucleic acid, an extremely long macromolecule that is the main component of chromosomes and is the material that transfers genetic characteristics in all life forms. DNA is constructed of two nucleotide strands coiled around each other in a ladderlike arrangement with the sidepieces composed of altering phosphate and deoxyribose units and the rungs composed of the purine and pyrimidine bases adenine. Guanine, cytosine, and thymine: the genetic information of DNA is encoded in the sequence of the strands bases and is transcribed as the unwind and

14

replicate. It says that all the biological information is stored there. I say it is also the place where the spiritual information is stored. The spiritual evil inheritance called iniquity must be cleansed and uprooted out of us through the cleansing of our DNA.

In Joel chapter 3:20–21, it speaks of the Lord cleansing the blood. It reads, *"But Judah shall remain and be inhabited forever, and Jerusalem from generation to generation. And I will cleanse and hold as innocent their blood and avenge it, blood which I have not cleansed, held innocent, and avenged, for the Lord dwells in Zion"* (AMPC). Through bloodline cleansing, the Lord is avenging our bloodline, redeeming and restoring us to wholeness, releasing His glory in us!

We know that God made man a triune being: spirit, soul and body. Upon our salvation, we become one with the Lord in spirit. 1Corinthians 6:17 says, *"But the one who joins himself to the Lord is one spirit with Him."* In the realm of our soul (our mind, will and emotions) and this physical body, one needs to be cleansed from the earthly contamination through the fallen man. Jesus came to restore humanity back to wholeness through His finished work of the cross. The word says Jesus poured out His soul unto death. We know He poured out His blood for humanity. Through the blood of Jesus, our bloodlines can be cleansed and made whole. Hebrews 9:14 speaks of the blood of Jesus, *"How much more will the blood of Christ, who through the eternal Spirit offered Himself without blemish to God, cleanse your conscience from dead works to serve the living God?"*

Concerning the victory we have in Jesus in our generations, Hebrews 4:12–13, it says, *"For the word of God is living and active and sharper than any two-edged sword, and piercing as far as the division of soul and spirit, of both joints and marrow, and able to judge the thoughts and intentions of the heart. And there is no crea-ture hidden from His sight, but all things are open and laid bare to the eyes of Him with whom we have to do."* The writer is saying the Word goes into the heart (soul) deep in the joints and marrow. We know that marrow is in the interior cavities of the bones as a major site of blood cell production. This is where the iniquity is rooted in our spiritual DNA and works its evil through our spiritual and physical health. The Greek word for creature is *ktisis* meaning building, ordinance, formation or creature. These creatures can be bloodline familiar spirits, infirmity, contracts, covenants or altars of evil that are living and active from the unrepented sin of our ancestors. These things are the legal accusations being spoken or used by our accuser in the spirit realm that must be dealt with. The Word (Jesus Christ) will divide, cut asunder, destroy and uproot the things of darkness that are hidden to our natural eye.

In Job's distress, in Job 16:19, he cries, *"Even now, behold, my witness is in heaven, And my advocate is on high."* 1 John 2:1–2 says, *"My little children, I am writing these things to you so that you may not sin. And if anyone sins, we have an Advocate with the Father; Jesus Christ the righteous, and He Himself is the propitiation for our sins; and not for ours only, but also for those of the whole world."* An advocate is one who speaks or writes in support or defense of a person. You could say Jesus is our defense attorney in the bloodline of our generations when we become born again, and He is the Victor of every case the accuser brings against us!

It says in Colossians 2:13–15, *"When you were dead in your transgressions and the uncircumcision of your flesh, He made you alive together with Him, having forgiven us all our transgressions, having canceled out the certificate of debt consisting of decrees against us, which was hostile to us; and He has taken it out of the way, having nailed it to the cross. When He had disarmed the rulers and authorities, He made a public display of them, having triumphed over them through Him."* The enemy comes to steal, kill and destroy, but Jesus has come to give us abundant life which is a life of health and peace. The blood of Jesus has disarmed and defeated our enemies, making us victorious through Him over every evil plan of darkness. There is available the application of Truth for the believer to experience all the Lord has purchased for us.

God admonishes His people to repent and be free of generational iniquities. In Leviticus 26:40–42, He says, *"But if they confess their own and their fathers' iniquity in their treachery which they committed against Me—and also that because they walked contrary to Me* [41] *I also walked contrary to them and brought them into the land of their enemies—if then their uncircumcised hearts are humbled and they then accept the punishment for their iniq-uity,*[42] *Then will I [earnestly] remember My covenant with Jacob, My covenant with Isaac, and My covenant with Abraham, and [earnestly] remember the land."*(AMPC). Repentance strips the veil and tears down the barriers and any petitions erected against us in the spirit, bringing breakthrough and blessing.

Romans 4:6–8 says, *"Thus David congratulates the man and pronounces a blessing on him to whom God credits righteousness apart from the works he does: Blessed and happy and to be envied are those whose iniquities are forgiven and whose sins are covered up and completely buried. Blessed and happy and to be envied is the person of whose sin the Lord will take no account nor reckon it against him."* (AMPC)

In the bloodline, generational curses, demonic cycles of bondage, and iniquities are what is behind the death structures we find working within our hearts. The spirit of iniquity keeps records of unrepented generational cycles of bondage and curses. All these work through unconfessed sin, rebellion and ignorance. A cycle is any complete round or series of occurrences that repeats itself. These cycles of generational bondages and curses will continue until iniquities are repented of, broken, and dealt with. Psalms 106:6 says, *"We have sinned like our fathers; We have committed iniquity, we have behaved wickedly."* In Ezekiel 16:44, it says, *"Behold, everyone who quotes proverbs will quote this proverb concerning you, saying, 'Like mother, like daughter.'"* God's people are destroyed for lack of knowledge and the enemy can visit us with bondage.

The Psalmist rejoices in Psalms 32:1–7, *"Blessed [happy, fortunate, to be envied]) is he who has forgiveness of his transgression continually exercised upon him, whose sin is covered. Blessed [happy, fortunate, to be envied] is the man to whom the Lord imputes no iniquity and in whose spirit there is no deceit. When I kept silence [before I confessed], my bones wasted away through my groaning all the day long. For day and night Your hand [of displeasure] was heavy upon me; my moisture was turned into the drought of summer. Selah [pause, and calmly think of that!] I acknowledged my sin to You, and my iniquity I did not hide. I said,*

I will confess my transgressions to the Lord [continually unfolding the past till all is told]—then You [instantly] forgave me the guilt and iniquity of my sin. Selah [pause, and calmly think of that]. For this [forgiveness] let everyone who is godly pray—pray to You in a time when You may be found; surely when the great waters [of trial] overflow, they shall not reach [the spirit in] him.[7] You are a hiding place for me; You, Lord, preserve me from trouble, You surround me with songs and shouts of deliverance. Selah [pause, and calmly think of that]! (AMPC)

In Mark 9, we find a good example of a generational iniquity curse in a young boy who was brought to Jesus. Jesus was on top of the mount of transfiguration and came down to find a severely demonized boy whom the disciples were unable to help. The boy was severely demonized and tormented. The father said he had a spirit that causes him to be mute. His speech impediment was due to demonic activity that stole it. The spirit was a seizing spirit, an epileptic type spirit, causing continual seizures. It dashed him to the ground, causing him to foam at the mouth and grind his teeth and then stiffened him. In Matthew 17:15, it is recorded that the boy was a "lunatic" and very ill. The word lunatic is *seleniazo,* a Greek word meaning "moonstruck," translated lunatic or epileptic. Jesus at times healed other epileptics, being biological, but this was demonically rooted, which both still refer to a curse somewhere within the bloodline.

This spirit caused him to scream. Mute spirits can scream. Jesus addresses him as deaf and dumb, mute spirit. Deaf spirits can hear, and dumb spirits are intelligent, because as recorded, it listened, understood and obeyed Jesus! The boy was mute, deaf, and the spirit had indwelt him since childhood, according to the boy's father. The Greek word for childhood is *paidon,* which denotes infants, probably from birth, meaning he was born with this within him. It threw him into the water/fire. This was not suicide attempt, but an iniquitous curse sent to murder the boy, thus a demonic generational assignment through bloodline inheritance. Jesus, of course, had great compassion and freed him of it completely, bringing healing and restoration. The boy's goods, which included understanding, speech, and hearing, were stolen from him, and Jesus restored him to wholeness. He defeated the demonic strength or power over him, and returned to the boy what was rightfully his, canceling any tormenting, murderous contract on his life. Jesus says later to his disciples that this kind cannot come out by anything but prayer and *fasting*. The Greek word for kind is *genos*, which means family or kindred. Placing this definition in the content of the scripture text is means it was a generational curse (Mark 9:14–29).

Some strongholds will require us to fast with prayer due to the strength of the structure we are up against. I believe the disciples looked at the severity of the manifestation of the enemy and it brought some doubt and fear of failure. Jesus calls them an unbelieving generation. Fasting will not only crucify our flesh, taking it off the throne of the heart, but it will uproot doubt and unbelief in our hearts. It puts Holy Spirit in the place of ruler of our will, not us. It brings a deeper surrender of the Lordship of Jesus within us, which causes our spiritual ear to hear more clearly. Then in turn, it causes our faith to arise and be demonstrated through deed! We must utilize this supernatural weapon of the kingdom to see greater works released. As a child of God, fasting should become a lifestyle worship practice while waiting for the return of our Beloved Lord Jesus.

Bloodline Iniquity

The word iniquity is a Hebrew word *avown*, meaning perversity, (moral) evil, faulty, mischief, and sin. The Greek word for iniquity is *anomia,* meaning a violation of the law, transgression, wickedness or unrighteousness. It is anything that turns us away from God's perfect path. In Ezekiel, the Word says that iniquity and guilt were found in Lucifer. Lucifer was trading his goods for self-exaltation and worship. His pride and rebellion got him kicked out of glory! It is no different today when we trade the blessing of the Lord to enjoy sin for a season. We are told each day to choose life or death. Our actions impact our life and can affect our eternity. Our sin behavior can and does give demons legal right to traffic our bloodline. We must deal with iniquitous behavior and not make excuses for it. We must learn to repent quickly, apply the blood of

Jesus to our sin behaviors, change our thinking in that area, and take a new course of action.

Ezekiel 28:15–17
   "You were blameless in your ways from the day you were created until iniquity and guilt were found in you.[16]* Through the abundance of your commerce you were filled with lawlessness and violence, and you sinned; therefore, I cast you out as a profane thing from the mountain of God and the guardian cherub drove you out from the midst of the stones of fire. Your heart was proud and lifted up because of your beauty; you corrupted your wisdom for the sake of your splendor. I cast you to the ground; I lay you before kings, that they might gaze at you."* (AMPC)

In Psalms 51, David said he was shaped in iniquity in his mother's womb. He speaks of his mother's iniquity and his desire to be cleansed of it. This speaks of the iniquity being passed down in the womb. David had written this after his fall into adultery with Bathsheba. In verses 1–7, *"Have mercy upon me, O God, according to Your steadfast love; according to the multitude of Your tender mercy and loving-kindness blot out my transgressions. Wash me thoroughly [and repeatedly] from my iniquity and guilt and cleanse me and make me wholly pure from my sin! For I am conscious of my transgressions and I acknowledge them; my sin is ever before me. Against You, and You only, have I sinned and done that which is evil in Your sight, so that You are justified in Your sentence and faultless in Your judgment. Behold, I was brought forth in [a state of] iniquity; my mother was sinful who conceived me [and I too am sinful]. Behold, You desire truth in the inner being; make me therefore to know wisdom in my inmost heart. Purify me with hyssop, and I shall be clean [ceremonially]; wash me, and I shall [in reality] be whiter than snow* (AMPC).
   In Psalm 58:3, it says, *"The ungodly are perverse and estranged from the womb; they go astray as soon as they are born, speaking lies."* Jesus says in Matthew 15:18–20, *"But whatever comes out of the mouth comes from the heart, and this is what makes a man unclean and defiles [him]. For out of the heart come evil thoughts*

[reasonings and disputings and designs] such as murder, adultery, sexual vice, theft, false witnessing, slander, and irreverent speech. These are what make a man unclean and defile [him]; but eating with unwashed hands does not make him unclean or defile [him]" (AMPC).

The iniquities living in the soul of a man will, if gone undealt with, cause him to sin. Jesus also said you will know a tree by the fruit it bears. Generational iniquity is the root system and source of the sin bondage and evil fruit we produce. There is repentance and cleansing with the blood of Jesus that is needed as well as a crucifying of the flesh to walk free in victory. One must fill that place of the soul that was cleansed with the Word of Truth. In addition, one must build spiritual muscles by walking in their authority in the very area where freedom was gained. We must crucify the works of the flesh with its affections and lusts of sin choices and behavior. The more one puts an ax to the root of the works of the flesh, the easier it becomes to walk in obedience to Jesus. As we yield to Holy Spirit's leading and say no to our flesh, there comes a deeper circumcision of the heart, a fresh cutting away of things that bring death to us, and an easier walk of holiness in Christ. Galatians 5:24 says, *"Now those who belong to Christ Jesus have crucified the flesh with its passions and desires."*

When the flesh becomes a slave to demonic bondage, one no longer has control in that area of sin behavior, the will has been taken over. That sin nature now controls, overpowering one's will and there is no choice but slavery. Romans chapters six and seven speak of whomever you yield yourselves servants to obey, one becomes its slave. We see many struggling in bondage to generational strongholds and cycles of sin behavior until complete freedom is received. That iniquitous bondage is the twisted evil and rebellion that is passed down from one generation to the next, warring in the flesh of humanity, and going against God's righteousness.

Paul writes of the internal struggle in Romans 7:14–25, *"We know that the Law is spiritual; but I am a creature of the flesh [carnal, unspiritual], having been sold into slavery under [the control of] sin. For I do not understand my own actions [I am baffled, bewildered]. I do not practice or accomplish what I wish, but I do the very thing that I loathe [which my moral instinct condemns]. Now if I do [habitually] what is contrary to my desire, [that means that] I acknowledge and agree that the Law is good (morally excellent) and that I take sides with it. However, it is no longer I who do the deed, but the sin [principle] which is at home in me and has possession of me. For I know that nothing good dwells within me, that is, in my flesh. I can will what is right, but I cannot perform it. [I have the intention and urge to do what is right, but no power to carry it out. For I fail to practice the good deeds I desire to do, but the evil deeds that I do not desire to do are what I am [ever] doing. Now if I do what I do not desire to do, it is no longer I doing it [it is not myself that acts], but the sin [principle] which dwells within me [fixed and operating in my soul]. So I find it to be a law (rule of action of my being) that when I want to do what is right and good, evil is ever present with me and I am subject to its insistent demands. For I endorse and delight in the Law of God in my inmost self [with my new nature]. But I discern in my bodily members [in the sensitive appetites and wills of the flesh] a different law (rule of action) at war against the law of my mind (my reason) and making me a prisoner to the law of sin that dwells in my bodily organs [in the sensitive appetites and wills of the flesh]. O unhappy and pitiable and wretched man that I am! Who will release and deliver me from [the shackles of] this body of death? O thank God! [He will!] through Jesus Christ (the Anointed One) our Lord! So then indeed I, of myself with the mind and heart, serve the Law of God, but with the flesh the law of sin."* (AMPC)

We must realize that we have a spiritual inheritance, both good and evil. We often experience curses that manifest in the same cycles and pattern of the previous generation. These things maintain its legal right to continue in bloodlines through ages of unconfessed sin and repeated generations of rebellion against God's righteous standards. The generational cycles and bondage get repeated through unbroken curses and the familiar spirits that travel down through the family bloodline living within. When we become born again, we get the revelation that they are illegal squatters blocking our inheritance and wholeness. Often they can get left unnoticed until they become active in one's life manifested through struggles, sickness and cycles of bondage. They can lie dormant, inactive or skip a generation. These evil spirits can stay hidden and unnoticed until later in one's life, or they could show up in a family member whom they have chosen to manifest through. They may even decide to show up in the next generation around the same cycle of age. We see this happen often when adult children get the diseases of their parents at the same age, or when death tries visiting at the same age. That is not a coincidence, but a spiritual curse that needs to be broken. Who keeps the evil scorecard? The enemy does. He is one that continues to use his legal rights to visit, until the blood of Jesus is applied and annihilates his evil plans!

We ministered to a lady during a mass cleansing whom we never mapped out. We knew nothing about her life. We will call her Lynn. She was of an Asian descent. I was led by the Lord to break generational curses in the bloodline and curses on their conception, to deal with birth defects, (ADD) Attention Deficit Disorder and any hiding learning disabilities. I commanded all things hiding within bloodlines of those in service to come out and loose the people. Lynn, who was healthy, was manifesting deliverance from these bloodline curses and spirits. Later she explained to us that her children had grown up with ADD and learning disabilities, and that her grandchild was born with half a brain. Although she herself did not have these issues, the spirits of these curses were within her bloodline and had manifested themselves through her seed. There was some legal right in place because there was no repentance within the family history; this gave these things a place and a right to manifest. Proverbs 26:2 says, *"Like a sparrow in its flitting, like a swallow in its flying, so a curse without cause does not alight."* Through her renouncing the generational iniquities and sin, it lost its right to stay attached to her. She also shared that as curses were being broken of spirit guides and familiar spirits in the bloodline she saw in the spirit realm. She said she saw and was able to describe the face of a spirit guide as it was leaving. Lynn had no idea it was still following her. She received a glorious deliverance and cleansing. To God be the glory!

In Jeremiah 17:1, it states that, *"The sin of Judah is written with a pen or stylus of iron, and with the point of a diamond: it is engraved on the tablets of their hearts and on the horns of their altars"* (AMPC). The iniquity, if left unrepented, is judged by God. In Exodus 34:7, it says of the Father, *"Who keeps lovingkindness for thousands, who forgives iniquity,* transgression *and sin; yet He will by no means leave the guilty unpunished, visiting the iniquity of fathers on the children and on the grandchildren to the third and fourth generations."* This iniquity must be dealt with, cleansed, and uprooted out of the hearts of men to stop the continual cycling of evil and sickness. When the children of Israel were going in to possess the land of promise, He warned them in Deuteronomy 7:5–6, *"But thus you shall do to them: you shall tear down their altars, and smash their sacred pillars, and hew down their Asherim, and burn their graven images with fire. For you are a holy people to the Lord your God; the Lord your God has chosen you to be a people for His own possession out of all the peoples who are on the face of the earth."* It is still the same charge today, though we do it in the spirit realm through cleansing the house of God, His temple.

We ministered to a girl we will call Mary. Mary was half Liberian. Her father was from Liberia and her mother was American and raised her in America. Even though she had not been raised within that culture, the cultural spirits from her Liberian father were in her. Many of the curses she was dealing within her blood were from his ethnicity. They were, we discovered, the cause of her current issues. In her family, she was given the tribal name of her grandmother, who had a strong matriarchal spirit. Upon being given that name which was supposed to be a blessing for her life, she received all the demonic assignments attached. The name and the so-called blessing was, in reality, a curse. When we did her cleansing, she had strong spirits of witchcraft, Jezebel, barrenness, and a nest of many other things that were passed down in the women. We had to call out spirits of the Liberia bloodline. At one point in her cleansing, we witnessed a spiritual manifestation where Mary began to speak fluently in another language. I believe it was an African dialect. At another point, the spirit within Mary began looking over in the corner of the room speaking in its tribal language. That spirit began motioning with her hands to whatever it was looking at and talking to come and help. (I discerned it was another spirit watching us, and that had been summoned for help.) I'm sure it was something from her tribal ancestors. Still, at another time in her deliverance, a spirit of barrenness spoke saying Mary was not having any children for the Lord. It was very angry that Jesus was evicting it. It said her womb belonged to Satan. As revealed in Mary's deliverance story, generational strongholds are very real within the bloodline. Many demons will stay hidden until challenged with the Truth or the anointing. Mary was gloriously set free from the curses and later conceived a child. To God be the glory!

We do a lot of cleansing from the spirit of Freemasonry, one of which I recall vividly. There were several family members that were going through cleansing together. As we were breaking Masonic curses and calling out the demons from each degree, we notice that, at one level, demons were speaking in another tongue that sounded Latin. Quite interestingly, a father and the son had the same unlearned language coming out of them at the same time. It was the same spirit operating in the father and son because of the curses of the occult passed down from the grandfather. Neither of them had personally been involved in the Masonic, but their fore-fathers were highly active.

We had another man whose grandfather was a high-ranking Mason. This man had many curses and much demonic oppression that he was unaware of until he sat through a cleansing and experienced many hiding things of freemasonry were in him because they came out of him. This happens a lot with Freemasonry curses. It is not uncommon to hear demons speak of legal rights they had from years prior, even before the people receiving deliverance were born. Sin doors we open can affect our children and grandchildren. There are many names still on Masonic altars from one's ancestor's rebellious participation in this witchcraft. Freemasonry is all through our nation and I believe all need cleansing from this demonic structure, even if it is renouncing with prayers.

We must note demons are not all-knowing. They learn from studying humanity's behavior in the bloodline they have been assigned to live in. I believe these untaught languages spoken under the deliverance anointing by victims of bondage are of the ethnicity of their ancestors from past generations. Demons who came in that past generation sometimes speak out in these languages unknown to the person. Possibly, it was a language learned during the time of their stay in that body, or a cultural spirit in operation.

Iniquity brings temptation

In the book of James, chapter 1:12–15, it says, *"Blessed (happy, to be envied) is the man who is patient under trial and stands up under temptation, for when he has stood the test and been approved, he will receive [the victor's] crown of life which God has promised to those who love Him. Let no one say when he is tempted, I am tempted from God; for God is incapable of being tempted by [what is] evil and He Himself tempts no one. **But every person is tempted when he is drawn away, enticed and baited by his own evil desire (lust, passions).** Then the evil desire, when it has conceived, gives birth to sin, and sin, when it is fully matured, brings forth death"* (AMPC). This explains that it is our own evil desires that draw us away into sin behavior. One can see that which we desire inside our soul snares us. Those desires often have a voice that tempts us to do evil. I am amazed after a cleansing how many people say their mind is quiet and clear. When the Lord frees us from other voices, we can hear Him so much clearer. The stranger's voice will never lead us to life or peace. It will always lure us away from obedience and the will of the Lord. Whether it is a bondage to fear, doubt or unbelief or maybe an addiction of some kind, it is always out to steal, kill, or destroy one's purpose. Those voices can be the evil of generations past still using the same schemes and speaking the same accusations attempting to destroy another generation.

The Word tells us that blood has a voice. In Genesis chapter 4:9–10, it says, *"Then the Lord said unto Cain, 'Where is Abel your brother?' And he said, 'I do not know. Am I my brother's keeper?' He said, 'What have you done? The voice of thy brother's blood is crying to Me from the ground.'"* The Lord heard the voice of Abel's blood crying out for justice. The shedding of innocent blood from murder and abortion stills cries out in the spirit realm for judgment. Therefore, cleansing of souls and even the land is important for breakthrough and revival to come and for the kingdom of God to flourish.

In Hebrews 12:24–25, it says, "*and to Jesus, the mediator of a new covenant, and to the sprinkled blood, which speaks better than the blood of Abel. See to it that you do not refuse Him who is speaking. For if those did not escape when they refused him who warned them on earth, much less will we escape who turn away from Him who warns from heaven.*" Humanity's blood has a voice and it is speaking things spiritually about our personal history. That voice is the voice of generational iniquities. Only through the blood of Jesus do we receive our redeemed inheritance that blots out the cry of guilt and curses. Through the blood of Jesus, the Spirit of God will destroy the works of darkness and cursed inheritances that have been passed down fallen bloodlines. Revelation 12:11 says, "*And they overcame him because of the blood of the Lamb and because of the word of their testimony, and they did not love their life even when faced with death.*" In Romans 3:23–25, it says, "*for all have sinned and fall short of the glory of God, being justified as a gift by His grace through the redemption which is in Christ Jesus; whom God displayed publicly as a propitiation in His blood through faith.*" All victory is ours in obedience to Jesus.

Iniquity is also connected to the condition of our health. Psalms 31:9–10 says, "*Have mercy and be gracious unto me, O Lord, for I am in trouble; with grief my eye is weakened, also my inner self and my body. For my life is spent with sorrow and my years with sighing; my strength has failed because of my iniquity, and even my bones have wasted away*" (AMPC). The body can waste away because of iniquity. This is very true concerning sickness and diseases. Some sickness can be due to bloodline curses. Others can come in through open doors of sin or bad health choices, too. Often during cleansing sessions, when dealing with curses of sickness, disease or infirmities, the evil spirit will speak out telling us its assignment. For instance stating that it was in a parent or grandparent, taking their life, and that it plans to take the life of the one getting deliverance also. Sometimes it will even say the same of the next child, too. That is valuable information for us concerning familiar spirits and their plans to stay active within bloodlines.

We were ministering to a woman we will call Sherry, who had cancer, and we were dealing with its evil nest of darkness. It spoke and was very angry as we were breaking its assignment against her and calling out spirits. The spirit spoke out and said she belonged to him and it took her grandmother and was going to take her son, too. That is a generational curse telling us its intention to cycle down the family line. In her case, it had rights to manifest itself through sin doors of bitterness, witchcraft and the occult. We took authority over the spirit and its assignment and she was set free, healed, and is still alive today. Sherry had renounced and repented of it, so all legal rights were broken off her. This is an example of the blood speaking or having a voice within of death and destruction to generations.

I have seen these bloodline curses and cycles manifest in many areas. I ministered to a young girl we will call Emily, who was raped in her freshman year of college by a man from another country who was a student at that time. She was afraid and never reported it. Emily got pregnant and secretly had an abortion. She had never revealed this to her mother. The Lord healed her of the trauma of the rape and the abortion. Sometime later, her mother came for ministry and I learned that the mother was also raped her freshman year of college, had gotten pregnant, and had a secret abortion. The mother was raped by a man from the same country! All this sounds too far out to believe, but it is true, to the glory of God and the testimony of these ladies, evidenced by their freedom through cleansing. This is an example of a wicked cycle of darkness and its assignment to stay within a bloodline. Ezekiel 16:44 says, *"Behold, everyone who quotes proverbs will quote this proverb concerning you, saying, 'Like mother, like daughter.'"* I am so thankful for freedom and the power of the cleansing of the blood of Jesus.

Children receive cleansing rather easily and are set free from generational or familiar spirits traveling down the bloodline. Parents are a spiritual gateway to their children. Once, while ministering to the youth at a fellowship, many very young and innocent children came up for cleansing. They received much freedom from hiding generational and familiar spirits. One girl I recall was set free from a spirit of fornication. She was thirteen, still a virgin, very chaste. Her parents, however, had both been in fornication when they were young. This spirit entered through the womb, and, if left undetected, I am sure at some time in this young girls' life, the spirit of fornication would have troubled her mind, trying to lead her away into that sin behavior. Now, because it was broken off of her, she will no longer be an easy target for this spirit! She will need to keep doors closed by living holy. I truly believe because of the cleansing, it will be much easier for her to remain pure in her sexuality. The demons we allow to traffic our lives as parents will visit our children. Therefore, parents must themselves repent and take authority over the spirits that traffic their children through bloodline inheritance.

A generational curse spirit will, at times, tell us it has a right through the blood to remain, oftentimes mentioning a parent or grandparent. There may have been a sacrifice of shedding of blood, a blood covenant of witchcraft, or vows made in the family history unknown to the one receiving its curses. Because the enemy is a legalist, the curse will hold its ground until the blood of the covenant of Jesus Christ is applied and breaks the evil legal contract that Satan has in the spirit realm. People then can become healthy and whole.

Psalms 103:2–5 says, *"Bless (affectionately, gratefully praise) the Lord, O my soul, and forget not [one of] all His benefits—Who forgives [every one of] all your iniquities, Who heals [each one of] all your diseases, Who redeems your life from the pit and corruption, Who beautifies, dignifies, and crowns you with loving-kindness and tender mercy; Who satisfies your mouth [your necessity and desire at your personal age and situation] with good so that your youth, renewed, is like the eagle's [strong, overcoming, soaring!]"* (AMPC). Jesus can and does renew our health! That is a covenant promise of the Kingdom, so we must never accept sickness and disease but stand against it. The Lord can reveal the hidden things and bring it into the light showing us what we must deal with. His will is and will always be freedom, healing and wholeness for His people.

King David wrote in Psalms 51:1–3; *"Be gracious to me, O God, according to Your lovingkindness; according to the greatness of Your compassion blot out my transgressions. Wash me thoroughly from my iniquity and cleanse me from my sin. For I know my transgressions, and my sin is ever before me.* In verse 5, *"Behold, I was brought forth in iniquity, and in sin my mother conceived me."* This was written after David fell into the adultery with Bathsheba. It is a great example of the spirit of iniquity working through bloodline curses. Whatever you are warring with externally is a sure sign that you are called to defeat it internally. And when it raises its ugly head, cut it off! Don't allow bloodline assignments to continue. If you have fallen prey to one, rise in repentance and cleansing and move forward in victory. In Proverbs 24:16, it says, *"For a righteous man falls seven times, and rises again."* Never allow guilt and condemnation to come when the blood of Jesus can wash it all away.

The Lord is releasing to us more revelation concerning sickness and disease as we continue in cleansing. We have learned what is in the blood from generation to generation could be hiding inside the bodies of the children. It can be lying dormant, waiting to manifest itself at any time it chooses through a compromise in the body due to stress, weakness, or maybe another open door of sin behavior. It was quite a surprise to hear Holy Spirit tell us to call out the spirit of a disease that had not yet manifested in a person and find it is there hiding without any known symptoms. I believe we can stop sickness before it gets a chance or opportunity to cause illness in bodies. We can go down the parts of the body and take authority of things hiding in the organs and call out those as led by Holy Spirit. We do this in cleansing and many get freedom from spirits they did not know were dwelling in them. Jeremiah 17:9 says, *"The heart is more deceitful than all else and is desperately sick; who can understand it?"* This is so true, as sometimes we don't realize the depth of all that is working within us. Also, through the family spiritual mapping, we can investigate the areas of generational sickness and cycles and get cleansed from it before it decides to manifest itself in our health.

Hidden iniquity (spirit) curses can also block healing from flowing in the body. We were ministering to a Navajo man and who had set through a mass session. It was not revealed to anyone that he was in severe physical pain the whole night in need of a miracle in his spine. He sat through all the cleansing prayers and then after the mass cleansing, we called for anyone who felt they still needed prayer for healing. He comes forward and tells us he had been receiving twelve shots in his spine for pain just to be able to function. He said he would have to have surgery and rods in his spine or he would lose mobility of his body. We ministered to him by the laying on of hands and prayed until all pain was gone and the Lord released a creative miracle and he received a new spine! It was glorious, he now could bend and move and do things he could not do before, pain free. I believe the repentance and renouncing of iniquities and generational sins broke any legal hindrance of the miraculous for our brother to be whole. Healings come rather easily after the demons are evicted!

There can be hiding infirmity spirits in people who have had addictions of cigarettes, drugs or alcohol. Their bodies can have hiding infirmities inside lungs, liver and other organs and they have not yet been diagnosed with anything. For instance, while ministering to a young man we will call Jack, who had done hard drugs years earlier, along with a current cigarette addiction, the Lord had us go through his body and organs calling out diseases that are usually attached to these types of bondages. He had the spirit of emphysema and the spirit of cancer. He had been a heavy drinker, so we dealt with spirit of infirmities of liver disease and sickness. There was a deep cleansing of the organs that he had no diagnosis of from a doctor. I believe this revelation can stop Jack from manifesting the disease later in life as he keeps the sin doors to the enemy closed. Many people become born again after a life of sinful activity and need cleansed from the residue of their past and physical healing to their organs. 1 Corinthians 3:16–17 says, *"Do you not know that you are a temple of God and that the Spirit of God dwells in you? If any man destroys the temple of God, God will destroy him, for the temple of God is holy, and that is what you are."* These temples need to be restored after one has damaged them through sin doors of rebellious activities. We can call it a spiritual renovation!

The Word also tells us in Galatians 3:13–14 that, *"Christ redeemed us from the curse of the law, having become a curse for us-for it is written, 'Cursed is everyone who hangs on a tree'-in order that in Christ Jesus the blessing of Abraham might come to the Gentiles, so that we would receive the promise of the Spirit through faith."* Many diseases are spiritually rooted by curses within the body and need to be cast out, so healing can come to the body. A good example is when Jesus ministered to the church-woman of His day who had a crippling infirmity. In Luke 13:11–13, it says, *"And there was a woman who for eighteen years had had a sickness caused by a spirit; and she was bent double, and could not straighten up at all. When Jesus saw her, He called her over and said to her, 'Woman, you are freed from your sickness.' And He laid His hands on her; and immediately she was made erect again and began glorifying God."* Jesus loosed the evil spirit of infirmity from her, and then He laid hands on her and released healing. If you find there is a block in receiving healing within the body, there could be an evil spirit hindering the healing. That spirit needs to be evicted first. This is the meaning of a sickness being spiritually rooted.

Just as we go to the doctor for a checkup and we are asked what is in our family line of sickness and disease, we should do this spiritually, uprooting these curses before they decide to manifest physically. We do this through cleansing, calling the hidden things out of our bloodline. The Lord Jesus is a healing God and He desires us to be whole. Once we call out sickness and disease, we can then release the healing oil of Holy Spirit through these areas of the body. One also needs to command the chemicals and hormones of the body to be restored to perfection. Many we have found after receiving deliverance of addictions, need healing to the brain and endocrine system. We command those systems to come back into divine order. We have received great revelation in dealing with the health of the body, and we will continually gain more. I believe most sickness and diseases are rooted in a spiritual stronghold of bloodline iniquity.

CHAPTER 3

THE UNHEALED REJECTED SOUL

*"He is despised and rejected by men, a Man of sor-
rows and acquainted with grief. And we hid, as it
were, our faces from Him; He was despised, and we
did not esteem Him."* Isaiah 53:3 (NKJV)

The spirit of rejection

JESUS CAN IDENTIFY WITH THE EMOTIONAL
pain of humanity, for it says in Hebrews 4:15, *"For we do
not have a high priest who cannot sympathize with our weaknesses, but One who has been tempted in all things as we are, yet
without sin."* The spirit of rejection, many teach, is at the root of
all things. I believe it could very well be a bloodline curse due to
the fall of man and the rejection in the garden due to disobedience
and sin. To reject is to refuse to take, agree to, see to, use, believe
in, to discard, to throw out as worthless or useless, to deny acceptance, care and love, etc. The word rejection means the act or process of rejecting or being rejected. Rejection can come in when
one is rejected, denied love or acceptance. If one even thinks he
is being rejected, it is real to him regardless of the intent of the
other person. It is real even if it happened in fact or not. Real or

33

perceived rejection happens many times in childhood experiences and cane even come in through the womb of the mother, especially if the child was not wanted or if the child is conceived out of wedlock. Being conceived out of wedlock also brings a curse of illegitimacy upon a child in the womb. It says in Deuteronomy 23:2, *"No one of illegitimate birth shall enter the assembly of the Lord; none of his descendants, even to the tenth generation, shall enter the assembly of the Lord."* This is a curse that makes it difficult for people to receive the spirit of adoption and it must be broken off. Many have multiple places of rejection that need to be cleansed and healed. Whether it is real or not, we must deal with it as such, meaning that if the person believed a lying spirit of rejection and allowed it in to rule in their heart, the pain must be healed at the root and then the spirit cast out.

Rejection hurts people and hurting people will hurt others. Simply put, those rejected will reject others. We must learn to forgive quickly and not receive the evil that is in others. After one gets healed and delivered from this spirit, they must learn not to receive it again. Rejection brings with it abandonment, the fear of rejection, and self-rejection. It will cause one to have difficulty receiving or giving love. Being healed and delivered from the spirit of rejection will enable one to receive the perfect love of our heavenly Father. Fear of rejection is an open door to allow the spirit of fear to come in. One must deal with this spirit to fully understand their sonship in Christ and to be able to receive their inheritance from their heavenly Father.

In William G. Null, M.D.'s book, *REJECTION: Its Fruits and Its Roots,* he describes the root system of the strongman of rejection. He reveals in his diagram the entry points from society and family. (These root diagrams are found in the Spiritual Cleansing Handbook.) This brings an excellent understanding of this death structure's operation.

Rejection will always blame someone else and will never take responsibility for its actions. It acts as a repellant. It will cause you to be rejected by others and to reject others, working inwardly and outwardly. People who suffer from rejection cannot retain healthy relationships. It will isolate, causing you to feel lonely, unloved, and unvalued. It will also open doors to bitterness. It is like a poison that feeds emotional pain and contaminates other relationships in your life. This spirit is a real issue in the body of Christ, bringing much division and broken relationships. It is responsible for many wrong perceptions of situations. It may keep you paralyzed in insecurities, stuck in spiritual adolescence, or locked in spiritual arrested development.

"Arrested development," according to the online Collins English Dictionary, is a physical development that is not complete and a psychological development that is not complete. In the 1983 Mental Health Act of UK, it was considered a mental impairment resulting in a lack of intelligence. Today, some researchers now call it a development disorder, or a learning disability of the mind. I believe it can be a spiritual problem to consider when one has suffered emotional pain or abuse as a child and has not been spiritually healed. When one is experiencing blocks in emotional development to maturity, or find themselves stuck in childlike or adolescent behavior, that is a good indicator that this spirit of arrested development needs to be broken off of them, so they can move forward in spiritual development and maturity within their soul. We treat this as a curse of demonic hindrance connected to a damaging childhood/adolescence experience of the soul. The area and stage of development wherein one gets damaged emotionally or spiritually can be identified as the time the spirit of arrested development entered in causing delays in normal development (stunted behavioral, emotional, spiritual, social and/or relational maturing). We describe it as being stuck at a certain age, in certain identity or place in one's mind. This behavior will persist until healing and freedom comes. In 1 Corinthians 13:11, it says, *"When I was a child, I used to speak like a child, think like a child, reason like a child; when I became a man, I did away with childish things."* When the body of Christ gets healed in the soul, they can walk in spiritual maturity, manifesting mature fruit in life experience. It is not unusual to find this spirit in the hearts of God's people during a cleansing. Healing of the inner child is very common need in most people. This is especially true in traumatic childhood experiences, which we will discuss deeper in a later chapter.

A spirit of rejection will convince you that God does not accept you because men reject you. It feeds the fear of man, bringing in a man-pleasing spirit. One who is oppressed by this spirit will always be challenged to fit in and feel accepted, and often one will pattern their life after another, striving for an identity. Our identity must be complete in Christ and His love and acceptance for us. We were all created as God's masterpiece, not a carbon copy of another!

To overcome a spirit of rejection, one must discern the roots by which it began to grow, identify the weak areas and allow the Word of God to replace the lies of the enemy. Be honest with self-evaluating, allowing hidden hurts to be exposed, dealt with and even discussed if needed. Once the roots are exposed and pulled up, healing can come to our foundation. One then must prevent any more seeds of rejection (lies) to be planted in your heart, become dead to your flesh and no longer receive the evil in other people. Resist any rejection, forgive quickly and repent for harboring offense. Learn to press in to Holy Spirit when others hurt you, because He is your comforter and you are always accepted in Him.

Rejection brings false identity

Understanding who you are in Christ is receiving the sonship through the adoption in Christ. With this truth in place, one can accept who God created them to be. He will reveal in you His plan and purpose. When a man tries to create his own identity, it will be out of fear and rejection. The enemy will always try to get you to receive a false identity. Spiritual false identity is psychological. It is caused by confusion about one's goals and roles in society and not functioning according to God's plan and purpose. There are many ways in which one can develop a false identity.

We are to take on the mind of Christ Jesus and learn of Him, not our cultural traditions, ways or beliefs we learned that are contrary to Truth. 1 Corinthians 2:16, *"For who has known the mind of The Lord, that he will instruct Him? But we have the mind of Christ."* Our biological family influences our identity. It is not all bad, of course, but it can at times limit what God is calling us to if we allow generational curses and barriers of our bloodline to shape us. Word curses are another area of identity crisis, which we will discuss more deeply in a later chapter. Jesus said in John 6:63, "It *is the Spirit who gives life; the flesh profits nothing; the words I have spoken to you are spirit and are life.*" Many live out the lies that were spoken over them which shape their personal identity. The first part of Proverbs 23:7 says, *"For as he thinks within himself, so he is."*

If one is filled with rejection and has a bad self-image, one will have a false identity. For example, one who always identifies as a victim has a false identity shaped by wrong perceptions of life's difficult circumstances. It becomes how he perceives himself in all situations. The Word of Truth, along with all the limitations and restrictions that were placed on you, can tear down any false identities that life has created in you. The Greater One lives in you. Allow Him liberty to transform your life!

You should evaluate these areas of influence that could affect your personal identity below. Some of these influences may have hindered you from receiving and walking in the fullness of your sonship in Christ.

Areas of influence that affect one's personal identity
- rejection
- cultural traditions
- one's biological family
- generational bloodline iniquities
- life experience
- religious/traditional beliefs
- word curses/inner vows

The disciples of Jesus tried to make Him an earthly king. In John 6:15, it says, *"So Jesus, perceiving that they were intending to come and take Him by force to make Him king, withdrew again to the mountain by Himself alone."* Later, in chapter eighteen, when He was before Pilate, He says in verse 36, *"My kingdom is not of this world. If My kingdom were of this world, then My servants would be fighting so that I would not be handed over to the Jews; but as it is, My kingdom is not of this realm."* If one doesn't know who they are in Christ, others will define you according to their design. In the book of Judges, chapter six, Gideon was full of rejection, insecurity and fear. When God called him to be a deliverer to his people, he had excuses of his inability to obey God. He says to the Angel of the Lord in verse 15, *"He said to Him, 'O Lord, how shall I deliver Israel? Behold, my family is the least in Manasseh, and I am the youngest in my father's house.'"* What a great example of a false identity woven into him due to family rejection and poverty. The rich young ruler in Matthew 19 could have left and followed Jesus, but he had his false identity of success rooted in his wealth. Jesus was calling him to follow him and become a disciple, but instead it says in verse 22, *"But when the young man heard this statement, he went away grieving; for he was one who owned much property."*

The acts of abandonment can open the door to the spirit of rejection. The word abandoned means to be forsaken or deserted. These spirits of abandonment and rejection can be interwoven together. Usually at the root of the inner feeling of rejection is an outward act or action of abandonment. The act of abandonment is a root issue that will cause many to feel like an orphan. With many children raised outside of a home with biological parents, abandonment and rejection are very common issues we are facing in the church today. This is a generation curse in many bloodlines. There are too many absent fathers and mothers, abandoning their children, leaving them vulnerable to the enemy.

Some acts of abandonment:
- having been adopted
- having been left by a parent or guardian; illegitimacy
- having been left to raise yourself as a child
- going through a bad divorce or breakup
- thoughts that the Lord has left you, especially if one has been through a crisis
- being constantly ignored by those you love
- betrayal of a spiritual leader or friend

The feelings of rejection:
- feeling that you don't belong or ever fit in
- feeling you are worthless and of no value, always accusing yourself
- feelings of failure, uselessness and being invisible to others
- feelings of not being loved, accepted or able to have friends
- feelings that you are not important, nor are your needs
- feelings of never being good enough
- fearing man
- being a perfectionist
- driven to performance mode to be loved or to measure up to others' standards

This spirit of rejection can be so severe that it can be a root issue to sickness or disease. We worked with a woman I will call Ann, who was now in her older years and had an unknown sickness in her body. The doctors did not know what it was, and they continued running tests on her. Ann was in starvation and her body was very thin; it would not receive any of the nourishment that she struggled to eat. She was on a feeding tube through her stomach when we went to minister to her; she was still up and about, but very weak. Ann was a spirit-filled believer and had many seeking God for her healing. We were asked to come and work with her to see if we could get to the root of the illness. We did a quick mapping and learned Ann had suffered with severe rejection, self-rejection, and self-hatred from some traumatic experiences as a little girl. I addressed these issues and told her I felt that was the root of her starvation. These things deep within her were still there and were on assignment now trying to kill her body. She did not believe it at first, saying she had dealt with all that years ago. But clearly, her body was in self-rejection and self-hatred, trying to take her life. I told her we needed to let the Lord have His way. Ann was encouraged to write some healing letters of forgiveness to the one who had abused her, which she did. As I had expected, the anointing of God brought up a suppressed, rejected, angry, and hurting little girl spirit with a nest of evil that was locked up within her soul. It was on assignment to reject life and nourishment so that Ann would die. The demons manifested. They were all intertwined within her organs and were evicted by the power and the love of Jesus. Ann could now receive the physical healing needed and be restored back to good health, and she did. To God be the glory! Great things He is doing!

The spirit of fear

John 14:27
Peace I leave with you, my peace I give to you; not as the world gives do I give to you. Let not your heart be troubled, neither let it be afraid (NKJV).

Fear is the inward manifestation that rejection is operating within the soul. The fear of rejection opens the door for the spirit of fear to enter, which has many manifestations. People who are afraid have not been loved perfectly. 1 John 4:18 says, *"There is no fear in love, but perfect love casts out fear, because fear involves punishment, and the one who fears is not perfected in love."* There is a breach somewhere in relationships of not being loved perfectly by others, of not loving oneself, or of feelings that God hasn't loved them perfectly. Most of the breaches come through soul wounds of abandonment, betrayal, rejection, abuse, or areas of trauma. Fear is often a bloodline root issue passed down through generations. It is a witchcraft, mind control spirit with many functions, including causing feelings of low self-esteem and insecurity. The longer it is in operation, the stronger it gets stronger within its structure. Fear can infiltrate every area of one's life. Whatever influence it has on you, that is what you call it, and that is what name it will answer to as it is evicted!

In Matthew 25, when Jesus taught about the parable of the talents that were given out according to the ability of the people. All gave the master increase, except for the one who was full of fear. He hid it in the ground and produced nothing. Verses 25–29 say, *"And I was afraid, and went away and hid your talent in the ground. See, you have what is yours. But his master answered and said to him, 'You wicked, lazy slave, you knew that I reap where I did not sow and gather where I scattered no seed. Then you ought to have put my money in the bank, and on my arrival, I would have received my money back with interest. Therefore take away the talent from him, and give it to the one who has the ten talents.' For to everyone who has, more shall be given, and he will have an abundance; but from the one who does not have, even what he does have shall be taken away."* As one can see in this teaching, fear is a spirit that works opposite of faith and it will steal the fruit of the kingdom and the increase the Lord has called us to bring to Him. This man felt inadequate, so he hid his talent, he did not even put it in the bank. This speaks of him throwing away even the thought of doing anything; it was out of the question for him to use it, rejecting his purpose. If he would have chosen the bank, it would have been in the faith incubation of possibility, receiving interest on it, and at least the master would have had something to work with. But this man, being full of fear, was afraid to take a risk in faith to produce anything for the master, so he tossed it away. This is what fear does in our life, it paralyzes our potential, steals our inheritance and hinders personal destiny.

Fear is witchcraft, a mind control spirit, and an enemy of our faith. You must refuse to allow it to rule your heart. If it gets within you, it can weaken and breakdown the immune system. Fear, anxiety and stress are demonic structures that can cause sickness and many infirmity diseases to incubate and contaminate our physical health. It is a common root issue to many undiagnosed syndromes, to allergies, heart disease and high blood pressure. One's spiritual health is connected to their physical health and finances. In 3 John 1:2, it says, *"Beloved, I pray that in all respects you may prosper and be in good health, just as your soul prospers."* Fear and bitterness is a cause of much of the sickness and disease within people's bodies. Bloodline iniquity and poor diet can also be a cause of sickness and disease. (A list of spiritual roots of diseases can be found in the glossary of this book.)

We have seen many receive healing in their body as their soul became healthy. Many no longer have the need for prescription medications for anxiety, depression, and blood pressure issues after receiving their healing through cleansing.

To become free, one must become honest about what is working within their heart, deal with it and not tolerate it. When this happens, the process of being renewed in the mind and restoration of the body to good health can begin. When one only deals with the fruit of the sickness and not the root cause, it will usually be a short-lived victory. Spiritual cleansing is needed when fear is present. It must be uprooted, and Truth replaced on the throne of the heart in that area. In Proverbs 3:7–8, it says, *"Do not be wise in your own eyes; Fear the Lord [with reverent awe and obedience] and turn [entirely] away from evil. It will be health to your body [your marrow, your nerves, your sinews, your muscles-all your inner parts] and refreshment [physical well-being] to your bones."* (AMP)

There was a man we will call Ted. Ted had recurring seasonal depression at the same time each year. Every year he fought against getting on the prescription medication prescribed by his physician. He came for personal ministry. It was revealed that he had a suppressed area of childhood pain that was the root cause of his depression. As a young child, during this same season, he experienced a shocking and traumatic event in his life that was never dealt with spiritually. The sorrow and pain he had experienced that day was still locked in his mind or subconscious. In that place, he was still bound in sorrow, and although he was now an adult, he was reliving it each year through a season of depression. Once the root cause was revealed and dealt with through forgiveness, and after receiving inner healing and cleansing, freedom came. Many like Ted are trapped in areas of emotional pain and suffering and are oppressed with the manifestation of sickness in their mind or body.

Another lady we will call Jan had been diagnosed with severe clinical depression and could not keep her a job in her profession or function in normal life activity. It was to the point where suicidal thoughts beginning to plague her mind. She had spent over a decade being in psychiatric therapy, counseling and medications, learning only how to cope with the illness. Through spiritual mapping, Holy Spirit led us to the root of the issue of her mental oppression. She was then set free and able to function again. In an area of a traumatic unhealed soul wound of betrayal, the enemy was able to set up his death structure of clinical depression to keep her bound in a prison of sorrow. Jesus came so we could experience freedom, and Jan received what was rightfully hers through the finished work of Jesus. Psychology may have some good coping tools to medicate or suppress systems, but it is unable to deal with the spiritual root issue that is deep within. 1 Corinthians 2:14 tells us, *"But a natural man does not accept the things of the Spirit of God, for they are foolishness to him; and he cannot understand them, because they are spiritually appraised."* One doesn't have to suffer with mental oppression or spend years in expensive counseling. The Spirit of Counsel and Wisdom of Jesus should use counseling to find a solution to the problem at hand. Hebrews 4:15–16 says, *"For we do not have a High Priest who cannot sympathize with our weaknesses, but One who has been tempted in all things as we are, yet without sin. Therefore let us draw near with confidence to the throne of grace, so that we may receive mercy and find grace to help in time of need."*

In 1 Kings 19, it tells the story of Elijah fleeing in fear from the witch Jezebel. This is after God used him for great accomplishments and victories. It says in verse 2, *"Then Jezebel sent a messenger to Elijah, saying, 'So let the gods do to me, and more also, if I do not make your life as the life of one of them by tomorrow about this time.' And when he saw that, he arose and ran for his life, and went to Beersheba, which belongs to Judah, and left his servant there"* (NKJV). Notice that when Elijah saw the message, fear had painted an illusion of Jezebel's declaration of death and defeat. He allowed the witchcraft spirit of fear to get in his imagination or meditation, painting a wrong picture, which caused him to retreat from the enemy he was called to defeat! Paul writes to us in 2 Corinthians 10:5–6, *"We are destroying speculations and every lofty thing raised up against the knowledge of God, and we are taking every thought captive to the obedience of Christ, and we are ready to punish all disobedience, whenever your obedience is complete."* As you overcome your enemy, you are now ready to bring punishment to those things by setting others free. Guard the eye and ear gate and do not allow the enemy of fear to use your mind as his canvas for his lying illusions. If he has been busy releasing images from within, evict him so faith can rule and create the right imagery of vision and destiny.

It says of Jesus in Isaiah 53:5, *"But He was pierced through for our transgressions, He was crushed for our iniquities; the chastening for our well-being* (peace) *fell upon Him, and by His scourging we are healed."* Jesus not only made the way for our physical but also for our emotional well-being. Some that have soul wounds can get emotional healing and move forward in victory, but there are many others that must go deeper with deliverance. Soul wounds can be a door to check for demonic oppression, but not all who are wounded have evil spirits attached. Our lives are unique, as is the journey we experience, all affecting us differently, and our deliverance is also tailored-made for each of us.

CHAPTER 4

DOUBLE-MINDEDNESS AND MENTAL ILLNESS

*"Draw near to God and He will draw near to you.
Cleanse your hands, you sinners; and purify your
hearts, you double-minded." James 4:8*

I N THE BOOK OF JAMES, CHAPTER ONE, THE
Word speaks of a double-mindedness believer. It reads in verses
1–16, "*James, a servant of God and of the Lord Jesus Christ, to
the twelve tribes scattered abroad [among the Gentiles in the dis-
persion]: Greetings (rejoice)! Consider it wholly joyful, my brethren,
whenever you are enveloped in or encounter trials of any sort or
fall into various temptations. Be assured and understand that the
trial and proving of your faith bring out endurance and steadfastness and patience. But let endurance and steadfastness and
patience have full play and do a thorough work, so that you may
be [people] perfectly and fully developed [with no defects], lacking
in nothing. If any of you is deficient in wisdom, let him ask of the
giving God [Who gives] to everyone liberally and ungrudgingly,
without reproaching or faultfinding, and it will be given him. Only
it must be in faith that he asks with no wavering (no hesitating,
no doubting). For the one who wavers (hesitates, doubts) is like
the billowing surge out at sea that is blown hither and thither and*

tossed by the wind. For truly, let not such a person imagine that he will receive anything [he asks for] from the Lord, [For being as he is] a man of two minds (hesitating, dubious, irresolute), [he is] unstable and unreliable and uncertain about everything [he thinks, feels, decides]." (AMPC)

As you see, the fruit of double-mindedness is much instability, causing one to be unreliable and uncertain about everything in life. It all comes from doubting God. Doubt means one has a divided judgment and this steals one's spiritual resources because there is no faith. Without faith it is impossible to please God. Faith is the supernatural substance that causes us to receive from the hand of God. Double-mindedness will create a tormented soul that is tossed about like the surf of the sea in a spiritual storm, and that is no way to live as a child of God. James begins by warning that tests and trials will come, and you need wisdom or else you will doubt God and have this divided judgment, becoming double-minded. This will cause you to contradict yourself and withdraw from the presence of God and His work. People who are halfhearted toward God will yield to this spirit, experiencing inner turmoil and conflict. They backslide into the old man and into sin habits, because there is no conviction of the heart when this is in operation. Double means two, so this spirit will conflict with the Spirit of God within, vacillating between two opinions and causing you to reason away the voice of the Lord causing you to be unable to walk in the Spirit.

Proverbs 25:28 says, *"Like a city that is broken into and without walls is a man who has no control over his spirit."* There is no safety from attacks with double-mindedness. One must be healed and renewed in the spirit of their mind with the truth of God's word. Psalms 119:113 says, *"I hate those who are double-minded, but I love Your law."* Double-mindedness can begin rather subtly, but it can develop into a real spiritual problem in the hearts of men.

Believers who have this are people who live by what they see instead of by faith. They will have a hard time trusting the Lord and will live a life of worry. This stronghold has produced many worldly, carnal Christians who have no power and are in a backslidden condition towards God because of its deception. If it continues, it can become witchcraft, rebellion and bring in infirmity spirits of mental illness.

King Saul was one of the greatest examples of a double-minded man. He had two minds, that of rebellion and that of rejection. He was rebellious against God and His commands, and he had the fear of man's rejection. He was always in confusion and disobedience. This caused him to continue in sin cycles. He eventually became fragmented and lost his mind to the nest of demonic torment. He lost the throne and ended up taking his own life. That is a sad story of a double-minded man! The enemy wants us to falter between two opinions, so he can gain access through personal doubt and unbelief. We must pray as David did in Psalm 51:10, when he cried out saying, *"Create in me a clean heart, O God, and renew a steadfast spirit within me."*

Mental illness and spiritual schizophrenia

I believe double-mindedness can become a root issue of mental illness strongholds. Spiritually speaking, mental illness can also manifest through fear, roots of rejection, witchcraft, mind control structures, trauma, or bloodline generational curses. I have found this to be true when working with those with mental illnesses. One woman, who we will call Amy, had a family who had strongholds of mental illness. Many of them were medicated for bipolar and schizophrenia. Amy was a believer and had only used mild antidepressants for depression. The first time I met her, she was sitting on my sofa weeping, very weary, and unable to focus. Amy had been married several times and had been battling a spirit of depression and suicide, which is common with mental strongholds. I had many sessions with her dismantling the lies of the enemy. She had suffered trauma as a child, molestation and deep rejection and abandonment. She had all the symptoms of the double-minded spirit of schizophrenia, both rejected and the rebellious personality behaviors. She had much torment in her mind with what I call spiritual schizophrenia. A doctor did not diagnose her, but she clearly had all the symptoms actively tormenting her. We know a spirit by its nature and assignment and that is what we call it.

During one cleansing session, while we were ministering to Amy concerning her childhood, a little girl spirit of fear begins to manifest. Amy crumbles out of her chair and begins to act like a child. She curls up in a ball and tries to hide. She begins talking as if she is a child and asks us if we see them? She kept repeating herself and tells us "they have come." We had found out that when Amy was a child and when her parents would fight, she would hide under the bed and have imaginary little people (demonic spirits) that came to keep her company. She had become fragmented in her mind because of the trauma of all the fighting. It was a way of escaping reality at a very young age. The enemy had taken advantage of her and multiple spirits had come in. This area was now being brought to light and the Lord was dealing with this stronghold. It was one root issue that was feeding the mental oppression. We had to break curses of trauma and call out all the supporting spirits. There was a whole nest of evil in Amy's childhood. The Lord delivered her, and we called back all the fragmented pieces of her soul and released healing. She was restored in that area and never affected by that childhood pain again. Later, she had shared how she was in and out of herself, listening, and seeing the little people as we were praying. The spirit realm is very real and active in our lives whether we believe or not.

We often use the illustration from the book *The Pigs in the Parlor* by Frank Hammond, (found at the end of this chapter). It speaks of a rejected and rebellion personality. It is very accurate with a diagram that is quite helpful in understanding the fragmented soul. Amy's family had this stronghold, so we went down through the list of supporting spirits of this double-minded spirit, commanding them to loose her. I found out by revelation of Holy Spirit concerning Amy that there were many more supporting spirits than what was on the list. We called out the unnamed spirits of schizophrenia, witchcraft, mind control and mind bondage and broke the generational cycles in the bloodline. Since her mother and all her sisters were living with this evil structure, it was a strong probability that it was also in her, and it was. The Lord teaches us that we can know a tree by its fruit. Well, the fruit was there, and she became free, restored, and received a fresh infilling of Holy Spirit.

It was glorious! Amy had testified that she had never felt so free and clear in her thoughts. The chatter and oppression were gone. She had the peace of God within. Keep in mind that she was not medicated except with mild antidepressants. She was born again with Holy Spirit working in her and fighting that stronghold, keeping it from getting deeply seated within. It did take more than one session to dismantle the nest of evil dwelling in her through the many generations. The process is far worth the glorious victory, no matter how many sessions it takes, each person is different. There have been other sessions with Amy that we walked through concerning another area of that stronghold which had also been set up in her heart. The results have been glorious and she has become a strong team intercessor for the kingdom, healthy and whole and in her right mind. She is a far different woman than the one who came to us scattered, tormented and full of despair.

In Deuteronomy 7:22, it says, *"The Lord your God will clear away these nations before you little by little; you will not be able to put an end to them quickly, for the wild beasts would grow too numerous for you."* Sometimes, the Lord will peel off things little by little in spiritual layers and at other times there is an instant deliverance. I do believe we must develop spiritual muscles in spiritual warfare on our journey to wholeness. The Lord knows the heart of His people and He will mature them as He sees fit. One must learn their weapons of warfare to be able to maintain the freedom they receive. People sometimes think the process of deliverance of cleansing is not working because the change is very subtle due to the fact that there are so many supporting spirits that need to be dismantled. Do not allow discouragement to come in. Sometimes even after several spirits are evicted it can take a while to recognize the ground that was taken back. It saddens me when people give up the fight before full victory. We must realize we did not get in that degree or depth of bondage overnight, and unless the Lord does an instant miracle, which is very possible, we must exercise patience as we walk on our road to wholeness. People need to learn discipline and accountability to maintain the freedom they receive. We live in a quick fix society, therefore, taking up your cross and walking a thing out is foreign to most. Jesus never promised us a life that was void of trial and suffering; He did, however, promise us authority to overcome all the schemes and works of darkness. Weapons will form against us, but they will not prosper if I choose to continue to walk with Him!

This spiritual schizophrenia is more common than we realize in people. It gets its entry through a double-minded spirit that will bring instability. It works through bloodline generational curses, trauma doors, fear and rejection. When I speak of one having hidden mental infirmities or generational strongholds, these are ones with some symptoms but no diagnosis. These people could possibly have others in their family line who had suffered from the illnesses. The same is true with the bipolar disease. Many have had generational depression, chronic anxiety, depression or bipolar in families. It is often hiding inside the DNA and people can free of it before it is deeply seated and manifests through an open door of some kind.

We find this spiritual schizophrenia stronghold can also be drug-induced. Drug addictions can fracture or split the soul or mind of a person. It fragments them, causing this death structure to set up in them. Those evil spirits take advantage of the fragmenting and get in rather easily through this door. After they enter, they will begin to build their false identities within the person. In the false identity, one can develop an alternate personality spirit. In these cases, we break curses of multiple personality disorder of mental illness and call out the false personality spirits and their supporting spirits. Depending on the degree of darkness and the length of the bondage, it may take a while to dismantle those supporting spirits from the real person. Holy Spirit filled counselors, through discernment, can usually identify what is the real and what is an intruder. We have seen the Lord free and heal people of hidden multiple personality spirits.

The Lord gave us one mind, one of power, love and soundness (2 Tim. 1:7). The Lord can deliver and bring wholeness. I ministered to a girl we will call Holly. She was hearing voices telling her to do evil things of violence to her children and husband. She had acute anxiety and depression with a whole nest of evil tormenting her. She refused to listen to the voices and knew they were demonic. She loved her family and wanted to be free. Each time we dealt with her, we would break the generational bipolar disorder that would manifest. It took some time to get to the root of it, but freedom did come. There are countless numbers of poor souls locked up in prisons in their minds or worse yet in mental institutions needing the freedom from demonic torment that only Jesus can give. Demonic chatter is very common in believers and it will continue until the demon is cast out. It can be different depending on the stronghold within them. Most demonic chatter demons carry voices of accusation, hate, paranoia, and suspicion towards self and others. Many suffer from the torment of demonic chatter and just believe that hearing other voices is normal. God said we could and have a sound mind. We should not settle for anything less than this.

The Lord is releasing revelation to His body to deal with any inherited demonic structures, disease or sickness in a family line. Bondage can be stopped before it starts to manifest. We don't have to accept becoming sick as we get older. The Lord can cleanse the DNA in us before any symptoms begin to set up in areas of mental illness, sicknesses and disease. Wholeness can be accomplished through the finished work of Jesus Christ.

A (spiritual) schizophrenia stronghold list taken from *Pigs in the Parlor* by Frank Hammond and Ida Mae Hammond. A rejected personality (inward) spirit will have these demons attached:

- rejection, self-rejection, fear of rejection
- perversion
- fantasy lust
- self-accusation
- compulsion confession
- insecurity/inferiority
- envy/jealousy
- fear of judgment
- self-pity
- false compassion/false responsibility
- depression/despondency/despair/hopelessness
- suicide
- guilt/condemnation/unworthiness/shame
- perfection

- pride/vanity/ego
- intolerance/frustration/impatience
- unfairness
- withdrawal/pouting/unreality
- fantasy
- daydream
- vivid imaginations
- self-awareness
- timidity/shyness
- loneliness
- sensitiveness
- talkativeness
- nervousness/tension
- fears/phobias

A rebellion personality (outward) spirit will have these demons attached:
- bitterness/unforgiveness/resentment/retaliation/anger/hatred/vilence/murder
- distrust
- fears
- suspicion
- persecution
- confrontation
- accusation of others
- rebellion
- self-will
- selfishness
- stubbornness
- self-deception/self-delusion/self-seduction
- judgmental
- pride
- unteachableness

This list is an excellent beginning point to use when ministering to one with this structure. But I have found it is just the beginning, most will need more sessions. You will need to cast out all hiding schizophrenia spirits—and many more. How long the spirit has been within them and how deeply seated it is will dictate the number of follow-up sessions. One must break the generational cycles of it within the bloodline, witchcraft mind control/bondage, loss of soul, mental illness, insanity, double-mindedness, and multiple personality disorders. The person will then need ongoing counsel to discover who they really are in Christ. Their minds need to be renewed in the Word of God. They will need encouragement on their journey with affirmation and godly spiritual guidance.

CHAPTER 5

CLEANSING TRAUMA
AND THE VICTIM

*"For God has not given us a spirit of fear, but of
power and of love and of a sound mind." 2 Timothy
1:7* (NKJV)

I N THE STORIES OF AMY AND HOLLY, IT WAS
noted that both had areas of trauma in their childhood. Trauma
is not just a terrible event, but it is a spiritual attack and it affects
the whole person. It can bring damage to the mind, emotions and
physical body. It affects behaviors and how one thinks about themselves, others and the world around them. It can cause one to have
a wrong self-image, one contrary to what the Word says about
them, due to the depths of fear that dwells deep within. It says in
1 John 4:18, *"There is no fear in love; but perfect love casts out
fear, because fear involves punishment, and the one who fears is
not perfected in love."*

The definition of trauma is a serious injury to the body, as from
physical violence or accident. It is severe emotional or mental distress caused by an experience. The event is tragic itself due to
the nature of the experience and many times it involves a fear of
death or physical or emotional injury. Different people can and are
affected differently as trauma gets stored in their brain. If traumatic

situations happen to one as a child, it can shape the person at the core, giving them a wrong identity. They can become fractured, fearful, vulnerable, and develop a victim mentality. One can have a spirit of arrested development, and if left unhealed, it will alter the view of basic human needs. Things will often be distorted and can and will open the door of torment in different areas. One's perception is their reality, whether it is true or not. Unhealed soul wounds distort perception and will have a negative impact upon relationships and personal destiny. This spiritual problem will delude one's judgment with themselves and others. The way one views their self will cause others to draw the same conclusions about them. Jesus said in Matthew 7 verses 11–2, *"Do not judge so that you will not be judged. For in the way you judge, you will be judged; and the standard of measure, it will be measured to you."* This does not only happen outwardly but also inwardly against yourself. To become spiritually healthy and have positive relationships, one needs to have the mind of Christ concerning who they are in Him!

Like spirits will attract and the unhealed soul will connect with those who have the same spirit, or with familiar or comfortable situations. This can cause one to be locked in cycles of repeated abuse and dysfunctional relationships and unhealthy soul ties. Trauma images that are suppressed can surface while the anointing is present in counseling or the cleansing. They may begin to see images and slowly recall things that happened that were previously stored away. God sometimes allows things to be stored away to keep them one remembering the pain of the experience. I believe sometimes the Lord keeps the memory stored until He has one in a safe place and made them ready to receive the healing and freedom from the traumatic experience.

One can experience traumatic pain of trauma as they are ministered to. The pain of their broken life can come to the surface as the root is being exposed. While ministering to a young teen male who was full of anger and rebellious behavior, he begins to have flashbacks while we were breaking curses of trauma from his childhood. Traumatic spirit images surface in his mind and he felt it within his emotions. He said later, as he testified, that he was seeing his dad beat his mother and he was feeling the terror of it as if it was real, happening at that moment. He became that little boy in elementary school in those few moments. The Lord delivered him of all the demonic spirits that came into him during the trauma. Jesus was the Lamb slain before the foundation of the world! *(Rev. 13:8)* His blood goes all the way back to Adam in our lives and avenges our enemies.

Medical science would call these spirit images PTSD or post-traumatic stress disorder. PTSD is defined as a mental disorder, as battle fatigue, occurring after a traumatic event outside the range of usual human experience, and characterized by symptoms such as reliving the event, reduced involvement with others, and manifestation of autonomic arousal such as hyperalertness and exaggerated startle response. These symptoms may include disturbing thoughts, feelings or dreams related to the events, mental or physical distress to trauma-related cues, attempts to avoid trauma-related cues, alterations in how a person thinks and feels, and an increase in the fight-or-flight response. These people are at a higher risk for suicide or self-harm. This is a spiritual attack and the fear spirit images can be dealt with spiritually. Medically, counseling and medication is used, but neither can deal with the spirit of fear and its tormenting images that entered through the door of trauma. Medication only deals with the flesh but not the spiritual problem at the root. These spirit images can be cast out and healing and wholeness can be experienced within the soul and body of the traumatized individual.

We worked with a girl who we will call Diane. Diane came to me very shattered and broken. She was full of trauma and had sickness also in her body with severe kidney and bladder issues due to severe rejection and fear. Diane was now an adult who had been severely abused sexually and physically as a child and several years prior by her father. The abuse was so severe that she would manifest in intense shaking and PTSD symptoms during counseling and often end up in the corner of the room on the floor. She would never look me in the face, having a difficult time concentrating as she saw trauma spirit images during our meetings. It took many sessions and a lot of patience to build her trust. Diane had an eating disorder and was also a cutter and she had often cut her arms, legs, and stomach. She was also on psychiatric meds for the PTSD. After weeks of counseling, she was prepared to begin the cleansing prayers. We worked as a team to get her set free from all the demonic torment. There were intense battles with demons scratching and clawing at her cuts to shed more blood and to cause her physical harm. There were many threats from the demons saying they were going to kill her when she left us, but they could not because the Lord Jesus prevailed over every enemy of Diane on the cross of Calvary. Demons will many times challenge one's authority and try to get one to back off from the battle. Do not give in but press through in confidence in Christ. The Power of God prevailed in each prayer session, dismantling demonic structures within, and Diane gained more and more freedom. As time continued, we saw the effects of the cleansing, the good fruit of peace, love and joy as she gained authority over her own life. Her health began to change as demonic assignments were broken off her body, too. As the Word says in Matthew 11:12, *"From the days of John the Baptist until now the kingdom of heaven suffers violence, and violent men take it by force."* Today, by the grace of God, she is living a healthy, productive life in victory.

In severe trauma, especially of sexual abuse, one can be so tormented that they will turn to cutting on the body, eating disorders or other means of escape to relieve the emotional pain by inflicting physical pain instead. The demon sees this as a bloodletting sacrifice to Satan. It is a spirit that tortures its victim. This is a wicked network with an unloving spirit, self-hatred, unforgiveness, shame, rejection, and rage at its root. There will be a nest of evil lies connected that will need to be dismantled with much inner healing that will need to be done. One who is in this bondage believes the lie that physical pain is easier to deal with than emotional suffering. Eating disorders have much of the same roots and causes with lies of self-rejection and hatred. It is important to get the emotions healed as we get people set free and that lies are replaced with the Truth of God's Word. There should be accountability and follow up with them if possible.

There is hope for those who have suffered traumatic experiences to become whole. A Korean woman who we will name Lee came to a cleansing who had been molested and raped repeatedly as a little girl of four years old. She told us a man in her village used to take her into the woods and violate her and no one knew it was happening. She was clearly arrested in her development and needed freedom. During her session, as she chose to forgive her perpetrator, all the tormenting spirits who took advantage of the sin door that was open to her were dealt with by Jesus. He destroyed the hold it had upon her and not only took out all the pain that was locked in her emotions from the trauma, but he also freed her of the pain in her physical body. Lee was freed of all the fear and rage connected to the repeated abuse. Jesus lovingly and completely cleaned childhood trauma out the abused four-year-old and brought healing and wholeness to her. She later testified that during this process she felt as though she was protected within a "love bubble" of Jesus. How beautiful is the love of God for His children!

Trauma can also be a root issue of sickness. We ministered to a young mother we will call Sally. Sally grew up a sickly teen with a lot of health issues. She developed asthma and it tormented her up into adult life. The spirit came into her lungs after she was raped at eleven years old. It was then that she was diagnosed with asthma, and no one knew of the rape. Sally told no one because of it being a family member, and she was full of fear and shame. She also had a multiple personality spirit that was a bloodline, generational curse, (her mother had the same mental illness), which manifested in Sally after this traumatic event. She at times would change into a childlike personality. Her voice would also change into a child's and she exhibited childlike behavior. Keep in mind she was now a married woman with a family. This would cycle from time to time when things got out of hand or she became too stressed. She also had a generational alcoholic demon that worked with these other demons to keep her in bondage. We did cleansing, breaking the trauma curse, trauma bonds, and soul ties with her perpetrator.

I would describe a trauma bond as a loyalty to someone who is destructive in a relationship. It can be the result of ongoing cycles of abuse followed by the reinforcement of reward and punishment, bringing a double-minded conflict with the perpetrator. This creates demonic oppression of emotional bonds that are resistant to change without deliverance.

This sexual abuse didn't just happen one time but other times, and as a rejected little girl, Sally begins to feel like she was accepted and being loved by her family member. All of this was connected to this molested little girl spirit personality we called out of her, which was a fruit of this childhood trauma. One can also say Sally dissociated from her real self because of the pain of the traumatic experience and the enemy took advantage of her need to escape a horrible reality she was powerless to stop. He then sets up a demonic playground of bondage within her mind. This dissociation can open one to multiple spirit personalities. God created us with one mind. He said a double-minded man brings bondage and instability (James 1:8).

Sally did get freedom from asthma, the alter personality demon, a nest of bondage, and the spirit of alcoholism. Sally also had a generational structure of a bloodline, a reprobate mind curse working against her that needed to be dismantled. (Reprobate will be discussed in a later chapter.) Sometimes it is necessary and good to understand how demons enter a spiritual door so one can know what is needed to get them out. One could say that Jesus did pre-deliverance counseling. We read many times He asked questions concerning those in bondage to demons. If Jesus is our perfect model, we can do as He did and follow His example to victory.

There was another young woman we will call Sasha. Sasha was raised by a single mother who was an addict and very dysfunctional. Sasha had gotten into gangs with all the violence, cutting, homosexuality, drugs, and alcohol at a young age and went through much sexual abuse. She was another one who was traumatized by a life of gang violence. She had a bloodline generational stronghold of mental illness with a multiple personality altar spirit from the gang life that set up within her. It was very manipulative and controlling. It had a homosexual spirit attached to it and she struggled with sexual purity and holiness even after being filled with Holy Spirit and working in her gifts within the church. This personality spirit was hidden for some time until the Lord Jesus said it was time to deal with it. It was affecting her personal relationships and was out to destroy her witness. This personality had a name, which was her gang name. Sasha needed deep healing to the inner child and teen and deliverance from the demons who were trafficking her through her past life.

In one of her sessions, Holy Spirit spoke to me and said, *"silly woman curse."* I knew this to be spoke of in 2 Timothy 3:6. This was an apostate curse on her bloodline that needed to be broken. I will discuss this more deeply in a later chapter. Both bloodline reprobate and apostate curses were present within her. Jesus, true to His nature is faithful to finish the work that He begins in us. Needless to say, Sasha received freedom from this bondage and is growing in great grace in the kingdom, another one snatched by the hand of God and now working for Him!

When ministering to those who have trauma, I found that many who come out of cleansing and begin their positive journey to a new normal life may experience a low level of anxiety due to the loss of the rush of release of internal morphine called endorphins. Flashes of spirit images of trauma and constant conflict triggered this rush. An endorphin is defined as any of a group of peptides occurring in the brain and other tissues of vertebrates, and resembling opiates, that react with the brain's opiate receptors to raise the pain threshold. The principal function of endorphins is to inhibit the transmission of pain signals. They produce a feeling of euphoria very similar to that produced by other opioids. They are naturally produced in response to pain, but they can be triggered by various human activities, including trauma. We must release healing to the brain and ask the Lord to heal and restore the proper balance of chemicals in the body. This should be done to those coming off addictions and cigarette smoking also in which dopamine rush is increased by the nicotine addiction. That increase brings damage to the natural function and release of dopamine to the brain. The brain needs to be healed and restored to health. Jesus is a healer and He can restore all the organs to proper function as He created and intended them to be. This may take more than one prayer session. Pray until the complete healing manifests.

At times we will meet people who love to live in war and conflict. These people will stay in a place of turmoil or will even sabotage their own peace because the euphoria is gone. This is an indication that one has become addicted to the adrenaline rush. Sad as it is, they believe the lie that life is boring when there is peace. Believing that lie, and not being content in a life of peace, they are pulled them back into a cycle of chaos. If someone lives in constant confusion and drama even after cleansing, this should be considered a topic of discussion. There could also be an attention-seeking spirit or a spirit of arrested development at work. People are starved for love and acceptance today in such a dysfunctional society. Always try to direct them to Jesus and His unconditional love for them as you help them grow past their pain into new life. There is a chance one could become co-dependent on the counselor if not careful. Be reminded, one cannot counsel demons. A good counselor should discern demons present in the one they are counseling for cleansing, being careful not to allow demons to wear one out emotionally or spiritually.

In Mark 5, the story of the demoniac paints a similar picture of a severely tormented man whom Jesus set free and healed. The Word says the man was bound with chains and that he would cry out day and night among the tombs, beating and cutting himself, breaking the chains and no one could restrain him. When confronted by Jesus and asked what the demon's name was, it said Legion, because it was many.

The Greek word *memeion*, meaning grave, and its root word *mnemneuo*, meaning to remember, tell us that his memory was full of stored spirit images of torment, pain, death, and some traumatic natural experience. One could say he lived in the physical graveyard because he was living out a spiritual death in his soul. These traumatic spirit images will disrupt one's thoughts and keep one chained in pain. The nature of the experience, if it is sin, can manifest as a demonic oppression. The enemy will use these disruptions in one's soul to recall and reinforce the prison of pain, causing them to remain immersed and sealed in that experience, reliving it repeatedly until they find healing and freedom. Counseling will be needed with inner healing as well as deliverance of the supporting demonic spirits. Close follow-up these severe cases is essential.

This passage about the demoniac in Mark 5 reveals some things concerning trauma:

- It can be deep, tormenting pain that can be suppressed, causing outward manifestations of destructive behavior or mental oppression of sin cycles of bondage.
- It can be suppressed or forgotten, can still manifest, damaging fruit in one's emotions and physical health.
- It can bring bitter roots, producing unforgiveness and hatred towards oneself or others through soul ties or trauma bonds.
- It can manifest spirit images within the memory, keeping one living in the experience, unable to move forward.
- It can work with a nest (legion) of tormentors to try to destroy one's soul/body
- It can be the root cause to addictive behaviors, enforcing its death structure within
- It can be unhealed and be a root to sickness or disease if left untreated

When dealing with trauma, one needs to be healed from the inside out, in the place where the hurting child or painful experience is locked up. The root source of this death structure of trauma is deep within. The trauma bond (the strong emotional demonic attachment) between the abused and the abuser that was formed as the result of the cycle of violence needs to be broken. A good example of an unbroken trauma bound cycle is see in spousal abuse, when the abused partner continues to cycle back to their abuser. These soul ties must be broken and the spirits trafficking the union cast out. Concerning physical trauma, it may be necessary to check to see if inner healing in the soul is needed. If needed, the healing needs to take place first so physical healing can more easily be received.

I ministered to a deeply tormented man I will call Jon. When Jon was young, he was involved in drug trafficking and gang violence. He had been in and out of jail, physically and sexually abused, and extremely rejected as a boy. He raised himself on the streets and grew up at the mercy of who would take him in. He began using the drugs that he was trafficking. He did many things that opened him up to many demons. Jon was now born again but was struggling with PTSD, demonically tormented with many nightmares containing images of his horrendous crimes. He held all this inside for fear of the church rejecting him. His marriage was in trouble, and he feared he would slip into a rage and hurt his wife. Jon would wrap himself up in a sheet at night so not to hurt himself or his wife while he was being tormented by demons.

While mapping him out, there were many manifestations that would surface as we talked. Holy Spirit was with us as we walked through dismantling the lies of the enemy. He was full of guilt, shame, grief and hatred towards himself. He saw and participated in much darkness and the darkness was now trying to kill him. I heard Holy Spirit say he had a psychopath stronghold within him. I had never mapped anyone of this nature. The definition of psychopath is a person with a psychopathic personality that manifests with immoral and antisocial behavior, a lack of ability to love or establish meaningful personal relationships, extreme egocentricity, and failure to learn from experience. These personalities oftentimes display criminal behaviors, lacking a sense of moral responsibility or social conscience. This described his old life of sin and destruction.

As we counseled, others were in the building, which was wisdom. I felt the strongest presence of the love and shield of God around us. Jon would experience anxiety when the Lord allowed the spirit images to surface and I would assure him he was now a new creature in Christ and that the blood of Jesus washed his old life away! I would tell him that Jesus makes the vilest sinner clean. It can be a very draining experience to listen to the broken souls in their anguish of heart. It says in Leviticus 6:25–26, *"Speak to Aaron and his sons, saying, 'This is the law of sin offering: in the place where the burnt offering is slain the sin offering shall be slain before the Lord; it is most holy. The priest who offers it for sin shall eat it. It shall be eaten in a holy place, in the court of the tent of meeting."* It is important as a spirit-led counselor to stay filled up with Holy Spirit and maintain good soul health. They must stay spiritually strong and balanced with hearing all the painful stories of broken and bruised souls. It is the grace and the wisdom of the Lord that sustains them.

I had to research the characteristics of psychopathic behavior to understand the demonic influences attached to his life. I took good notes and made a list of characteristics as revealed by Holy Spirit. It was an intense battle, but Jesus is, as always, the Victor over darkness! Jon received the grace of Jesus to be set free from this structure.

You know a demon by its nature, how it makes you feel. In Jon's case, the nature (characteristics) of this personality disorder were examined, spiritually identified, and named. Those demons were cast out by name and freedom came. We cannot heal anyone without the supernatural power of God. We can counsel and help people with coping methods, so they can function, but getting them whole is what Jesus died and was raised to life for! Isaiah 53:4–5 says of Jesus, *"But He was pierced through for our transgressions, He was crushed for our iniquities; The chastening of our well-being fell upon Him, And by His scourging we are healed."* This promise was for Jon and he received what was his through the covenant he had with his Father. Glory!

If you find yourself a victim of an accident and in need of a physical healing, you may experience blocks or a delay in receiving that healing. It would be wise to discern if inner healing in the emotions from the shock and fear of the accident are needed. There may be a need to break the curse of the accident and cast out the spirit of trauma. Trauma goes through the entire being of a person and can at times block the physical healing because trauma is first spiritual and then natural/physical. Someone who experiences recurring accidents needs to pray against the curse of accidents.

If nothing is happening or moving in a session, and there is bloodline occult practice or participation of witchcraft in the persons spiritual history, those seals and ties may need to be broken to open spiritual doors for deliverance to occur. If a bitter or grief soul tie is in place, the spiritual door to get inside may be through the breaking of those ties. As deliverance starts to take place, continue with the inner healing and cleansing process. Many times in sessions we go in and out of inner healing and deliverance as led by Holy Spirit.

A traumatized person may need to identify *when* the negative feelings began in order to track the source. Unhealed trauma can be a root issue of addictions and can open one up to a victim mentality. I find people coming out of these relationships need a strong support system of love, encouragement, and accountability to stay free.

John 14:27 says, "Peace I leave with you; My peace I give to you; not as the world gives do I give to you. Do not let your heart be troubled, nor let it be fearful."

Spiritual victim mentality

The word victim is defined as one who is harmed by or made to suffer under a circumstance or condition; one who is tricked, swindled, or taken advantage of. Proverbs 23:7 says, *"for as he thinks in his heart, so is he"* (AMPC), meaning the place one finds themselves today is because of their thought process. How one views himself affects everything about him, as well as all the relationships around him. A spiritual victim will take on a mentality or death structure that will hinder them from entering into the fullness of their purpose. One who is victimized will need inner healing from the wrong suffered, and oftentimes need deliverance from the demonic oppression that took advantage of them in their circumstance. The definition of a victim is a person who suffers from destructive or injurious action or agency. Mentality means the set of one's mind, view or outlook. One with a victim mentality has a wrong way of thinking of oneself as a victim. It can begin when the soul is damaged by the lying roots of the seeds planted by the enemy through victimization. I call this a spiritual victim mentality and it will cause one to stay stuck in failure.

Some roots of the spiritual victim mentality:
- unforgiveness/bitter root judgments of the wrong suffered
- unhealed soul wounds of past abuse/trauma
- a wrong response to bad circumstances
- negative mindset which results in negative confession
- negative word curses/lies received that were spoken against you

- a wrong perception of the Father/always thinking He is a punisher
- false identity with the sickness/attention-seeking spirit

A person with a spiritual victim mentality will have a negative self-image and will be unable to see himself or herself as the Father sees them. Their decisions will be based on wrong assumptions, which are coming out of the resource center the enemy has built. These wrong perceptions will cause more pain and failure to come. Pain and repeated failures will reinforce the death structure, causing the person to believe they will always be a victim. One will feel powerless, trapped and believe there's no way out and the cycles will be repeated.

An extreme spiritual victim will believe they are being punished and deserve to be victimized, believing life has not treated them fairly. One with this mentality will be easily angered and carry an offended spirit, blaming others for problems and failures and will be unable to take responsibility. This can bring in a spirit of entitlement due to past suffering. As one continues in this way of thinking, they will continue to look back into past pain and be unable to move forward. One will be stuck living in that old man because of the unforgiveness. Living in the past, one will take no risk. This becomes an escape from new challenges or new levels of faith, keeping one enjoying the false comfort of self-pity bondage.

A spiritual victim's focus is inward. They are takers and not givers. Self-pity is connected to this structure and is most destructive. It gives momentary pleasure to self and separates one from reality. The spiritual victim creates their own reality within a false world in their own mind. One will have little or no control over one's life, and believe life revolves around them, making one a prisoner of sadness and often depression. This can become deeper and in time could bring suicidal tendencies. One living like this will never reach their potential or walk in their purpose, as self becomes an idol/god.

Also, in the extreme, a victim who doesn't get healed can become a narcissist. Narcissism is an inordinate fascination with oneself, excessive self-love and vanity. One will be self-centered and operate in egocentrism. We ministered to a man who was victimized with abuse as a child. He was married and had continual marriage issues, but it seemed everything evolved around him. Both needed healing, but this was a spiritual root in him that was blocking the victory in the whole family. We did a session and broke the curse of narcissism off him and cast the spirit out of him along with the demonic network that was connected to it. He was set free and then later he could see much clearer and recognize things were not as they appeared. He now had greater patience and grace to love his family the way he and knew he was supposed to.

A perpetrator spirit will hook up with a victim spirit. A perpetrator is one who is responsible for or commits a crime. It's a spirit that knows how to play on one's weakness and confirm one's worst feelings, which reinforced the lies the victim believes to be reality. They understand this because they were once victims themselves. Unhealed victims often become the perpetrator. When one chooses not to forgive, one can become what one hates. There can be co-dependent behavior due to demonic soul ties or trauma bonds with one's abusers or the one that they abused if they are the perpetrator. These ties need to be broken and cleansed.

To become free from the spiritual victim mentality, one must give up the unrealistic, lying benefits of being victim:
- self-justification of bitterness
- attention-seeking behavior
- self-absorbed living
- life without any risk
- entitlement spirit

Self must come off the throne and Jesus must be allowed in His rightful place as the Lord of one's life. It tells us in Ephesians 4:23, *"and that you be renewed in the spirit of your mind,"* meaning, there must be a transformation in one's mindset which comes through a renewing by the Word of God. This will keep one from going back into familiar negative behavior. Romans 12:2 says, *"And be not conformed to this world: but be ye transformed by the renewing of your mind, that ye may prove what is that good, and acceptable, and perfect, will of God"* (KJV). A victim can never know the will of God for their life until revelation comes.

The spirit of familiarity can cause a victim to resist the new identity God has for them. Spiritual newness is not always comfortable to one's flesh. The flesh will always war with the Spirit when God desires to change us into His image. Jesus taught this in Luke 5:37–39, *"And no one puts new wine into old wineskins; otherwise the new wine will burst the skins and it will be spilled out, and the skins will be ruined. But new wine must be put into fresh wineskins. And no one, after drinking old wine wishes for new; for he says, 'The old is good enough.'"* One's spiritual palate can be accustomed to bondage and stay in false comfort and complacency while continually resisting what God has for them. One must continue in the new the Lord has offered, and eventually it will begin to taste good and one will desire it even more!

Paul said he disciplined his body (flesh) and made it his slave (1 Cor. 9:27). He writes in Romans 8:5, *"For those who are according to the flesh set their minds on the things of the flesh, but those who are according to the Spirit, the things of the Spirit."* He further explains that the mind set on the flesh is death, but the mind set on the Spirit is life and peace, because the mind of the flesh is hostile toward God. Because the mind of the flesh is hostile toward God, it will require a disciplined effort to set one's heart to come out of bondage to any kind of wrong thinking or wrong behavior. The grace of God will empower one to walk it out according to the truth which Paul writes, *"For I am confident of this very thing, that He who began a good work in you will perfect it until the day of Christ Jesus"* (Phil. 1:6).

Jesus Christ has plundered the strong man and has defeated everything that kept one's mind chained in lies. The road to wholeness is different for everyone, as is everyone's bondage. It says in Deuteronomy 7:22–23, *"The Lord Your God will clear away these nations before you little by little; you will not be able to put an end to them quickly, for the wild beasts would grow too numerous for you. But the Lord your God will deliver them before you and will throw them into great confusion until they are destroyed."* This is the process of spiritual muscle development through personal spiritual warfare. It is time for those who have been wounded to live in victory over this spiritual victim mentality. It is time now to change the negative thinking to positive action! It begins here in Philippians 4:8, *"Finally, brethren, whatsoever things are true, whatsoever things are honest, whatsoever things are just, whatsoever things are pure, whatsoever things are lovely, whatsoever things are of good report; if there be any virtue, and if there be any praise, think on these things"* (KJV).

CHAPTER 6

REPROBATE AND WHOREDOM STRONGHOLD

"And even as they did not like to retain God in their knowledge, God gave them over to a reprobate mind, to do those things which are not convenient"
Romans 1:28 (KJV)

Reprobate society

THE LORD HAS RELEASED REVELATION concerning the bloodline reprobate death structure. This revelation that helped many be set free from this root of bondage in their generations. It all started when I was ministering to a young lady a few years ago we will call Jody. Jody was in and out of homosexual activity and relationships throughout her teen and adult life. Jody was first molested as a young girl by an aunt. Multiple episode of dysfunctional sexual activity followed. This caused this evil structure of reprobate to set up within her. Jody was now a spirit-filled believer and loved the Lord, but even then the struggle with this reprobate homosexual spirit was strong in her mind. In one of her sessions, I heard Holy Spirit say to break the curse of reprobate off her mind.

So, I obeyed Holy Spirit and broke the curse of reprobate, calling it out. As I did, it immediately speaks out of her and says, "I am strong in her." I believe the Lord allows these manifestations, so He could teach us some things. Anytime demons get vocal, there is usually a lesson involved. Of course, the Lord Jesus already broke the reprobate curse and stronghold when He defeated it on the cross. It declared how strong it was, but Jesus, we know, is the Stronger man, and it had to bow to Him. I went to Romans, chapter one, and I began to read the scripture concerning this revelation. It reads as follows:

"For the wrath of God is revealed from heaven against all ungodliness and unrighteousness of men who suppress the truth in unrighteousness, because that which is known about God is evident within them; for God made it evident to them. For since the creation of the world His invisible attributes, His eternal power and divine nature, have been clearly seen, being understood through what has been made, so that they are without excuse. For even though they knew God, they did not honor Him as God or give thanks, but they became futile in their speculations, and their foolish heart was darkened. Professing to be wise, they became fools, and exchanged the glory of the incorruptible God for an image in the form of corruptible man and of birds and four-footed animals and crawling creatures. Therefore God gave them over in the lusts of their hearts to impurity, so that their bodies would be dishonored among them. For they exchanged the truth of God for a lie, and worshiped and served the creature rather than the Creator, who is blessed forever. Amen. For this reason God gave them over to degrading passions; for their women exchanged the natural function for that which is unnatural, and in the same way also the men abandoned the natural function of the woman and burned in their desire toward one another, men with men committing indecent acts and receiving in their own persons the due penalty of their error. And just as they did not see fit to acknowledge God any longer, God gave them over to a depraved mind, (reprobated) to do those things which are not proper, being filled with all unrighteousness, wickedness, greed, evil; full of envy, murder, strife, deceit, malice; they are gossips, slanderers, haters of God, insolent,

arrogant, boastful, inventors of evil, disobedient to parents, without understanding, untrustworthy, unloving, unmerciful; and although they know the ordinance of God, that those who practice such things are worthy of death, they not only do the same, but also give hearty approval to those who practice them."

I began to pray according to the scripture and call out every reprobate demon of this death structure that was in Jody's bloodline. As you can read, it is a curse of idolatry, and that it says that after they are turned over, they are filled with other things. In verses 28–31: *"And just as they did not see fit to acknowledge God any longer, God gave them over to a depraved mind, (reprobated) to do those things which are not proper, being filled with all* **unrighteousness, wickedness, greed, evil; full of envy, murder, strife, deceit, malice; they are gossips, slanderers, haters of God, insolent, arrogant, boastful, inventors of evil, disobedient to parents, without understanding, untrustworthy, unloving, unmerciful."**

These other things are demonic spirits, meaning the door of rebellion was wide open for other demons to enter. This was a nest of demons within her bloodline because it was a generational stronghold. I find most of these bloodline curses of idolatry are generational, at this point of strength and activity. That is why it said it was strong in her. Many in her family had idolatry with drug addictions, whoredoms and the like and this was passed down to her. This stronghold can be connected to all whoredom and idolatry practices, such as false religions, occults, drug addictions, alcoholism, or even backslidings. It says in verse 21, *"that they knew God, but they did not honor Him as God or give thanks, but they became futile in their speculations, and their foolish heart was darkened."*

This is a bold statement, but I believe that the whole body of Christ needs repentance and cleansing from this stronghold within each personal bloodline. I believe it can pull our children into idolatry, and if you look at society today, we see much idolatry. We do corporate cleansing on this stronghold and find it is hiding within many. Anyone coming out of homosexuality, any bondage of addictions or idol worship needs this cleansing. Many cycle back into their sin behavior because the reprobate curse was not dealt with.

It is still hiding within one's mind and operating freely. Demons always try to pull one back into sin cycles. Cleansing from this stronghold many times comes in layers. We are always to be led by Holy Spirit.

The Greek word reprobate is *adokimos* meaning unapproved, rejected, worthless, or castaway. In Romans chapter one, it describes the condition of humanity that causes them to be rejected by God. It states the consequences of idolatry and all the immoral sins that come with it. The root issue of this whoredom stronghold is idolatry, which are bloodline iniquities. Anytime we see idolatry there will be sexual immorality. God is love and will always love people, but He cannot condone idolatry. God doesn't make someone become reprobated. Their sin behavior causes this destructive structure to set up within the heart. He gave them up to, or gave them over to, meaning He granted them what their hearts lusted after. I believe conviction lifts off and the mind in that area is seared and has no desire to change. The spirit of perversion cannot be satisfied and will continue to take people into deeper acts of perversion. It will work throughout the entire man as it spreads.

Some believers may initially have wrestled with this behavior, desiring to be in line with God's word, but because there was no teaching of truth, and no cleansing or deliverance power available in one's life, many lost the battle and continued to sin. God will allow them to be released to their own desires and passions, but His love for them doesn't change! The enemy, because of the open door of sin rewards them with more darkness and demonic oppression. I have found that the cleansing of one's bloodline must be done, especially in homosexuality. Today, Jody is completely set free today from this curse, the mind battles, activity and warfare within her soul. Glory to Jesus who does a complete work! This is an area of cleansing we do on most everyone who comes in for bloodline cleansing.

Here is the downward spiral to a reprobate mind according to scripture:

- the person knows, or has known God but rejects God (verses 18–22)
- they exchange the glory for idols (verses 21–22)

- they exchange truth for believing lies of the enemy (verses 24–25)
- they embrace and practice sexual perversion (verse 26–27)
- they are released by God to their heart's desire and evil passions (verse 28)
- demonic destruction comes into a society, bringing pain, suffering and destruction to it and defilement to the land

In Hosea, chapter four, it reads, *"Hear the word of the Lord, you children of Israel, for the Lord has a controversy (a pleading contention) with the inhabitants of the land, because there is no faithfulness, love, pity* and *mercy, or knowledge of God [from personal experience with Him] in the land. There is nothing but [false] swearing and breaking faith and killing and stealing and committing adultery; they break out [into violence], one [deed of] bloodshed following close on another. Therefore shall the land [continually] mourn, and all who dwell in it shall languish, together with the wild beasts of the open country and the birds of the heavens; yes, the fishes of the sea also shall [perish because of the drought] be collected* and *taken away. Yet let no man strive, neither let any man reprove [another—do not waste your time in mutual recriminations], for with you is My contention, O priest. And you shall stumble in the daytime, and the [false] prophet also shall stumble with you in the night; and I will destroy your mother [the priestly nation]. My people are destroyed for lack of knowledge; because you [the priestly nation] have rejected knowledge, I will also reject you that you shall be no priest to Me; seeing you have forgotten the law of your God, I will also forget your children"* (AMPC).

We understand that the bloodline reprobate curse is connected to the whoredom stronghold, and there is always an idolatry problem when there is sexual immorality. In Hosea, chapter four, it warns us that the curse of whoredom/harlotry will cause them to be unable to return to God. It says when that spirit is operating in them, they do not know God. They become their own gods as they violate God's laws. It speaks of destruction coming upon them and chastisement from God. It speaks of hypocrisy in churches and people perishing for lack of knowledge. There is a downward spiral when whoredom begins to reign in the hearts of people. It will affect the health of the land and the people. In chapter four of Hosea, it sounds very similar to the reprobate stronghold. In chapter five, it says their deeds will not allow them to return to their God, that a spirit of harlotry is within them and they do not know the Lord. Thus, we see that there is a reprobated mind curse in place keeping them in generational bondage.

This reprobate stronghold can be connected to
- apostasy
- whoredom/idolatry practices
- homosexuality
- false religions/teaching
- witchcraft
- drug addictions
- alcoholism
- backslidings/spiritual adultery

We see, because of the darkness, that we are in the last days before Christ returns. It is a dark hour, but there is a promise of greater glory for the remnant of God. There is a downward spiral when whoredom begins to reign in the hearts of people. It affects the land by bringing curses on it. All creation is groaning and desiring the righteousness of the Lord to come alive in the land. A nation does not get to destruction overnight; it is a process of looking the other way and compromising Truth. Maybe you have been guilty in the past of being distracted and not discerning times and seasons of the Lord, but not anymore! In this season we are in, I believe the righteous remnant is awakening and walking in revelation of their authority. The keys are given to those who understand their authority. The downward spiral of reprobate is being broken and many are coming out of bondage. Where sin abounds, grace does much more abound, in Jesus' name.

Below is a list of sexual bondage spirits and some will be discussed in greater detail within this chapter. Note that all whoredoms are connected to the reprobate stronghold.

Common whoredom sexual unclean spirits/practices:

- adultery (voluntary sexual intercourse between a married person and someone other than a lawful spouse)
- fornication (voluntary sexual intercourse between two unmarried persons)
- homosexuality (of or pertaining to sexual relations of the same sex)
- sodomy (anal sex)
- oral sex (sexual contact between mouth and genitals)
- pornography (sexual explicit videos, photographs or writings for sexual arousal)
- masturbation (sexual self-gratification)
- bestiality (sexual relations between a person and animal; sodomy)
- exhibitionism (the compulsion to exhibit genitals in public)
- sadomasochism (sexual gratification gained through inflicting or receiving pain)
- molestation (assaulting sexually, making sexual advances)
- rape (any unlawful sexual intercourse without the consent of the victim)
- incubus (male type sexual tormenting demon)
- succubus (female/animal type sexual tormenting demon)

Homosexuality

The word homosexuality appears in the New Testament with the word *porneia* or immorality (Gal. 5:19, 1 Cor. 5:1, Eph. 5:3, Col. 3:5). Homosexuality is a demon spirit that denotes uncleanness, impurity, and filthiness in a moral sense. It covers a wide variety of sexual practices and is condemned like all the other sin practices. It is a stronghold that produces much pain and suffering in humanity. It is very destructive, carrying curses of sicknesses and diseases. Homosexuality, as well as adultery and fornication, were widespread in the Old Testament and in the New Testament church. Sadly, is very active in much of the church today. Much of the present-day culture views sexual immorality as the norm, and desires everyone to accept and adapt to this view. God will not change His thoughts toward sexual purity. The church has abandoned sexual holiness according to Truth, and the curses of idolatry will remain within the church, bringing personal defeat and destruction within the body. This will continue until there is repentance, cleansing, deliverance, and a return to righteousness.

The word "homo" means alike or equal to. I found that everyone who we have ministered to with a spirit of homosexuality has had root issues that needed to be healed and the spirits attached uprooted out of their life. They can and do get delivered and walk in wholeness in a normal, happy heterosexual lifestyle. Man was not created to be a homosexual, murderer, drunkard, a thief, or any other thing contrary to the Father's design. They were created with purpose to be a part of God's blessed family. People can have an identity crisis because of deception. The enemy works diligently to reinforce the deception by taking advantage of the open door. The enemy is always trying to destroy humanity. It becomes easy for him to do so as we cooperate with him by replacing the once safe boundaries of God's word for our own. Homosexuality cannot reproduce life, natural or spiritual. The Lord told male and female to replenish and multiply in the earth from the very beginning.

We have ministered love and grace to many who have desired to be free from this death structure, and the Lord was faithful to do just that. I have found that a homosexual spirit can come in through many different doors, which are listed below.

Homosexual doors of entry:
- generational bloodline reprobate curses from the womb
- rape or molestation from the same sex in which the spirit transfers, bringing confusion of sexuality
- unhealed soul wounds or rape from the opposite sex, causing one to change sexual preference
- through moral depravity or sexual looseness
- pornography
- occult practices
- rejection of sexuality as a child from the parent
- sodomy in a marriage
- fornication soul ties
- curiosity through peer pressure/relationship

Homosexuality has a reprobate bloodline curse attached as I have explained earlier. In the condition of a person's soul, it can be a process of healing and wholeness. But the Lord does heal the broken and He frees those in bondage, doing a perfect work. His love is beyond our earthly comprehension, but it is eternal and full of power to restore humanity. John 3:17 says, *"For God did not send the Son into the world to judge the world, but that the world might be saved through Him."*

We ministered to a young man who was very gifted and grew up in the church. We will call him Larry. His family was strong in ministry and so was he. He was another soul that battled a secret homosexual lifestyle and was upset with God for not freeing him. He was doing all he knew to do but to no avail. He heard of Spiritual Cleansing and came to see, if he could find freedom through this ministry. He had sat through his spiritual mapping and counseling. He had been molested as a little boy and always felt rejected by his father. He had no healthy father-son bonding. This rejection reinforced the confusion of his sexual gender, and he was now an adult with a long history of pain from the rejection and confusion. The whoredom and bloodline reprobate death structures were in operation while he was involved in a ministry. He battled this secret life of shame. He was so full of condemnation, and the long battle caused unbelief. The enemy was telling him he would never be free. He was brought up in traditional beliefs that a reprobate person would go to hell without any hope of repentance. He felt condemned by God and unloved, deserving punishment. Thank God that the love of Jesus is stronger than religious spirits! Larry had to get freedom from the stronghold of reprobate before lasting freedom came. He had told us, even in his sin bondage, he always wanted to do right, that he wanted a wife and children, a normal family. It is through the power of deliverance and cleansing of the bloodline that people can find freedom and restoration to their foundation. The Lord has given us keys to His kingdom, telling us in Isaiah 61:4 that, *"Then they will rebuild the ancient ruins, they will raise up the former devastations; and they will repair the ruined cities, the desolations of many generations."* We must continue to release those who are in prison, and repair and restore the generations using the weapons He has given us!

In Galatians 5, the Word speaks of the "workings of the flesh" and uses the word "*immorality*" which is the Greek word *akatharsia*, meaning impurity, uncleanness. It appears again with the word *pornia*, meaning immorality, and we know it is the English word we use for pornography. This word covers a wide variety of impure sexual practices. It is the same root word for idolatry and fornication. It means filthiness and unclean. The word says to flee fornication; it causes us to sin against our own bodies, inviting sickness and disease, and defiles God's temple. When people turn their hearts to other gods, sexual immorality will come in.

It is very important that one has a strong support system and breaks away from soul ties of past relationships when coming out of sexual immorality practices. We have found when one wants to stay free, Jesus will keep you free. We ministered to a man we will call Gene, who received much cleansing from homosexuality, so much so that even his voice, print, mannerisms, and taste in clothing was different. He had a notable identity change. The longer this spirit is in place, the stronger the manifestations can be, either effeminate with a male or masculine with a female. We call out spirits of the homosexual death structure with confusion of sexuality, rejection of sexuality, the effeminate or masculine spirit and command a release from their voice, emotions and will. For a long time Gene did well, and then I noticed he had begun to hang out again with his old associations who were practicing homosexuals. He told me that he believed he could pull them his direction towards the Lord. These men, however, had no desire for change, and sadly, instead of Gene pulling them toward the Lord, he began to slowly slip back into some old behaviors. He eventually was pulled back into the practice, opening sin doors again, although he was once cleansed and delivered of reprobate. It was his choice to be disobedient to the word and reconnect to old relationships without any accountability to any spiritual authority. I still pray for him today to be set free and walk in the truth of whom he really is. One must hate their chains to be set free, and hate the sin activity that got them chained, to maintain personal freedom.

A very young girl asked me at a cleansing conference if "homo-romanticizing" was wrong. She was very innocent in her question and thought it would be okay because she wasn't doing the act of homosexuality. I had to explain that Jesus warned us not to lust in our heart, that He knew if we thought it, we would surely do it. It was no different than pornography. Pornography has spirit images that get lodged in the imagination. This fantasy is not uncommon with the media and television shows that project images to desensitize our kids to believe it is normal behavior. The eyes are the windows to the soul. We have a responsibility to teach the truth at home and guard them from the deception that is in the airways. Parents must become the example of a living God and be the guardian of their seed; they are not to be a friend but a parent. I find the same demons that torment the parents will torment the children.

Reprobate working with apostasy

We should not be surprised at the boldness of Satan in this hour when a society embraces lawlessness and rebellion against the Word of God. The discerning between good and evil must be done through Holy Spirit and the Word of God. I have been directed to put a chapter on discerning of spirits in this book to bring more understanding of this spiritual weapon. There is a warning throughout the Word of God against mixing the holy with the profane and the consequences that will follow. When the people of God begin to compromise truth and not love and embrace it, a spirit of delusion comes, and it will open them up to a spirit of error that works the curse of apostasy.

The word apostate means a betrayer, a renouncer or double-crosser. The Lord says we will be known by the fruit that we produce, meaning our actions in life tell all. The things we love and embrace must line up with the kingdom. In 2 Thessalonians, chapter two, it speaks of apostasy, the man of lawlessness and the Antichrist spirit. It speaks of the abomination taking his seat in the temple. I believe spiritually when homosexual marriage was acknowledged as a legal marriage in our nation, this spirit did just that and took its seat across the nation in every church sanctuary that allowed these marriage ceremonies and practices, standing very prideful declaring it is God. One must not compromise Truth for the cultural norm, taking pleasure in unrighteousness, which means I cannot partake of both evil and good. The power of God has been limited due to the compromise, which produces weak believers with no power who are unable to stand against their enemy.

"Let no one in any way deceive you, for it will not come unless the apostasy comes first, and the man of lawlessness is revealed, the son of destruction, who opposes and exalts himself above every so-called god or object of worship, so that he takes his seat in the temple of God, displaying himself as being God. Do you not remember that while I was still with you, I was telling you these things? And you know what restrains him now, so that in his time he will be revealed. For the mystery of lawlessness is already at work; only he who now restrains will do so until he is taken out of the way. Then that lawless one will be revealed whom the Lord will slay with the breath of His mouth and bring to an end by the appearance of His coming; that is, the one whose coming is in accord with the activity of Satan, with all power and signs and false wonders, and with all the deception of wickedness for those who perish, because they did not receive the love of the truth so as to be saved. For this reason God will send upon them a deluding influence so that they will believe what is false, in order that they all may be judged who did not believe the truth, but took pleasure in wickedness" (2 Thess. 2:3–12).

Titus 1:16 says, *"They profess that they know God, but in works they deny Him, being abominable, and disobedient, and unto every good work reprobate"* (KJV). We cannot make a holy God become like us. We are to become like Him, a lover of Truth. We must examine ourselves and line up with righteous living. Paul says in 1 Corinthians 4:2, *"Moreover; it is [essentially] required of stewards that a man should be found faithful [proving himself worthy of trust]."* Verse 4 says, *"I am not conscious of anything against myself, and I feel blameless; but I am not vindicated and acquitted before God on that account. It is the Lord [Himself] Who examines and judges me"* (AMPC).

Demonic traffic in marriage

Whoredom spirits desire to traffic marriages. The enemy hates the marriage covenant and he is always looking for a way to enter to destroy the union that God called blessed. As we stated earlier, in Genesis 2:23–25, it reads, *"The man said, 'This is now bone of my bones, and flesh of my flesh; She shall be called Woman, because she was taken out of man.' For this reason, a man shall leave his father and his mother, and be joined to his wife; and they shall become one flesh. And the man and his wife were both naked and were not ashamed."* The sanctity of marriage has been under attack and we must see a shift of godly kingdom examples of marriage that God desires for His church. The generation coming up must see the marriage model God intended restored and blessed. Notice in the first union there was no shame in nakedness, a transparency without any fear, a perfect love. Many marriages have been shattered, fractured, and broken by the sin damage that has occurred and not been restored. Demons will traffic the marriage and cause continual suffering until the couple becomes so worn out that they give in and break the union. The lies the demons speak are often half-truths of despair and disappointment filtered through a rejected, hurt soul. Hebrews 13:4 says, *"Marriage is to be held in honor among all, and the marriage bed is to be undefiled; for fornicators and adulterers God will judge."* The Lord Jesus is more than able to restore marriages from the pain of fornication and adultery. There is a healing and forgiveness in Christ that is available to broken marriages.

Many have opened the door to sexual immorality with pornography and other bondages that have brought defilement into the covenant. In cleansing, we have cast out many unclean sexual spirits that were called out by the name of the behavior. Meaning people were in bondage (slavery) to the behaviors of the demonic uncleanness in marriage or fornication relationships. These spirits fall under the whoredom stronghold, many of which are bloodline curses.

There are often old soul ties that are still in place from former relationships that will open doors to demons. Sexual intimacy and emotional intimacy can create soul ties to the one you gave your soul to. Any intimate spiritual union outside of a marriage covenant creates curses of adultery or illegal marriages. Sexual relationship is an emotional, physical, and spiritual linking to the one you gave yourself to. It works in the whole being to bring life or death to one's soul. It says in 1 Corinthians 6:18, *"Flee immorality. Every other sin that a man commits is outside the body, but the immoral man sins against his own body,"* meaning this sin against their own body is defiling it and opening one's body to curses of sickness and infirmity. Many curses are in the sexual organs where the demons are lodged. We also see demonic traffic of sickness and disease because of the marriage union. This means whatever is in one can traffic the other because they are one. An example of this could be when one spouse manifests the same mental disorder as the other, with no known generational history of that illness in their bloodline.

Fornication and pornography

Fornication is the Greek word *pornia*, meaning harlotry, adultery, incest, unlawful lust of either sex; to practice idolatry. It covers sexual sin practices that many have fallen prey to when pure sexual boundaries are not kept. The word is clear on sexual purity; the marriage bed is to be held in honor. *Pornia,* as stated earlier, is the word we get pornography from, which opens the mind to spirit images of pornography and defiles hearts even within marriage. Jesus warned in Matthew 5:28 that, *"everyone who looks at a woman with lust for her has already committed adultery with her in his heart."* Pornography will bring in shame, insecurities, perversion, and more bondage. It also opens the door for the acts of seducing and adultery spirits to work.

If one spouse is involved in pornography and the other is not, the same unclean seduction that is working through the pornography will have a place to traffic the other causing them to have feelings of uncleanness. The traffic of these spirits can even seduce the other into the act of adultery. The spiritual union is an entry point to one another, because the two are one flesh. When one's conscious feels condemned, that is a good indicator that the enemy is at work. These sexual demons will bring shame and defilement that hinder true intimacy, not only in the marriage, but also one's personal intimacy in relationship to Jesus. If pornography is watched secretly, the other spouse can still feel unclean during and after intimacy. Many spirits of masturbation and unclean spirits can enter into those who have opened themselves to sexual impurity. Masturbation or auto-sexuality steals the intimacy that was supposed to be for one's spouse and gives it to demons. This is a very addictive behavior, as those unclean spirits reside within the sexual organs, constantly pulling one into temptation. We cast many spirits out of the sexual organs and out of the womb of women.

Adultery spirit

The spirit of adultery has no gender and is a spirit of witchcraft, mind control that hunts and steals the soul of a person. In Proverbs 6:26, it says, *"For on account of a harlot one is reduced to a loaf of bread, and an adulteress hunts for the precious life* (soul)." The spirit of whoredom works with reprobate bloodline curse and poverty curse. Proverbs 7:21 says, *"With her many persuasions she entices him; With her flattering lips she seduces him."* It is a perpetrator demon and hunts for its victims. It is a demonic network that has a system of deception, with an assignment of evil to work against its victim and God's established marriage covenant. It can operate as a generational curse of covenant breaking that continues to cycle through bloodlines in the generations. James 1:14–15 says, *"But each one is tempted when he is carried away and enticed by his own lust. Then when lust has conceived, it gives birth to sin; and when sin is accomplished, it brings forth death."* It can come in through perversion and lust by influence or curiosity. It is a rebellious spirit, full of pride, and will often justify its behavior. It brings much demonic bondage and soul ties that one will need to be delivered from.

An adultery spirit can seduce when one spouse feels unfulfilled within a marriage. The deception comes in the mind through a door of a lie. The lie is that there is no healing available within the marriage for one's loneliness or emptiness. It can be very convincing as it appeals to one's flesh in flattery and false comfort, and it presents a way of escape from one's sad reality. Adultery cannot fulfill anyone; it only steals from its victim. Be wise and understand when a after demon uses your body for their pleasure, they bring guilt, shame, condemnation, infirmities and more added pain to the suffering you're trying to escape. It will seek to punish one in their failure and steal any hope of restoration in one's marriage.

Fornication and adultery are seducing spirits that can also be a bloodline generational curse of idolatry. Proverbs 6:32 says, *"whoever commits adultery with a woman lacks understanding; He who does so destroys his own soul"* (NKJV). Notice the lack of understanding. This is an evil spiritual assignment! I find that most people usually do not plan to fall into this temptation or even desire to hurt their spouse. It is a seducing deception, a working of witchcraft, and mind control that will seduce one to bring destruction to the marriage covenant. If a spouse has unhealed soul wounds and is looking for their mate to heal them and they are not receiving the healing and wholeness they desire and believe should come from their mate, the enemy will deceive them into thinking someone else has what they need. The enemy will send someone their way to make them stumble. Understand that the enemy is not all-knowing, but he does watch for ways in which to tempt us to fall. Jesus, the healer of our soul is the only one who can bind up the brokenhearted. The healing and wholeness that they seek can only come from the Lord! Many put too much pressure on the spouse to be to them what only God can be to them! Spouses are a gift from the Lord to enjoy a oneness and covenant relationship of blessing in the Lord. We must demonstrate this blessing to the next generation. Some statistics say approximately 40 to 50% of marriages end in divorce. Some conclude it is higher within the church than in the world. These spirits are behind the covenant breaking. When there is infidelity within the church, Jezebel is working her witchcraft. We will discuss her in a later chapter.

Demons will and do communicate information they have learned concerning your life. In the spirit realm, nothing is hidden. They know your weaknesses by your words and your behavior, and what will cause you to fail in your weaknesses. Demons will try the same strategy they used on your ancestors. Do not let flattery overtake you and be diligent to keep your heart free of unforgiveness toward your spouse. Be wise and cast down all negative seed thoughts concerning your spouse and marriage. This spirit of offense will open your heart for darkness to send harassing thoughts to you concerning your spouse. When we hold unforgiveness towards our spouse, we are holding them in that sin they committed, and they will continue to cycle in it. One cannot pray effectively for their spouse to be set free if you have not forgiven. 1 Peter 3:7 says, *"You husbands in the same way, live with your wives in an understanding way, as with someone weaker, since she is a woman; and show her honor as a fellow heir of the grace of life, so that your prayers will not be hindered."* Unforgiveness blocks anyone, husband or wife, from getting prayers answered.

In a marriage covenant, one must always allow the Potter to break the mold of past seasons and place you back on His wheel to reshape you. Seasons in marriage change and so do people. Marriage is a love relationship that can only thrive within the boundaries of Love. God is Love. The only one that is unchangeable in the marriage union is the Lord. As the years pass, we must decrease so He can increase in our marriages. If we do not become self-less, we will not be able to maintain healthy marriages. The union of marriage must be based on an internal love and commitment just as our relationship with the Lord. The loving Potter will reshape us on His wheel into His purpose for our marriage as often as is needed. All should do a spiritual housecleaning on your marriage, ridding it of the influence of the world. After it has been cleansed follow up by guarding what is precious to you and the Lord. Repent and release forgiveness for the traffic that has been allowed. Allow the Lord to release His love and grace into the covenant relationship.

Romans 12 says, *"Be affectionately kindly to one another with brotherly love, in honor giving preference to one another; not lagging in diligence, fervent in spirit, serving the Lord; rejoicing in hope, patient in tribulation, continuing steadfastly in prayer; distributing to the needs of the saints, given to hospitality. Be of the same mind toward one another, humble, and live at peace together, not repaying evil for evil."* This principle needs to be applied to all relationships, including marriage. It's never too late to begin again. May the grace of God fill every marriage and renew them again to the original plan and purpose for each union! We have been a witness as He continues to heal marriages through forgiveness and cleansing, bringing restoration and hope to many.

The joining of soul ties

The term soul/heart (psyche) pertains to the mind, will, and emotions. The term tie means to knit or bind together. After an intimate sexual relationship occurs, there is a binding together of the souls/hearts. Soul tie together is a term we use to describe when areas of our soul get yoked to another through sinful and/or intimate relationships. Soul ties will lock us into captivity or bondage to whomever we gave our soul, or it can bind us to a healthy relationship, which are godly covenants, life-giving bonds.

The one we have soul-ties with can have influence in or over us. In Genesis 2:24, it states, *"For this reason a man shall leave his father and his mother and be joined to his wife; and they shall become one flesh."* Jesus again quotes this in Matthew 19:6. The Greek word for being *joined* in marriage is *suzeugnumi,* meaning to be yoked together, joined together. The root word is *sun,* which can mean union, companionship, resemblance, possession, addition, and completeness. It is a spiritual union of meshing together, creating a tie or bonding. The breaking of soul ties and the calling out of the spirit of the other person would be described best as calling out the influence, nature, and spiritual part of the other person to whom the one being delivered was joined. It is very real, and many need soul ties broken from people they were joined to through fornication, adultery, divorce and other sins. The Hebrew word clave used in Genesis after Hamon defiled Dinah is *dabaq,* meaning to be joined or stuck. Genesis 34:3 says, *"And his soul clave unto Dinah the daughter of Jacob, and he loved the damsel, and spake kindly unto the damsel"* (KJV).

One can develop soul ties/trauma bonds to perpetrators. One can have grief, bitterness, rejection, domination, or witchcraft ties that need to be severed during deliverance/cleansing. We find many people are still soul tied to those that molested or raped them. When people forgive, the enemy loses the legal right to them. I have found from working with people who have been molested or raped that the breaking of the molestation, rape, bitterness, and victim soul ties is necessary. After those ties are broken, then the calling out of the molested child spirit, the spirit of rape, and/or the spirit of the perpetrator by name will set them free. Only after they are free can deep healing take place. These places in one's soul, left unhealed, can be a root of sickness later in one's life.

Many are still tied to those who are deceased, still holding onto a spirit of grief. There is a need to once and forever release these loved ones to the Lord. It does not mean you do not love them, nor that you are forgetting them. Holding on to a spirit of grief will cause depression, sorrow of heart, and possibly even sickness. Psalms 119:28 says, *"My soul weeps because of grief; strengthen me according to Your word."* Ecclesiastes 11:10 says, *"So, remove grief and anger from your heart and put away pain from your body, because childhood and the prime of life our fleeting."* The enemy steals our health with continued sorrow and emotional pain. Isaiah 53:4, the first part of the verse says that Jesus bore our grief. Deuteronomy 34:8 says, *"The sons of Israel wept for Moses in the plains of Moab thirty days; then the weeping and mourning for Moses came to an end."* Emotional pain, many times, is connected to physical pain. Proverbs 17:22 says, *"A joyful heart is good medicine, But a broken spirit dries up the bones."*

One can be in bondage to controlling parents, dominating spouses, or abusive relationships. Old relationships of drug use can cause witchcraft ties of control and manipulation. A good indicator that a soul tie is still in place is when one has moved forward, but find when they get around an old, past relationship, their mind is influenced, and again the old behaviors returns. Another example could be when a grown individual may feel like or act like a child when they are around their parents.

When there are soul ties, there is a loss of pieces of one's soul due to the sin. Unclean spirits have the legal right to come in through this spiritual bond and occupy the places that were opened up by sin. Various unclean spirits can now travel or oppress the individual with these ties. These ties can affect one's emotional, spiritual, and physical state. This oppression can make it difficult for one to make decisions on their own due to the other's influence upon them. One can project their soul upon another through soul ties. One can receive infirmities from the binding together and the exchange of soul. Satan can bind people in illegal marriages through fornication and adultery and use these ties to oppress them.

Soul ties bring loss of soul, whoredom and idolatry practices, witchcraft and occult activity, and drugs and alcohol intoxication.

One can develop soul ties to others through:
- bloodline curses (Ezek. 16:44)
- fornication/adultery/divorce
- rape/molestations
- physical/emotional abuse
- domination/witchcraft control
- trauma bond/grief soul tie
- bitterness/rejection

In holy matrimony, becoming one is a tremendous gift from God. There is a power of agreement in a covenant marriage. It was created by God and was intended to be a blood covenant of two virgins coming together it is a spiritual bond until death and a powerful weapon against the enemy on earth. Because of the sexual depravity of our society, many come together with unhealthy spiritual baggage of past soul ties. Many times, they experience warfare and defeat within their marriage from these former relationships. The Lord can break these ties and cleanse them, purifying the union. In Deuteronomy 30:1–4, it says that after repentance, that there is restoration of souls and a gathering of them back together, saying to us, *"If your outcasts are at the ends of the earth, from there He the Lord your God will gather you, and from there He the Lord your God will bring you back."* It says in Psalms 23:3, *"He restores my soul."* In Ezekiel 34:16, it says, *"I will seek the lost, bring back the scattered, strengthen the sick."* We serve the God of restoration and He can do a complete work of healing and wholeness in our sexuality.

Incubus/succubus

Because of sexual immorality many can also have sexually explicit dreams in which incubus (male type spirit) and succubus (female or animal type spirit) demons are involved. These can come in through bloodline, soul ties, occult, fornication practice and adultery. These sexual curses can bring many sexually transmitted diseases, infirmities, female problems, barrenness, and can even be a root to cancer. Jesus said in Matthew 24:28 that, *"Wherever the corpse is, there the vultures will gather,"* meaning demons gather to places of darkness and death.

These sexual dreams bring violation to the body. One will feel molested or raped in their sleep during sexual experiences. In extreme cases, depending on the soul ties of whom the person has slept with, it is actually possible that a witch or warlock may using a familiar spirit to seduce and have sex with that person through astral travel. These spirits may take ownership of one as a "spirit husband" or "bride," and become very jealous of any human relationship. People who have been victimized by these spirits have stated it feels like a real person in the bed with them.

If one is tormented with this demonic oppression, one can experience:
- difficulty in dating relationships/maintaining relationships
- an inability to stay sexually pure in thought or act
- continual marriage strife and conflict
- barrenness or fertility issues

We have had many come to us tormented with such things and they find freedom. Jesus defeated sexual demons, and by His authority they all must go. An example of this is a young native girl we will call Leah, who was receiving cleansing. As we broke soul ties of witchcraft and fornication, we found she was heavily oppressed with demons of the occult, addiction, perversions, and had watcher spirits and the spirit of a warlock (male sorcerer) within her. This spirit was projecting itself as we were doing her deliverance. We broke the incubus/succubus curses and the illegal marriages, (she had more than one). We called out the influences of these bonds and the girl was set free by the love of Jesus. She had multiple scars from cutting herself and we also heard by Holy Spirit, that the spirit of Legion was present. All the nests of demons were commanded to go, and she had a glorious transformation! Glory be to God! She was plugged into a local church for discipleship and testified that she was a new person and never wanted to go back to bondage.

We are very vulnerable while we are sleeping. It says in Matthew 13:25, *"But while his men were sleeping, his enemy came and sowed tares among the wheat, and went away."* We need to pray before we go to sleep, covering ourselves in the blood of Jesus and releasing the angels. If one has a lot of battles at night, taking communion is a great weapon, and anointing oneself with oil before bedtime will keep out the enemy.

Reprobate bloodline curse death structure:

(The list of spirits is taken from Romans 1:19–32)

- reprobate mind/ idolatry curse
- vain imaginations
- vile affections
- unrighteousness
- uncleanness
- foolishness
- lust: lust of the flesh, lust of the eyes, lust of the world, pride of life
- wickedness
- covetousness
- maliciousness
- envy: jealousy
- reprobate unforgiveness, resentment, retaliation, anger, hated, violence and murder
- debate
- deceit
- malignity
- whisperers
- backbiters
- inventor of evil things
- disobedience

- without understanding
- covenant breakers
- without natural affections
- implacable
- unmerciful
- haters of good
- homosexuality/ bi-sexuality idolatry
- sexual immorality
- fornication
- masculine/feminine spirit
- confusion of sexuality
- rejection of sexuality
- reprobate mind binding spirits
- reprobate bondage spirits
- reprobate witchcraft control
- break reprobate generational cycles

These demons listed above, even though one may have not acted upon them, most likely are within the bloodline. Call each one out and break their curse off the generations.

CHAPTER 7

INSIGHT INTO WITCHCRAFT

"Do not turn to mediums or spiritists; do not seek them out to be defiled by them. I am the Lord your God." Leviticus 19:31

A S I SHARE SOME THINGS WE HAVE learned concerning witchcraft, I first want to say that I believe this is the strongman over America. Through all the occult practices, false religions and pharmakia, prescription and illegal drug use in our nation, this is a vast power that is in operation that I will discuss in the next chapter. It is not the only one, but it is a strongman that the Lord is working to tear down through His church. The church must recognize that it is in operation within, even as a bloodline iniquity. We must stop giving it strength through personal participation. The Lord gave me a word that He was going to deal with the witchcraft over America, starting within the root of our nation. The root of our nation is our Native Americans or the first nations. The Lord is doing a deep work in them and we are watching the move of God as He restores the first nation people. He is bringing freedom and cleansing to their bloodline from their ancestral practices of witchcraft, also healing their bodies and their land.

All witchcraft activity has a lust for supernatural power and knowledge. It can operate through manipulation, intimidation, domination or control within the church. Any means to try to control another man's spirit is a form of witchcraft. Making one feel guilty is witchcraft manipulation. Holy Spirit convicts but does not bring condemnation or guilt on anyone. All witchcraft is forbidden and puts one under the curse of the law according to Galatians 5:19–20. One is guilty by association, occupation, and participation, which God equates as idolatry. This idolatry is spiritual adultery or prostitution (whoredom). Whoredom and witchcraft work together, and when you find one in operation, the other will be there, also, in some form. Any knowledge or information gained through witchcraft or the occult will be pregnant with spiritual poison. All supernatural knowledge should come from Holy Spirit or God's messenger. Jesus said in John 14:16–17, *"And I will pray the Father, and He will give you another Helper, that He may abide with you forever, the Spirit of truth, whom the world cannot receive, because it neither sees Him nor knows Him; but you know Him, for He dwells with you and will be in you"* (NKJV).

Galatians 5:19–21
Now the deeds of the flesh are evident, which are immorality, impurity, sensuality, idolatry, sorcery, enmities, strife, jealousy, outbursts of anger, disputes, dissensions, factions, envying, drunkenness, carousing and things like these, of which I forewarn you, just as I have forewarned you, that those who practice such things will not inherit the kingdom of God.

God forbids His people from seeking information from another spirit. In Isaiah 8:19, He warns us, *"When they say to you, 'Consult the mediums and the spiritists who whisper and mutter,' should not a people consult their God? Should they consult the dead on behalf of the living?"* Many believers today still call on and use other sources such as psychics, fortunetellers, Ouija boards, tarot cards, and horoscopes to get predictions. People who receive predictions from these other channels are receiving a demonic destiny. Satan can only give you a suggested destiny; it's up to you to receive it. If one has participated in any occult activity, it needs to be renounced and repented and cleansed from your life. The Holy Spirit is the only one who has revelation that flows from the throne of God to you. True destiny comes from God and it is good. Demons use information gained through familiar spirits and other demonic communication in the spirit realm to give you a reading or a false prediction.

The Hebrew word for medium is *owb*, meaning mumbling or a channeling with the dead. A necromancer is one who calls up the dead to seek information. They use mediums or familiar spirits. Necromancy is praying to the dead and seeking answers or information from them. It is only calling on demonic information from demons with information gained through channeling. The spirit of deception operates within the occult and will keep people coming back for more lies and curses. When one gets a false demonic prophecy and begins to dwell and meditate on it, the demons will work to cause things predicted to come together in that person's life. The scheme is to make one believe it was a word from the Lord. The word says *so a man thinks in his heart so is he*. We can attract what we meditate upon.

The word is clear and warns us in Deuteronomy 18:10–14, saying, *"There shall not be found among you anyone who makes his son or daughter pass through the fire, one who uses divination, one who practices witchcraft, or one who interprets omens, or a sorcerer, or one who casts a spell, or a medium, or a spiritist, or one who calls up the dead. For whoever does these things is detestable to the Lord; and because of these detestable things the Lord your God will drive them out before you. You shall be blameless before the Lord your God. For those nations, which you shall dispossess, listen to those who practice witchcraft and to diviners, but as for you, the Lord your God has not allowed you to do so."* When we practice these things, we are sacrificing our children to idol gods. Isaiah 47:13 says, *"You are wearied with your many counsels; Let now the astrologers, those who prophesy by the stars, those who predict by the new moons, stand up and save you from what will come upon you."* There is no revelation from demonic information and no protection from demonic deception gained through the occult.

There are many lessons concerning King Saul's life; in I Samuel 15:23, it says, *"For rebellion is as the sin of witchcraft, and stubbornness is as iniquity and idolatry"* (NKJV). This is the word the Prophet Samuel gave Saul when he had rebelled against God, fearing man more than Him. He chose to disobey the instructions the Lord gave him in the battle with his enemies. Proverbs 29:25 says, *"The fear of man brings a snare, but whoever trusts in the Lord shall be safe"* (NKJV). This snare was serious, and it cost him the kingdom. The Lord said He regretted that He made him king because of his disobedience to follow His commands. In Saul's stubbornness to obey was rebellion against the Lord and it stopped the voice of God from speaking to him, so he goes to a witch to try to get his answers. Rebellion sets aside true divine authority (God's authority) and finds a substitute (illegitimate) authority, which is witchcraft. God created and delegates authority and all must be submitted to it. The root of pride brings rebellion and its fruit is the many faces of witchcraft. A rebellious spirit will refuse to obey God, and a stubborn one will do it but only their way, making idols out of their own opinions! Partial obedience is really disobedience.

In *1 Samuel 28:7*, it says, *"Then Saul said to his servants, 'Seek for me a woman who is a medium, that I may go to her and inquire of her.' And his servants said to him, 'Behold, there is a woman who is a medium at En-dor.'"* Clearly the medium had no power to bring up Samuel; she was surprised and screams out in terror at the sight of him! It was prophesied earlier in 1 Samuel 15:35 that, *"Samuel did not see Saul again until the day of his death; for Samuel grieved over Saul,"* letting us know God sent Samuel to him. Later, after his inquiring of the witch, Saul died by his own sword at his own hand. It tells us in 1 Samuel 31:4, *"Then Saul said to his armor bearer, 'Draw your sword and pierce me through with it, otherwise these uncircumcised will come and pierce me through and make sport of me,' But his armor bearer would not, for he was greatly afraid. So Saul took his sword and fell on it."* This is a tragic ending for a king who started out knowing God. King Saul reigned forty-two years as king of Israel, but only in the beginning was the Spirit of the Lord resting upon him. In his later years, he suffered demonic torment, leading Israel without hearing the voice of the Lord. He forfeited his purpose and the throne because of his stubbornness to obey God. An obedient spirit is what will guarantee one's ability to complete the plan, purpose and call of God.

In Ezekiel, chapter eight, it speaks of Israel having idols in the walls of their houses and the elders burning incense to them. Verses 7–11 read, *"Then He brought me to the entrance of the court, and when I looked, behold, a hole in the wall. He said to me, 'Son of Man, now dig through the wall.' So I dug through the wall, and behold, an entrance. And He said to me, 'Go in and see the wicked abominations that they are committing here.' So I entered and looked, and behold, every form of creeping things and beasts and detestable things, with all the idols of the house of Israel, were carved on the wall all around."* It goes on to say that standing in front of them, the elders were burning incense. When God's children go to other things to find answers, it is building idols within our hearts, burning incense to them during our worship practices.

We are to come out from among these things and be separate, understanding that a little leaven will go through the whole lump. If the root of a thing is unholy, so will the branches be. When one comes into the kingdom of God, one must take on the identity of the kingdom. One must begin to learn of Jesus Christ, becoming His disciple, which is to be like Him in thought, word and deed. That takes a renewing of the mind by the Word of God, meaning I must come out of cultural practices and traditions that are rooted in idolatry. The children of Israel were told to tear down idols and their altars, smash their sacred pillars and burn them all with fire. Jesus said the greatest commandment of all is this in Mark 12:29–30, *"The foremost is, 'Hear, O Israel! The Lord our God is one Lord; And you shall love the Lord your God with all your heart, and with all your soul, and with all your mind, and with all your strength."* Loving God like this is to give up the idolatry and all its practices.

We have been blessed to work with some first nation tribes. They are a great example of what the Lord is doing in the restoration work of cleansing. Countless Native Americans have been set free and healed due to the finished work of Jesus. They are renouncing the ancestral witchcrafts and practices and forgiving all who have hurt them. Many have seen bodies healed and lives changed through their obedience of cleansing their bloodline and coming out from among the works of darkness and following Jesus wholeheartedly. They are doing house cleansing, getting those trinkets and ceremonial items out of their lives. God is doing a deep work in the first nations, bringing hope and restoration.

What many do not realize is as they come out of witchcraft and do not get cleansed and delivered from those demons that came in, they do often hide within the bodies in organs and bring infirmities and diseases. Many are still tied in witchcraft soul ties and demons can travel through these ties, bringing oppression or even sickness. Proverbs 5:22 says, *"His own iniquities will capture the wicked, and he will be held with the cords of his sin."* Psalms 129:4 says, *"The Lord is righteous; He has cut in two the cords of the wicked."* This area can be a root to sickness and disease. Infirmity spirits can hinder or block the healing anointing. Even yet, one can receive a healing and the sickness return because the spirit behind it was not dealt with. Jesus at times released healing and at times He cast out the spirit and then released healing to the body. We must be discerning to what is needed with each soul.

Tolerating Jezebel

"But I have this against you, that you tolerate the woman Jezebel, who calls herself a prophetess, and she teaches and leads My bond-servants astray so that they commit acts of immorality and eat things sacrificed to idols." Revelation 2:20

To tolerate something means to allow one to do as they wish; to allow the existence, presence, practice or act of without prohibition or hindrance; or to permit. The Jezebel structure that operates within the religious church is witchcraft control, manipulation, seducing doctrines, sexual immorality, soul ties and the usurping of righteous authority. When it is recognized, it should be addressed, or one could be in danger of being a victim of its rebellion, become one of its eunuchs, or take on an Ahab spirit, giving it more power. It has no gender, of course, being a spirit, and can operate in men or women. Jezebel needs an Ahab influence to support its harlotries and rise in power. Examples would be if a pastor has a Jezebel spirit, the deacons or elders would be Ahab. If the pastor has an Ahab spirit, the elders or deacons can have a Jezebel spirit. There is a wicked balance of power in operation to support the networking and its platform. Ahab is passive and tolerant to its wickedness, but it is also out for the personal gain and perks enjoying Jezebel's power to strengthen his rule. It says of Ahab in 1 Kings 16:31– 33, *"It came about, as though it had been a trivial thing for him to walk in the sins of Jeroboam the son of Nebat, that he married Jezebel the daughter of Ethbaal king of the Sidonians, and went to serve Baal and worshiped him. So he erected an altar for Baal in the house of Baal which he built in Samaria. Ahab also made the Asherah. Thus Ahab did more to provoke the Lord God of Israel than all the kings of Israel who were before him."*

Jezebel was a powerful, wicked queen, and wife of a passive king called Ahab. She was a false prophetess and a witch. She was killed by several eunuchs at the order of commander Jehu. Her spirit of witchcraft is still in operation today in the church, and in the world. Jezebel is an influencing power that operates over the occult, abortions, whoredom, false doctrines and the apostate church. It was the power behind homosexual bondage and its law-less marriage agenda, along with all sexual immorality, including the pornography industry. It understands that sexual immorality defiles one within and it desires to outwardly disqualify God's servants from ministry. Jezebel will pull one into spiritual adultery or the very act of adultery. One will have increased battles in their sexuality with ungodly sexual desires or lust in the imagination when influenced by its witchcraft. Jezebel always wants to defile God's holy ones and rise in authority.

It says in Revelation 2:20 that *Jezebel calls herself a proph-etess,* meaning she was self-appointed, not God called. Jezebel was a usurper of authority. Usurping authority is more than disobeying a man, it is also one that seizes and holds a position, office, power, etc. of another by force or without legal right. Spiritual leaders are never permitted to control another's will, gifts or their possessions as their own. Jezebel desires to control another's spirit and their anointing through any means necessary. It can be through money, emotional manipulation, sexual immorality through soul ties or unholy alliances, which are all built on lies and seductive tactics. Jezebel promises one something it cannot give. All stolen is for its personal agenda of self-promotion and power to build its kingdom. Jezebel's agenda will never be about the real Jesus, nor can it ever walk in the pure brotherly love of the Lord.

Jezebel when tolerated will work through a false honor system within relationships. It works through mammon and influence. Anytime one tolerates evil, it will surely come back to inflict pain and suffering upon them. Many tolerate the behavior due to financial increase or need, but this money gained will be tainted with a spirit of mammon and greed. Jezebel has a lust for power, dominion and control; it is a master manipulator and very seductive and uses false humility. Its gifts can be very impressive and can deceive even the elect. It will project its soul on you through soul ties in a relationship. Jezebel uses a spirit of witchcraft, mind control that will try to dominate through fear and intimidation or flattery and seduction, it can be passive-aggressive. This is what happened to Elijah in 1 Kings 19:2–3, *"Then Jezebel sent a messenger to Elijah, saying 'So may the gods do to me and even more, if I do not make your life as the life of one of them by tomorrow about this time. And he was afraid and arose and ran for his life and came to Beersheba, which belongs to Judah, and left his servant there."* Jezebel's messenger was a spirit of witchcraft mind control, operating though fear, and it caused Elijah to flee and hide out in a cave, in isolation, in depression, with thoughts of death.

Mammon plays a big role in Jezebel's attraction. One can shift their allegiance from serving God in holiness and righteousness because of mammon. Jesus warns us in Matthew 6:24 that, *"No one can serve two masters; for either he will hate the one and love the other, or he will be devoted to one and despise the other. You cannot serve God and wealth"* (*mammon*). Jezebel works with mammon and leviathan, the father of pride. The more authority the Lord Jesus gives one, it must be fully surrendered to Him. Tolerating Jezebel for the sake of peace is false peace. It cannot and will never please the real Jesus! Jezebel will twist communication because it is intertwined with Leviathan and will have a strong religious spirit working alongside, twisting the Word of God against you. If you are its friend, it will support you, but if you are unable to be controlled, it will try to destroy one's life through lies, slander and accusations. Jezebel will use half-truths to build its death structure against the righteous authority that it hates.

As Jehu was cleansing the land of Jezebel's wickedness, the Word tells us in 2 Kings 9:25–26, *"Then Jehu said to Bidkar his officer, 'Take him up and cast him into the property of the field of Naboth the Jezreelite, for I remember when you and I were riding together after Ahab his father, that the Lord laid this oracle against him: Surely I have seen yesterday the blood of Naboth and the blood of his sons,' say the Lord, 'and I will repay you in the property,' says the Lord. Now then, take and cast him into the property, according to the word of the Lord."*

The dead king of Israel was cast into Naboth's bloody vineyard, the land that Jezebel stole for Ahab. This was cursed land, which teaches us that any gifts, ground gained or personal favors from Jezebel will be cursed and never bring a blessing in any area of one's life. Don't be deceived by the flattery and seduction; it will poison one's spirit. Jezebel will often promise one a promotion or platform if one will only bow to her false authority. It will promise one new doors of opportunity to sink her talons deeper into one's soul, bringing further bondage.

A mature Jezebel spirit will usually carry a strong influence and have many alliances that feed its power base, all due to the soul ties of these relationships and the law of supply and demand it brings to them. It will stay in power until someone recognizes by Holy Spirit revelation the sad trail of devastation of the victims it has devoured. Or until the Lord raises up a Jehu bold enough and empowered by God to throw her down! When Jezebel is in power, it takes a high level of authority and anointing from God to deal with its false leadership. By this time the networking is so intertwined in the hearts of many followers. It's unfortunate many now are affected by its poisonous control. The early sprouts of fruit, which can easily be tilled out if caught early on and corrected, recognize Jezebel's eunuchs. But as it is undetected and promoted, demonic deception and its authority increase.

Jezebel likes to infiltrate the prophetic, it will target the gifted, but unhealed, or those who are operating without any accountability. The prophetic gift coming through these will be tainted with divination, because the heart is not pure. But it's unfortunate that Jezebel is tolerated because of its gifting. The evil fruit is overlooked due to its many influences and charisma. Jezebel is very charming and has a network of eunuchs it is grooming for its wicked kingdom. Its soul ties have witchcraft bonds and are very difficult to sever due to the deception of seduction within them.

Jezebel brings infirmities, sickness and diseases. Revelation 2:22–23 reads, *"Behold, I will throw her (Jezebel) on a bed of sickness, and those who commit adultery with her into great tribulation, unless they repent of her deeds. And I will kill her children with pestilence, and all the churches will know that I am He who searches the minds and hearts; and I will give to each one of you according to your deeds."* Many get set free from the sickness this spirit invites. I find it can be the root issues in the reproductive system such as barrenness, loss of children and could be a spiritual root of other diseases. It should be considered as a possible root if the Jezebel spirit has influenced you.

Whether soul ties are within the church through Jezebel or outside in the occult, they still must be severed. Witchcraft has many faces and hidden deceptions. It is very important that soul ties from evil witchcraft associations are broken. We were ministering to a Native American pastor who had come out of the medicine men practices, he was now very sick with severe kidney issues, possible cancer on his leg, and stomach problems. His leg had an open wound with sores that would not heal. He came in wearing a medical boot.

It is very common for us to see sickness come upon people after they come out of darkness. Demons are very angry that they lost a soul to Jesus and will use any door they can to bring death upon them, until cleansing comes. The pastor was full of bloodline iniquitous curses from his former life. He needed the curses broken and the ties from his brothers severed. They were still practicing the medicine men practices and were sending more curses to him because he had shifted into the kingdom of light. The channel was the soul tie and the unrenounced practices he did in his past. They were angry with him for coming out of the family traditions and serving the "white man's religion" as they called it. Such deception is the working of witchcraft. These blinding spirits will continue to deceive until exposed!

The pastor went through all the repentance, renouncing, and forgiveness prayers. As we prayed for him, by the authority of Christ, we broke off and severed all family ties of evil inheritances and any claims, contracts, dedications, rituals, ceremonies, blood covenants, ties or bindings that were attached to him. He was cleansed and purged from every evil curses attached to his life by the power of the blood of Jesus! We then commanded curses of sickness and disease to go with every assignment of darkness and death in his bloodline. We could then release the healing power of God to flow through his body and he was filled with the Holy Spirit. He felt Holy Spirit healing his kidneys and stomach by a cool tingling and he felt heat all down his leg where the infection was. Healing flowed through his body, GLORY!

As we left service that night, we had a dark visitation outside. It was well after midnight when we were through ministering to the people. We saw a skin walker witch fly across the road. These witches are very real. The spirit world is very real. We must do spiritual warfare with confidence in Christ that He is our victorious King who defeated all darkness. We give no place to the devil, but we fully surrender our lives to the Lordship of Jesus. God kept us, as we were under the blood of Jesus, and we continued with our mission, seeing many saved, delivered and set free, healed and transformed for the glory of God. Oh, how we love the First Nation people! My prayer is that a great awakening and revival continues to flow through these beautiful people and they receive full restoration of everything the Father has for them, in Jesus' name!

Jezebel can come in through open doors of:
- unhealed soul wounds or trauma
- insecurities and pride
- those who are seeking an identity
- those who are spiritually illegitimate, meaning they have no accountability

- the corrected rebellious
- generational inheritance through bloodline
- learned dysfunctional behaviors of families, (for example, a passive father, dominating mother or dominating father, passive mother)
- unrighteous alignment of a mature Jezebel authority (becoming a eunuch)
- ungodly fornication soul ties

When this Jezebel spirit has influenced you, you should always check your heart for any unhealed places that you might have. Repentance for allowing her access to your soul is a must. Seek cleansing. Soul ties with her need to be broken, allowing healing to come. Forgiveness is key to keep her curses from landing. Forgiving yourself may be difficult, but you must. Don't be snared by wound-edness. Be reminded that Jesus is the Healer and He is also able to deliver and is also the revealer of all truth. If one has been influenced by it or bound by it, one must be intentional to walk in the opposite spirit. One must walk in a spirit of love and humility and submit to righteous authority to keep her out. Remember, all have sinned and fall short of God's glory.

Jesus instructs us to pray for our enemies, for those who persecute you and say all manner of evil against you. Bless those to be saved, healed and delivered. Once you have survived and overcome Jezebel, you will inherit a blessing. Understand that your battle with Jezebel has given you a sharper sword to deal with her witchcraft and harlotry within the church and to discern its operation. It is all for the glory of God, so allow the revelation to be revealed and the fire to burn in your heart for righteousness. Revelation 2:26–28 says, *"And he who overcomes, and keeps My works until the end, to him I will give power over the nations—'He shall rule them with a rod of iron; they shall be dashed to pieces like the potter's vessels'-as I also have received from My Father; and I will give him the morning star"* (NKJV).

In the victory, one receives a new level of wisdom, authority, rule of influence and a deeper level of intimacy with Jesus. So, rejoice that you are always a victor and have overcome Jezebel's harlotries and witchcrafts. John 8:36 says, *"So if the Son makes you free, you will be free indeed!"*

The spirit of Python

In the book of Acts, we find a story of a slave girl who was delivered of a spirit of divination called Python. It says in Acts 16:16–18, *"It happened that as we were going to the place of prayer, a slave-girl having a spirit of divination met us, who was bringing her masters much profit by fortune-telling. Following after Paul and us, she kept crying out, saying, 'These men are bond-servants of the Most High God, who are proclaiming to you the way of salvation.' She continued doing this for many days. But Paul was greatly annoyed, and turned and said to the spirit, 'I command you in the name of Jesus Christ to come out of her!' And it came out at that very moment."*

This marketplace at Delphi was a seat of Satan for demonic information, which brought in much wealth and increase into that city. It was a place where people came to hear the oracle to get future predictions through false prophetic utterances. The Greeks called it "the center of the world." The word python from Greek mythology, believed to be the Pythian serpent that guarded the oracle of Delphi, until Apollo slew it. This word was applied later to soothsayers and diviners. The oracle was a surrendered priestess and was the most powerful woman of the classical world. This slave girl in Acts 16 was one of the best soothsayers of the city; meaning, she was chosen and one most yielded to the power operating in the land and could hear demonic sources very well. She brought in much money for her accuracy. Paul had enough of its interfering with his assignment and evicted the spirit of divination out of the slave girl. Notice she was saying the right thing but with a wrong spirit. Motives of the heart are what the Lord is discerning. The evil spirit was using her to bring a reproach on the message of the kingdom. All knew she was a soothsayer, and her promoting the kingdom would have put the men of God in the same category as her.

The spirit of python is a witchcraft divination structure. Not only is it in operation in the world through the occult structures, such as new age, crystals, psychics, fortune telling, mediums, Ouija boards and horoscopes, it can and does operate through the false prophetic and its mixture within God's people and His church. Python working in the false prophetic will use seduction, manipulation, flattery, mammon, fame and lying suggestions towards its victim. One can be easily deceived if one is not discerning by Holy Spirit. These false utterances will be mixed with half-truths that will cause one to believe a lie. It can say all the right things but in a wrong spirit, just as the slave girl did. The motive to prophecy had evil intentions. Isaiah 2:6 says, *"For you have abandoned Your people, the house of Jacob, because they are filled with influences from the east, and they are soothsayers like the Philistines, and they strike bargains with the children of foreigners."*

The spirit behind Python is out for self-exaltation, power, and control. It can use false humility and looks for places of alignment that will give it a platform to prophecy. People that are gifted in the prophetic and have unhealed soul wounds of rejection, insecurities or abandonment will be an easy prey for this spirit to operate. The corrected rebellious can also be a target. It is a predator and seeks to find a host to work through to release its poisonous venom into. It will often create soul ties and will keep the victims coming back for more predictions! When it is in operation, it gives worship to Satan.

One must stay pure in heart with gifts. One is accountable to keep their gifts operating in holiness. All will give an account of how we used them to help others come to know Jesus more intimately. Python will try to get one to prophecy on demand, under pressure or by manipulation of others. This will not be purely inspired by Holy Spirit, but by the will of man. Jeremiah 23:35–36 warns, *"Thus will each of you say to his neighbor and to his brother, 'What has the Lord answered?' or, 'What has the Lord spoken?' For you will no longer remember the oracle of the Lord, because every man's own word will become the oracle, and you have perverted the words of the Living God, the Lord of hosts, our God."*

One should have accountability when prophesying to others. Prophesying for profit or on demand can open your spirit to divination. Never prophecy or get in a money line to draw a crowd; you are operating in a wrong spirit and will yield to idolatry and mammon. In Acts 8:20, when Simon tried to buy the gift of God, he was rebuked: *"But Peter said to him, 'May your silver perish with you, because you thought you could obtain the gift of God with money!'"*

Never prophecy to prove you are anointed or gifted; it is out of a wrong spirit. This is a sign also of immaturity and pride, which will open you up to destruction and your platform will be faulty and fail. Those who use you for your gifts will never value who you really are in Christ. Never yield to flattery in your gift or you will take ownership of its power. God is to get all the glory. It is only He that can give revelation through Holy Spirit to flow through you. If one has been a victim of this python structure on either end by association or participation, repent and get cleansed of its poison. In Jeremiah 23:21–22, it says, *"I did not send these prophets, but they ran. I did not speak to them, but they prophesied. But if they had stood in My council, then they would have announced My words to My people, and would have turned them back from their evil way and from the evil of their deeds."*

To keep the prophetic pure

- do not prophecy without accountability
- do not prophecy under pressure or by demand
- do not covet another Prophet or do copycat prophecies
- do not prophecy to prove you can
- do not yield to manipulation or flattery in your gift
- do not take money or give money to buy a word (sowing a seed offering is not buying it)
- always operate in the fear of God when releasing the word of the Lord

Python is a restricting spirit that squeezes its prey slowly to suffocate life's breath out of them to bring death. It can wrap around the body and can bring in infirmity spirits. It doesn't just bring oppression in areas of health, but it will choke out one's finances under its curse. It can work in false prophecy, sorceries, drug addictions, and potions with pharmakia.

In Delphi, historians have noted people used a mild leafy plant to get false prophetic hallucinations, which is sorcery in operation. This can come through use of ancient healing arts, magic or divinations used to alleviate pain. One must get understanding of the root or spirit of the practices one participates to assure they are not giving worship to other gods. Drugs that bring addiction, a high, or hallucination, require a release of control of one's own spirit, leaving it open to a demonic playground of activity. Legalizing marijuana is not making it an acceptable practice in God's eyes! Drugs should not be a go to source of action for comfort, nor should they be the first choice of hope as a child of God. Jesus is the great Healer of our bodies. God has also created natural remedies with oils and foods concerning good diet to bring health to us. This along with faith, cleansing and prayer can work bringing healing and wholeness.

The spirit of python may have some similar entry points as Jezebel, but it is a different stronghold. Jezebel seeks to rise as a usurper of authority and desires to control to attain power at the top, at every level of operation. Python operates with some of the same characteristics, but I believe its main operation in the church is divination through seduction, using false prophecy and infirmity. Outside the church, its main operation is the occult. We find it in bloodline generational curses of open doors to divination. Many times, this stronghold can be mixed with seer gifts in the bloodline. Those in a church with this spirit will be unsubmitted to authority, rebellious, unteachable, gossipers, slanderers, and backbiters, much of which is done in secret. Those who have been poisoned by it can experience infirmities, depression, and a lack of vision and creativity in the body.

An example of this was a woman we will call Sherry, who was heavily oppressed through bloodline generational witchcraft, and the fruit was evident in the many curses of mental illness, learning disabilities and poverty. She had a deaf and dumb spirit that was hiding in her tongue, causing a speech impediment when she spoke. It manifested during a cleansing and the serpentine demon projected out of her face as the deaf and dumb spirit was being called out of her tongue. The Lord spoke to break curses of python and divination. As it began to come up, her tongue became thick and she was unable to speak for a few moments as it was leaving. This spirit came in through the generational witchcraft door that was opened and through the trauma of sexual abuse. Python was a stronghold in her. It was strengthened by the repeated sexual abuse as a little girl by her step dad, and was kept in place because of inner vows she made not to tell. This reinforced the deaf and dumb spirit. She "heard no evil nor saw no evil." This went on for years and she began to disassociate with herself as it was taking place. This curse had to be broken. Now older, as an adult, she was set free from this evil net-working of bondage and the trauma it had caused her. Sherry was also gifted prophetically, and she became consecrated in this area through cleansing and her speech impediment was gone. The inner working of these death structures can be intertwined. Holy Spirit can reveal how they are working within. In Matthew 6:22–23, Jesus said, *"The eye is the lamp of the body; so then if your eye is clear, your whole body will be full of light. But if your eye is bad, whole body will be full of darkness. If then the light that is in you is darkness, how great is the darkness!"* Jesus is speaking of the soul of a man being clean or full of darkness that affects the entire being. He also is saying if the light in one is dark, meaning when one is deceived in their heart, it is a stronger deception and working of darkness.

One definition says the occult means hidden from view; it always uses deception. Some are unaware that it is within them through bloodline curses, and some are very much aware of its working, even in the church. While ministering to a lady we will call Hilda, a spirit of divination was in her and she knew she had inherited it from a grandmother. But she was operating as a prophetess and did not want us to cast it out of her because she believed she would lose her seeing gift. She desired cleansing in other areas but not that one. Sad is this deception. The door left open to witchcraft will always bring in other demonic activity. The enemy can't steal any gift God has given us! If Hilda were truly a prophetess, being set free from this death structure would have released a greater dimension of her gift into the body of Christ. Instead, she is accountable for what she knows is within her and is in danger of being a false prophet. Balaam in Numbers chapters 22–24 is a good example of this. He was called a seer/prophet of God, but because of divination, his heart was not pure, and he died by the sword as a false prophet, in the end.

The evil one tolerates will never bring blessing to one's life and one is deceived if they believe it will. Don't ever believe, because of the anointing or gift, God is winking at sin and does not notice the motive behind one's actions. In Romans 11:29, it says, *"for the gifts and the calling of God are irrevocable."* People can be deceived into believing God is okay with sin behavior since He allows us to use these tools for the kingdom. The gift is for you to be a steward over, as Holy Spirit wills, to bring glory to Jesus. In Mathew 7:22–23, it says, *"Many will say to Me on that day, 'Lord, Lord, did we not prophesy in Your name, and in your name cast out demons, and in Your name perform many miracles?' And then I will declare to them 'I never knew you; Depart from me, you who practice lawlessness.'"* That is a strong warning of being a hypocrite and operating out of both kingdoms.

Cleaning the natural house

A spiritual housecleaning of one's natural dwelling is very important after personal cleansing. All witchcraft/occult, freemasonry, whoredom, or soul tie material must be removed and destroyed. It says in Acts 19:19–20, during a move of God, *"And many of those who practiced magic brought their books together and began burning them in the sight of everyone; and they counted up the price of them and found it fifty thousand pieces of silver. So the word of the Lord was growing mightily and prevailing."* Demons are attached to persons, places and things. Some things are cursed and can't be redeemed. God wants them destroyed.

In Joshua chapters 6 and 7, when the children of Israel were in battle to possess their promised land, God told them not to take certain things for spoil because it was devoted to idolatry. When they disobeyed, they were without courage and tasted defeat from their enemy. So Joshua inquires of the Lord and finds Achan guilty, and in Joshua 7:21, he says, *"when I saw among the spoil a beautiful mantle from Shinar and two hundred shekels of silver and a bar of gold fifty shekels in weight, then I coveted them and took them; and behold, they are concealed in the earth inside my tent with the silver underneath it."* His disobedience brought curses on the whole camp and, sadly, death to his whole house. In Deuteronomy 7: 25–26, God told His people to burn the images and not to covet the value of them, that they would be a snare to one's house. In 1 Corinthians 10:20, it says to not become sharers in demons.

We were ministering cleansing on a lady we will call Sue. She was under a curse of poverty, depression and sickness in her body. The Lord spoke to me that her ring was keeping her blocked from receiving freedom and healing. I shared this with her and she was at first unwilling to take it off. It was a gift from a former fiancé that broke off their engagement thirty years prior, which she was still grieving. She argued that it was solid gold and very expensive. She was soul-tied to him and the ring was a doorway to the oppression she was under. The former fiancé was a Wiccan, so her ring was devoted to idolatry and witchcraft, which was the seal of the evil covenant and the right for demons to enter her body. Only as Sue finally obeyed God and took off the ring did she get freedom, cleansing, and healing, as the cursed ties were broken. I heard from her a year later and she was well, prospering, and had begun a new business. That is only the work of Jesus and the blessing of God through restoration and deliverance.

We had another young mother who was going through cleansing who we will call Lizzy. She had come out of a life of whoredom and was now serving God and being discipled. She had moved out of a bad situation and moved into another area that was closer to the ministry and brought all her belongings with her. She was having a lot of demonic torment in her home. Lizzy would pray in her home, but continued hearing someone call her name. She unable to sleep at night, and at one point something physically pulled her out of her bed. Realizing this was some occult activity, I asked Holy Spirit what the open door and I heard Him say it was her bed. There was a spirit attached to her bed and it was cursed. There was no redeeming it or consecrating it with prayer and oil. The Holy Spirit said it had to go, so we carried it out to the dumpster, anointed Lizzy's house and then she had peace afterwards. Whatever was attached had brought defilement into her house, occult in nature, due to the physical activity of it. This bed was from her past life of whoredom and it had a demon that was tormenting her. Holy Spirit is the revealer of mysteries. We don't always have to know the details, just obey His voice. So, you see, it is very important to cleanse one's home of possible entry points of evil. We minister a lot to the first nation people and they understand this need very well. Getting free of articles of witchcraft that have been passed down through the generations, from medicine men and women and practices of traditional ceremonies is essential to freedom.

Some common witchcraft definitions and terms:

- magic—the use of charms, spells, and rituals in seeking to control people, or cause events, or govern certain natural forces by a supernatural means.
- sorcery—the practice of casting spells or use of charms, reciting verses, formulas, trinkets, enchantments, compelling one by magical force. Sorcery uses drugs, potions, musical elements, a ring or stone object/symbols which are supposed to bring good luck and ward off evil spirits. To conjure spells is also a sorcerer or charmer and includes a hypnotist.
- witchcraft—witches and wizards who use endowment of supernatural powers from a contact with evil spirits; it involves the use of curses and rituals.
- divination—gaining supernatural past, present, or future knowledge, trying to tell the future by unknown or occult means. An example is a fortune teller, card/palm reader, ouija board, water witching, E.S.P, reading tea leaves or other such things.
- soothsayer—a person who predicts the future, as one who interprets omens, also who practices divination and astrology.
- wizards—one devoted to black magic or sorcery.

- medium—one who has a familiar spirit in which he consults or allows to speak through his/her own body like a transmitter, such as a séance. This deceives one to believe one is talking to the dead but is talking to a familiar spirit.
- stargazers—are astrologers, monthly prognosticators, such as horoscopes.
- spiritism—the worship of spiritualism which is the belief that the spirits of the dead can communicate with the living.
- necromancy—a practice of praying to the dead and seeking answers or information from the dead. A necromancer is one who calls up the dead to seek information, using a medium or a familiar spirit.
- familiar spirit—a demon supposedly attending and obeying a witch, often said to assume the form of an animal.
- fetish—an inanimate object worshiped for its supposed magical powers or because it is thought to be inhabited by a spirit.
- transcendental meditation (T.M.)—a religious system that stems from Hinduism, whereby a mantra (a secret sound) is repeated during meditation and the mind is said to be in the deepest level of consciousness.
- translocation—the movement of a person from one place to another by supernatural means.
- telepathy—mind-to-mind communication without the use of any normal means of communication.
- astral projection—the act of one in the occult who travels outside of his or her own physical body and operates on a different level of consciousness. One who is adept at this technique can travel considerable distances and report accurately things one has seen in other places before returning to their bodies.
- Séance—a meeting at which people attempt to contact the dead conducted by a spiritist.
- trance form of ESP—a condition in which consciousness and all natural senses are withheld, the soul becomes susceptible only to a specific vision.

CHAPTER 8

CLEANSING OF ADDICTION

Romans 6:12–16

"Therefore do not let sin reign in your mortal body so that you obey its lusts, and do not go on presenting the members of your body to sin instruments of unrighteousness; but present yourselves to God as those alive from the dead, and your members as instruments of righteousness to God . . . Do you not know that when you present yourselves to someone as slaves for obedience, you are slaves of the one whom you obey, either of sin resulting in death, or of obedience resulting in righteousness?"

IN OUR NATION TODAY, WE HAVE A DRUG epidemic of illegal and prescription drugs. We must recognize the seriousness of this and take authority over this strongman of witchcraft in our nation. We must see a change to save the generations after us, but first our eyes must be opened to see what the enemy is really doing. The word addiction means a compulsive need for and use of a habit-forming substance with physiological symptoms upon withdrawal. Addiction is a spiritual problem and works with a spirit of bondage and witchcraft mind control. Addictions are rooted in rejection and fear, pride and rebellion. They can come down through the curses of iniquity in generational bloodline.

In the previous chapter, I mentioned the word *pharmakia*. It is a Greek word found in the Word of God in Galatians 5:20, Revelation 9:21 and 18:23. In Galatians 5, pharmakia is described in the working of the flesh, and it means sorcery. In verses 19–21, it reads, *"Now the deeds of the flesh are evident, which are: immorality, impurity, sensuality, idolatry, **sorcery,** enmities, strife, jealousy, outbursts of anger, disputes, dissensions, factions, envying, drunkenness, carousing, and things like these, of which I forewarn you, just as I have forewarned you, that those who practice such things will not inherit the kingdom of God."* It says in the Greek lexicon it is the use of or the administering of drugs, poison, sorcery, magic arts, often found in connection with idolatry and fostered by it. Also, it is the deception and seduction of idolatry. In Revelation 9:21, it says *"and they did not repent of their murders nor of their **sorceries** nor of their immorality nor of their thefts." In 18:23, it reads, "and the light of a lamp will not shine in you any longer, and the voice of the bridegroom and bride will not be heard in you any longer; for your merchants were the great men of the earth, because all the nations were deceived by your **sorcery**."* Note that the merchants who were bringing deception were great men of the earth. The spirit of mammon is at work partnering with and trading its goods and resources to pharmakia to keep the continued deceptive slavery to sorcery for their personal profit and gain. Both structures receive benefits and have a place to rule in the hearts of humanity. In Hosea 4:6, it says, *"My people are destroyed for lack of knowledge."*

We know that God does not view all medicine as evil because it is referenced in 2 Kings 20:7, *"Then Isaiah said, 'take a cake of figs.' And they took and laid it on the boil, and he recovered."* Hezekiah became mortally ill and he had to take a cake of figs and put it on his boil and then he got well. We know Luke was a physician and he was chosen as one of the twelve disciples. God is all wisdom and He uses medicine, but the issue is the idolatry behind the practice, one looking to it as a god, and the use of drugs that alter our person or destroy our bodies. We serve the Great Physician, Jesus Christ. One of His covenant names is Jehovah Rapha, God our Healer. Many believers do not believe that Jesus heals today. They accept living on medication for life, not even seeking, asking for or receiving any healing from Him. They only medicate the symptom but do not deal with the root source of the illness. It is easier to take a pill than to look deeper within and examine the physical or emotional problem one has. They believe a lie that it is easier to escape into a bad diet or habit for comfort or to take an anxiety pill rather than to be real with what is really going on within.

Many habits can begin very subtle and seem as not a big deal but can grow into spiritual bondage. 1 Corinthians 6:12 says, *"All things are lawful for me, but not all things are profitable. All things are lawful for me, but I will not be mastered by anything."* Some such examples could be workaholic, shopaholic, social media or gamer addict, gossiper or a glutton. These types of things get overlooked and are many times unnoticed, but reality is, it has become your master, controlling your life in slavery. Gluttony has become the norm in our nation where we live to eat instead of eat to live. The god of the belly rules many believers, and it has damaged our bodies. Many are critical of drug addicts, smokers and alcoholics in the church, but themselves are addicted to other behaviors that are accepted as okay or the norm.

I had a simple dream that a girl wanted to know if this man was in love with her. She said that her medicine would tell her if he did love her. The Lord began to speak as I awoke one morning that many medications have influence over the mind and can alter their emotions, and thereby, can influence their will. He continued to tell me that certain drugs have an assignment attached to them which is to cause what we call "side effects" to the individual. A few examples might be suicidal tendencies, depression, hallucinations, or organ damage. Certain drugs are working witchcraft over humanity. The spirit of pharmakia (sorcery) can operate through the art of practicing spells, drugs or potions, and it has demons assigned to its medications. It says in the Word that witchcraft hunts for the soul (Ezek. 13:18–21). Many of these created medicines have a spiritual assignment to fragment the soul and bring more bondage into the body. We know a spirit's name by its nature and that is what we call them. We have called out spirits of suicide, depression, compulsive behavior and many others that came in through side effects of pharmaceutical drugs. When the door is opened to allow demonic traffic, demons will do just that! Even in the physical body there can be side effects coming off these legal drugs. Staggering are the number of people reported to be addicted to opioids and other prescription drugs. This is a work of a demonic assignment of witchcraft mind control spirits set out to keep the people of God in idolatry to a false god over America.

We minister to victims of this pharmaceutical drug addiction spirit and have cast it out by name and it obeys. It will come out of the neurological and psychological system of a person who has been on prescription drugs a long time. We have had to call out any side effects and withdrawals. Some are immediately free, and some have had to walk out minimal adverse side effects of withdrawal. But freedom came! These people also need healing to the endocrine system with a balancing of hormones. Some will need to be weaned by a doctor's order and monitored. To be free and healed from this structure, each one must be led by Holy Spirit.

We ministered cleansing to a young woman who we will call Dawn. She was an addict, addicted to meth, crack and opioids. She said she was a meth cook, and during her cleansing, Holy Spirit said she had a sorcerer spirit within her, and I saw (discerned) a vision of an ancient cauldron and a witch dressed in a black cape. This was no new demon, of course. It was an ancient spirit with a different name: "meth cook." It was the sorcerer spirit within her still cooking its potions. It was using her to make wicked, evil potions of witchcraft, mind-altering drugs for demonic playgrounds of darkness and torment. So you can see that what we call legal or illegal drugs all have been a door of demonic oppression in people's lives. The root source of this is idolatry, humanity serving other gods and looking to them for false peace, comfort and healing. Chemical addictions work with a spirit of bondage. Below are some entry points or cause of participation.

Common entry doors of addiction:
- generational curses, sins, or iniquities in the bloodline
- abandonment/rejection
- unhealed trauma/fear

- bitterness/unforgiveness
- rebellion/pride
- long-term use of prescription medications

Addiction is a spiritual problem first, due to soul wounds or an unhealed body, in which the spirit of bondage finds a way to manipulate its victim. The word bondage is the Greek word *douleia,* meaning slavery, which is its job function and assignment. It works with a nest of evil to keep one in captivity, being a false comfort and a false peace that brings destruction and death to its victim. It can come in through generational iniquities, sins or curses passed down through the bloodline, which has its roots in rejection and abandonment, in those with an unfulfilled desire to be loved and accepted. When you are not loved and accepted, or nurtured as God intended, you will look to other things, trying to find love and comfort from the loneliness and empty feelings within. This searching can begin even as a child, looking for love or something to fill the void. Those with addictions will have self-worth issues, feeling all the areas of rejection, feeling unworthy of love, and can harbor unforgiveness towards themselves, God, and others. The longer a death structure rules, the deeper the bondage can become, and more sin doors are usually opened.

Addiction affects the endocrine system, which is a collection of glands that secrete hormones directly into the circulatory system to be carried towards the organs. When a body has been bound in chemical addiction, not only is a spiritual cleansing and deliverance needed, but most likely one will need physical healing to the endocrine system with the restoration of and release of proper hormones and chemicals within the blood. One's whole being (spirit, soul, and body) need to be restored and possibly healed from organ damage. Spirits of infirmities can and do hide in the organs through doors of addicted behavior. There are habitual behavior patterns that must be torn down and replaced with accountability of a new action. Demonic oppression is not only hidden within emotional pain but also in the will of a man. Bondage can be intertwined in the whole man and calling them out of the will is very effective.

It is very disheartening to see many believers with prescription drug addictions or substance abuse with no faith to come out of the bondage to this slavery. Many have believed a lie that it is acceptable to God for them to cut their life short by unhealthy habits. Many do not finish their course because of disobedience and rebellion connected to their addiction to nicotine, alcohol, food and anything else that is destroying the temple of God. Addiction will cause you to believe those things that are destroying the temple of God are your only source of peace and comfort.

1 Corinthians 6:19–20 says, "*Or do you not know that your body is a temple of the Holy Spirit who is in you, whom you have from God, and that you are not your own? For you have been bought with a price: therefore, glorify God in your body.*" Many believers do not finish their course because of an undisciplined life of poor habits that shorten the body's life span, bringing premature death. Escaping from empty feelings of loneliness or other emotional pain by using alcohol or drugs because of unhealed wounds brings death. In Isaiah 28:15, it says, "*for we have made lies our refuge, and in a falsehood we have taken shelter. (False gods are our hiding place.)*" (AMPC). False comforts and medication may treat the symptom temporarily but cannot heal the root issue of pain or illness. We belong to the Great physician who can bring restoration to the whole man. Have faith in God and believe Him for this!

Many who suffer with addiction have not had healthy relationships nor can they build any due to the internal dysfunction. This stronghold will damage whole families. Whether it is substance abuse, food or fantasy with sexual vices, all can be used to open addictive behavior. Trauma is another door that can invite addictive bondage. One will escape from pain to alcohol or drugs because of unhealed soul wounds. This becomes spiritual adultery and idolatrous. Whenever the children of Israel turned to other gods, bondage resulted because of their rebellion.

Whenever you have given authority over to a spirit of bondage, you now must go to a higher authority to get authority back. There's no higher authority than Christ, and at His name, every knee bows, in heaven, in earth and under the earth (Phil. 2:10). There is freedom from the curse of addiction through Him who defeated everything on the cross.

Many bound in bondage are blinded to the destruction it is causes themselves or others. Bondage will lie to you, speaking to you in first person, wanting you to receive its suggestions as your own thoughts! James 4:7 says, *"to submit to God, resist the devil and he will flee"* (NKJ). Unless one realizes bondage is speaking, "I need, I want, I desire, I must have," in this area of habit, there will be no spiritual warfare but a yielding to its servitude. Addiction is a coping method that keeps one in avoidance of the root issue within. It will convince you that it's too painful or shameful to handle, and as it grows stronger, the more powerlessness you will feel overcoming it. It usurps your will and will lead you into isolation. Proverbs 18:1 says, *"A man who isolates himself seeks his own desire; He rages against all wise judgment."*

Bondage usurps one's identity and has them in a false identity crisis in need of revelation of who they really are. A healthy self-esteem must be built on the unconditional love and self-worth according to the Word of God. As one has a serious desire to change their will and cooperate with Holy Spirit, He will release the grace to overcome all. Slaves who love their chains will never be free of them and whatever demon one tolerates will never leave them. There's no higher power or authority than Jesus Christ, who has plundered the strong man and has defeated every addiction that has bound one in shackles. In Matthew 12:28–29, Jesus said, *"But if I cast out demons by the Spirit of God, then the kingdom of God has come upon you. Or how can anyone enter the strong man's house and carry off his property, unless he first binds the strong man? And then he will plunder his house."* Jesus said this after he did deliverance. The road to wholeness is different for everyone, as is everyone's bondage. But the Lord will drive out all the enemies and He will develop your spiritual muscles in spiritual warfare as He brings revelation to you while freeing you!

With the addiction stronghold, one should also do the reprobate and apostasy cleansing, releasing the iniquitous curse from the bloodline. Many on illegal substances will need multiple areas of soul healing, cleansing and much support, accountability and discipleship. The souls belong to Jesus; the work is finished! However He chooses to minister to each soul and enforce the victory, we are to be Spirit led with each one.

CHAPTER 9

APOSTASY STRONGHOLD

*"Let no one in any way deceive you, for it will not
come unless the apostasy comes first, and the man of
lawlessness is revealed, the son of destruction, who
opposes and exalts himself above every so-called
god or object of worship, so that he takes his seat
in the temple of God, displaying himself as being
God."* 2 Thessalonians 2:3–4

THE WORD APOSTASY IS THE GREEK WORD
apostasia, meaning a defiance of an established system or
authority, or rebellion and abandonment or breach of faith.
To operate in apostasy means one is a betrayer, double-crosser or
traitor. It says in the book of Timothy that the time will come when
people will not endure sound doctrine, but they will want to have
their ears tickled and will accumulate for themselves teachers in
accordance to their own desires. It says they will turn away from
truth and turn aside to myths. They will have a form of godliness
although they deny the power of God. The Greek word form is
morphosis, meaning a semblance, sketch or form. Their religion is
only in their creed and formal confession of faith not in their hearts.
Jesus said men would honor Him with their lips, but their hearts
would be far from Him. An apostate abandons true faith and loyalty
to Jesus and turns to other things for their hope, faith and salvation.

In ministering cleansing to a woman who we named Sasha, whom we mentioned in an earlier chapter, Sasha had a life of sin rebellion mixed within her church life. She grew up with a religious heritage and was in church most of her life. She had been in a lot of religious circles but struggled with addictions, fornication and homosexuality. She was under generational curses as a single mother and had much bondage in multiple areas but also had a strong religious spirit. While doing her cleansing, I heard Holy Spirit say, "silly woman curse," so I immediately went to the Word in 2 Timothy 3:1–7 which speaks of this curse, *"But realize this, that in the last days difficult times will come. For men will be lovers of self, lovers of money, boastful, arrogant, revilers, disobedient to parents, ungrateful, unholy, unloving, irreconcilable, malicious gossips, without self-control, brutal, haters of good, treacherous, reckless, conceited, lovers of pleasure rather than lovers of God, holding to a form of godliness, although they have denied its power; Avoid such men as these. For among them are those who enter into households and captivate weak (silly) women weighed down with sins, led on by various impulses, always learning and never able to come to the knowledge of the truth."*

We broke the generational curse of apostasy off Sasha and I began to call out the spirits listed in the Word that were connected to it. The nature of an apostate was listed in the Word of God as described by apostle Paul. The demons were lover of self, lover of money, boastful, arrogant, reviler, disobedient to parents, ungrateful, unholy, unloving, irreconcilable, malicious gossip, without self-control, brutal, hater of good, treacherous, reckless, conceited and lover of pleasure. The Lord broke the curse of a silly woman, *"weak (silly) woman weighed down with sins, led by various impulses, always learning but never able to come to the knowledge of the truth, and having a form of godliness but denying the power thereof, off her."* All the years of Sasha's church history and the double life of sin, being here and there but no freedom or apprehension of truth. Why? This bloodline curse was in place over her life. We broke the curse of ever learning but unable to come to the knowledge of the truth, all which were attached to this woman's life. Each demon came out as commanded and she was set free from this generational curse and she began to grow spiritually very quickly afterward. 2 Corinthians 4:6 says, *"For God, who said, 'Light shall shine out of darkness,' is the One who has shone in our hearts to give the Light of the knowledge of the glory of God in the face of Christ."* As in Sasha's life, Light came and brought Revelation and truth set her free.

In 1 Timothy 4:1–2, it says, *"But the Spirit explicitly says that in later times some will fall away from the faith, paying attention to deceitful spirits and doctrines of demons, by means of the hypocrisy of liars seared in their own conscience as with a branding iron."* There is a warning for us to be wise concerning doctrine. We can be deceived by doctrine of demons, which is false teaching of seducing spirits through men. These teachings will always appeal to the flesh and cause people to fall away who do not love holiness, righteousness and truth. 2 Thessalonians 2:10–12 is a warning of the Antichrist spirit that is working in the earth now and that would also come in as the person of the Antichrist. Verse 11 reads, *"For this reason God will send upon them a deluding influence so that they will believe what is false, in order that they all may be judged who did not believe the truth, but took pleasure in wickedness."* Then it goes on to say that Paul gave thanks for those God had chosen from the beginning for salvation through sanctification by the Spirit, and faith in the truth. He commends them and encourages them to hold to the traditions that they had been taught, whether by word of mouth or by letter from them. He is saying hold to truth; allow what you spiritually eat to line up with scripture.

I find many believers have taken pleasure in unrighteousness by voting for abortion, by electing baby killers in government office. Abortion is murder and child sacrifice to Satan. In Psalms 106:37–43, *"They even sacrificed their sons and their daughters to the demons, and shed innocent blood, the blood of their sons and their daughters, whom they sacrificed to the idols of Canaan; and the land was polluted with the blood. Thus they became unclean in their practices, and played the harlot in their deeds. Therefore the anger of the Lord was kindled against His people and He abhorred His inheritance. Then He gave them into the hand of the nations, And those who hated them ruled over them. Their enemies oppressed them, and they were subdued under their power. Many times He would deliver them; they, however were rebellious in their counsel, and so sank down in their iniquity."* Whoever we cast our ballot for, we come into agreement with the spirit that is operating upon them. We must pray and seek God as His kingdom government in the earth for whom we cast a vote! It is apostasy; betraying the loyalty of Christ, when we say we are a child of God, and then willingly break His commandments being in agreement with sin. James 4:17 says, *"Therefore, to one who knows the right thing to do and does not do it, to him it is sin."* These things open the door to demonic oppression and deception in our lives and block the blessing of God.

If a believer voted in leaders that passed the same sex marriage in the USA, they need to repent of this. I believe as one aligns themselves in agreement with these evil spiritual agendas of abortion and homosexual marriage, the spiritual door for it enter your personal life or bring a curse on one's bloodline. The curse will have a right to traffic your life or generations. Do we really believe the real Jesus would stand in an abortion clinic and support the killing of the innocent? Do we really believe the real Jesus would attend and bless a homosexual marriage ceremony? I know He wouldn't. God is not double-minded, His word is clear on these issues. In Psalms 119:89 it says, *"Forever, O Lord, Your word is settled in heaven."*

Grace is never a license to sin, but it is power released for us to be able to live a life pleasing to God. Grace is there to cover me by the blood of Jesus when I fall short. Much of the hypergrace message today has watered down the gospel of salvation and taken away the cross. It tells people they can live any way they desire and God is fine with that. It is a lying deception and has no accountability to truth of crucifying the flesh to walk with Jesus. It has no power to make true disciples of Christ. To become a disciple means I become like Jesus in thought, word and deed. Jesus said in Matthew 5:48, *"Therefore you are to be perfect, as your heavenly Father is perfect."* The word perfect is the Greek word *teleios*, meaning to become mature, complete, of full age in mental and moral character. That can only be accomplished through sanctification by faith, not living a life to please our own fleshly appetites.

The church is full of demonic bondage due to crossing God's safe boundaries and thus walking in sin behavior. God's commandments do not restrict one; just the contrary, they give me a broad place in the Spirit!

This apostacy stronghold, I feel, should be repented of by all when you are dealing with cleansing of the bloodline. In everyone's family line, one can find apostasy somewhere. If one has ever turned one's back on God and backslid into old cycles of sin behavior, this could be a stronghold that is hindering current spiritual growth and development. These truths were put into the Word for us to bring revelation, life and freedom to the body. These letters were written to the church, not heathens who did not know God. We must, as the bride of Christ, stop hindering the work of cleansing and deliverance but embrace it. We will see the glory released and our sonship manifested in the earth when we are obedient to the completed work of Jesus.

The apostasy stronghold can operate through

- generational bloodlines
- reprobate
- leviathan (pride)
- whoredom (spiritual adultery)
- idolatry (homosexuality)
- witchcraft (Jezebel)
- false doctrines/teaching
- religion (traditions of men)
- mammon

The political-religious alliance apostate curse: *"For no man can lay a foundation other than the one which is laid, which is Jesus Christ. Now if any man builds on the foundation with gold, silver, precious stones, wood, hay, straw, each man's work will become evident; for the day will show it because it is to be revealed with fire, and the fire itself will test the quality of each man's work. If any man's work which he has built on it remains, he will receive a reward. If any man's work is burned up, he will suffer loss; but he himself will be saved, yet so as through fire."* 1 Corinthians 3:11–15

This evil apostate curse of the political-religious alliance came against Jesus many times while He was obeying His Father. Eventually it worked to crucify Him. It is a cord of three that is not easily broken because of the strength of its power base. One can see it operating in Pilate and the Sanhedrin, who had this alliance for the balance of power and false peace. Outward peace is not real when there is inner turmoil. A political spirit is defined as a spirit exercising and seeking power in government and in public affairs of a state or municipality, etc. It says concerning the trial of Jesus in Matthew 27:19–20, *"that while Pilate was sitting on the judgment seat, his wife warns him to have nothing to do with Jesus, the righteous man;" for last night I suffered greatly in a dream because of Him. But the chief priests and the elders persuaded the crowds to ask for Barabbas and to put Jesus to death."* Pilate released the thief because of a riot starting and his concern of losing his false political peace with the Sanhedrin. These spirits had an alliance because Pilate was the authority who could sentence death and they needed his power to fulfill their plan to kill Jesus. Pilate was known as a ruthless ruler and cared for no one. The religious spirit hired false witnesses against Jesus, as it always does, to lie about him paying taxes to Caesar and claiming to be king. Pilate knew Jesus was innocent, but he listened to the voice of the masses who were influenced by the religious spirit.

The political-religious spirit must stay in power by any means necessary, keeping control of its kingdom it has created. It will partner with a religious spirit that is not a threat but an asset to its agendas. A religious spirit doesn't mind this evil association because it knows it has no real power itself, but it is about the appearance of power. Jesus said in Matthew 23 concerning them in verses 3–6, *"therefore all that they tell you, do and observe, but do not do according to their deeds; for they say things and do not do them. They tie up heavy burdens and lay them on men's shoulders, but they themselves are unwilling to move them with so much as a finger. But they do all their deeds to be noticed by men; for they broaden their phylacteries and lengthen the tassels of their garments. They love the place of honor at banquets and the chief seats in the synagogues."*

This religious spirit doesn't want to be threatened but left to its own complacent, self-indulgent idolatry and its form of godliness that denies the real Power of God. Both it and the political spirit hate the authentic Power of the love of Jesus Christ, and it will do whatever it takes to kill a move of God. It realizes that the authentic love of Jesus exposes the alliance of its antichrist kingdom, which has misled so many. It then will lose its power to control people's lives, thus losing its seat of honor, finances and influence. Today, this goes on in the circles of unsanctified church government that desire the accolades of men instead of pleasing God. This structure has no holy fear of God and continues to build its own personal kingdom.

The political-religious alliance is a death structure that will work to try to shut down one's personal liberty in Christ and the liberty in Christ operating in the pure work of God. It unites together and will put demands and restrictions on Holy Spirit and the gift of God in you. It will become accusing if one doesn't submit to its control which is out to fulfill its personal agenda.

Being apostasy, it is full of defensive pride, fueled by leviathan, believing it should have authority over another man's stewardship of his own spirit and gifts. This opens the one operating in it to work witchcraft control which can also create evil soul ties to those under its power. It will use fear and intimidation or legalism and condemnation. Any time someone in power makes one feel guilty, there is witchcraft at work with a soul tie working with the fear of authority and fear of punishment. In Luke 13:14, it says, *"But the synagogue official, indignant because Jesus had healed on the Sabbath, began saying to the crowd in response, 'There are six days in which work should be done; so come during them and get healed, and not on the Sabbath day.'"* The religious leaders told Jesus He could not heal on the Sabbath. They even used the law to enforce their demands. They did not care about the ones who were sick and dying and in bondage, but the underlying motive was their lust for power, control and recognition of their own seats of authority. This spirit doesn't give Jesus His rightful place of Headship. When it is in operation, it demands ownership of everything one has.

We see this death structure working within church circles today when leaders care more about their titles and ministry instead of being concerned for the souls of humanity. Many have exchanged the truth of God for a lie, worshiping created things, knowing God but not honoring Him as God. Many have built or are building their own kingdoms centered around their personal visions and desires. It is the same spirit of pride operating in the people in Genesis 11 when the Lord God confused the language of the people. In verses 3–4, it says, *"Come, let us make bricks and burn them thoroughly." And they used brick for stone, and they used tar for mortar. They said, 'Come, let us build for ourselves a city, and a tower whose top will reach into heaven, and let us make for ourselves a name, otherwise we will be scattered over the face of the whole earth."* When one exchanges the foundation of Christ and abandons what Christ is about, they are building their own personal city, using their own created stones instead. The foundation must always be Jesus Christ, which will be tested by fire to be sure it is true and remains standing.

We must understand that there are not any new demons or principalities being created. Satan cannot originate anything, but he can imitate, masquerade and transform into false light. Jesus always continued to do what His Father was doing, never allowing this system to control Him. He learned obedience by what He suffered in life, some of which came from the rejection of the political-religious system of his day. It is no different today for those who choose His kingdom purposes. In Mark 13:9, Jesus says, *"But be on your guard; for they will deliver you to the courts, and you will be flogged in the synagogues, and you will stand before governors and kings for My sake, as a testimony to them."* This is the same spirit that slanders the brethren from the pulpits and sends out reports to destroy other ministries in the name of Christ because of personal disagreements, jealousy or offense. Character assassination is the work of the accuser; it will never be included or accepted in the pure work of Jesus.

We must discern the fruit of Christ from another spirit. This political-religious alliance is deceptive because it has a form of godliness and seems to have good intentions. This is where the seduction comes into play to entrap and entangle one in a web of half-truths and lies. It will always have personal agendas in place. This spirit will desire to expose their brother instead of covering them, even using the Word of God to justify judgment. It will use authority unrighteously, even wielding the sword against their brother to gain approval of man and an ungodly promotion in the ranks of church government. Paul warns us in 2 Corinthians 11:3–4, *"But I am afraid that, as the serpent deceived Eve by his craftiness, your minds will be led astray from the simplicity and purity of devotion to Christ. For if one comes and preaches another Jesus whom we have not preached, or you receive a different spirit which you have not received, or a different gospel which you have not accepted, you bear this beautifully."* If it doesn't look like Jesus, talk like Jesus or act like Jesus, it is most likely not the real Jesus!

Jesus showed us how to deal with this. He resisted its threats and continued to follow His Father's purpose. He stayed in prayer, walking and demonstrating the kingdom of righteousness. He was the Word that became flesh. He set His face like flint, understanding that His Father had His hand on His life, and it was not His will He was walking out, but His Father's. One must be obedient to the call of God on one's life and remember that one is a steward over all that He has put within. One will stand alone before the Father concerning the call and for the willful obedience to follow Him through all personal opposition. I believe all ministers of the gospel will at some point be tested by the political-religious alliance. The question will be, will one obey God or man when the pressure is on?

Those who can fall prey to this evil alliance are ones who:
- have a man-pleasing spirit
- have the fear of man spirit
- are seeking an identity in ministry
- have a lust for power and authority
- sit under Jezebel leadership
- have a mammon stronghold
- operate in a religious spirit
- do not honor the Word of God as truth
- are under the power of leviathan

We minister to many who have been poisoned by this evil alliance. Many are broken and full of woundedness. Wherever one eats spiritually, they partake of the spirit in the house coming within and resting upon them. We must break ungodly soul ties and get free from all its oppression. One will need healing to the soul from all the disappointment of the alliance when the veil of deception has lifted. One must forgive those who hurt them and then the cleansing can come. The bloodline apostate stronghold is listed in the glossary and should be used in cleansing when one has been on either side of its poisoning influence.

Doctrinal history within bloodline

I have ministered to many who have received false doctrine and teaching within the body of Christ. Many were bound in a spiritual struggle with understanding Truth. I believe all need cleansing from their church history. We should renounce all teaching that omits these truths of Jesus written below. Any omission of the atonement or sacrifice of Jesus is false doctrine or occult. We should renounce all false doctrines and religious limitations that we put on God through believing the traditions of men that are contrary to kingdom teaching. We need to renounce the limitations and restrictions we were taught concerning gender bias and that the operation of the 5-fold ministry work of Christ was only for the Bible times. Renounce any teaching that said Jesus doesn't heal or do miracles through His people today. Renounce any teaching that said speaking in tongues is of the devil. One needs cleansing from the demonic oppression of church history. These demons will hinder one from receiving revelation of the kingdom. They are fortresses and speculations as described in 2 Corinthians 10:4–5, which says, *"for the weapons of our warfare are not of the flesh, but divinely powerful for the destruction of fortresses. We are destroying speculations and every lofty thing raised up against the knowledge of God, and we are taking every thought captive to the obedience of Christ."* They are also seducing spirits and doctrines of demons as in 1 Timothy 4:1. They are blinding spirits, as seen in 2 Corinthians 4:4. All of which left alone will bring hindrance and stunt one's spiritual growth. Unhealed church history is a very common stronghold today. Many are bound and stuck in former church pain, fear, soul ties, old covenants, false doctrines or traditions of men that have not been broken. They are wearing an old wine skin and religious mantles, that they were not called to wear! Many are still bound to old covenants, oaths and ministry papers and obligations they signed in ignorance. They do not realize it can still be attached to them as they try to move forward. It is still affecting them spiritually even though its years later and they have changed locations. The demonic still can traffic.

Demons don't grow old or tire of oppressing God's people. I do not believe it was Jesus' intention that we would divide and be called a Baptist, Lutheran, Pentecostal, Assembly of God, Methodist, Catholic, *or any other* label that could be stamped on us. We are called to be a follower of Jesus Christ, working in His kingdom. All denominations have some truths in areas, but they can also limit one in believing and walking out the fullness of truth.

It would be wise to take some time to reflect on past ministries you have been involved in and to ask Holy Spirit of the damage that has been done through immature or unrighteous leadership. Places of spiritual abuse or control often lead to soul wounds, fear and bitterness. Revisit the places where you were wounded, betrayed or not loved perfectly like Christ. Make sure there is no ungodly soul ties, unforgiveness or judgments you may have made. These things can bring curses that you may be living under. Some may need to renounce false teaching and false gifts because of the receiving of another spirit. 2 Corinthians 11:4 says, *"For if one comes and preaches another Jesus whom we have not preached, or you receive a different spirit which you have not received, or a different gospel."* Unhealed church history is a very common stronghold today.

Seek the Lord concerning these areas:
- ungodly soul ties
- unforgiveness
- unhealed soul wounds
- repentance needed from breaking covenant/promises/vows, so you can move forward
- fear of ministry

- repentance of judgments concerning God's anointed
- any doctrine that you received
- being a vagabond believer
- distrust issues
- disobedience in operating in your gifts

I have ministered to many who have received false doctrine and teaching within the body of Christ. Many were bound in a spiritual struggle unable to understand Truth. I believe all need some cleansing in the area of church history. I ministered to one lady who I will call June. She grew up Jehovah's Witness. She was hindered in receiving revelation of the kingdom of God and felt stuck and very dry. June had expressed to us that she would try to read the Word of God and apply it, but she was blocked somehow. Even when listening to anointed teaching, she could not apply it to her life. She went through cleansing and was set free of the curses attached to false doctrine, false baptism, the spirit of error, legalism, formalism, deception, religion and many other things that are connected to religious strongholds. Her mind then was now clear and open to receive Truth and understand it. June was free to hear clearly without a network of demonic arguments within her mind. Those arguments got cast out, in Jesus' name! In 2 Corinthians 10:4–5, it says, *"for the weapons of our warfare are not of the flesh, but divinely powerful for the destruction of fortresses. We are destroying speculations and every lofty thing raised up against the knowledge of God, and we are taking every thought captive to the obedience of Christ."*

Biblical truths of sound doctrine concerning Jesus Christ:
- He was born of a virgin (Matt. 1:23–25)
- He is God (Matt. 1:23, John 1:1)
- He is the Son of God (Luke 1:35, John 3:18)
- He died and rose from the dead (Rom. 10:9)
- He was sinless (Heb. 4:15)
- He came to save us from our sins (Luke 9:56)
- He ascended to the Father (Acts 1:9–10, 2:34)
- He is presently seated at the right hand of the Father (Heb. 1:13)

132

- He is making intercession for us (Heb. 7:25)
- He is coming back again (1 Thess. 5:1–4)

Bloodline apostate curse death structure
(The list of spirits is taken from 2 Timothy 3:1–7)
- lovers of self
- covetous
- boaster
- proud
- blasphemer
- disobedience
- unthankful
- unholy
- without natural affection
- truce breaker
- false accuser
- incontinent
- fierce
- despisers of good
- traitor
- heady
- high-minded
- lovers of pleasure
- opposers of truth
- Break the curse of ever learning and never able to come to the knowledge of the truth
- Break the curse of the form of godliness but denying the power of God (call it out).
- Break (off men) the curse of captivating weak women
- Break (off women) the curse of the silly women of divers lust, of ever learning and never able to come to the knowledge of the truth.

These demons listed above, even though one may have not acted upon them, most likely are within the bloodline. Call each one out and break their curse off the generations.

CHAPTER 10

DISMANTLING LEVIATHAN

"In that day the Lord will punish Leviathan the fleeing serpent, with his fierce and great and mighty sword, even Leviathan the twisted serpent; and he will kill the dragon who lives in the sea." Isaiah 27:1

Leviathan's nature

THE FATHER OF PRIDE IS LEVIATHAN. JOB 41 describes this power and its nature. It is in operation in many areas within the earth, resting in places of government over nations, ruling with mammon and idolatry, whoredom and witchcrafts. These death structures will always use an evil networking to enslave humanity. Leviathan has many faces and manifestations that it produces in men that bring much torment to its victim. The operation of sin behavior gives Satan power to rule in regions and specific areas even within the church. Where there is continual sin, Satan can build a throne of iniquity and fortify its power base in that region. Demons then will rule in the hearts of men without resistance. Different nations and ethnic groups will have varying thrones of iniquities differing within them due to the strength of it within bloodline curses or through the sin doors of activity. Jesus speaks to the church of Pergamum in Revelation 2:13 saying, *"I know where you dwell, where Satan's throne is; and you hold fast*

My name and did not deny My faith even in the days of Antipas, My witness, My faithful one, who was killed among you, where Satan dwells." Tearing these thrones down must be done by releasing the kingdom, through intercession, preaching truth, casting out demons, healing the sick and cleansing the land through repentance. In Matthew 12:28, Jesus said, *"But if I cast out demons by the Spirit of God, then the kingdom of God has come upon you."* Only the kingdom of God will bring breakthrough and change regions and nations. 2 Chronicles 7:14 is the greatest kingdom weapon to tear down the throne of Leviathan over regions. It says, *"and My people who are called by My name humble themselves and pray and seek My face and turn from their wicked ways, then I will hear from heaven, will forgive their sin and will heal their land."*

Leviathan will always resist the Spirit of the Lord and will justify itself, desiring to be honored and builds its own platform. It is a bloodline iniquity and its strength will be determined by the power of its support system within and the continuous yielding of its demands. It was found in Lucifer and it was the fall of him. In Isaiah 14:13–15, it records the fall, *"But you said in your heart, 'I will ascend to heaven; I will raise my throne above the stars of God, and I will sit on the mount of assembly in the recesses of the north. I will ascend above the heights of the clouds; I will make myself like the Most High.'"* Ezekiel 28 also records his fall, telling us he was blameless in his ways from the days of creation until iniquity was found in him. He was found trading goods for the worship that only belonged to God, being corrupted by his own beauty (pride). God cast him down and he lost everything.

Listed here are but a few common manifestations of a leviathan spirit that can be seen in operation within the hearts of men. It works through the behavior of selfishness, ego, haughtiness, arrogance, boasting, stubbornness, rebellion, being unteachable, uncorrectable, bitter, offended, argumentative, and debating. It is critical and judgmental, unable to submit to authority. It will keep people in a vagabond cycle and cause restlessness, not allowing one to have rest and peace or to be established in Christ. It is at the root of a bitter stronghold and is behind church splits and other things I will discuss in this chapter ahead.

Areas of Leviathan operation:
- bloodline iniquity/generational whoredom
- idolatry/mammon/robbing God
- witchcraft/Jezebel/false doctrines
- offenses/unforgiveness
- word curses/slander/gossip/accusation
- bitter root judgment/inner vows
- church splits/covenant breaking rebellion against authority
- infirmity/bone disease
- addictions

In one cleansing, we were ministering to a church lady we will call Susan. She had a lot of generational, bloodline pride. The leviathan structure had caused bone issues of arthritis, curved spine and hip issues. While praying over her, a haughty spirit came up and she stuck her nose up in the air, and it speaks out of her and said, "She worships me every Sunday!" Meaning on Sundays, when Susan thinks she is worshiping the Lord, while also filled with this haughty spirit, her worship was not going to Jesus. John 4:24 says, *"God is spirit, and those who worship Him must worship in spirit and truth;"* otherwise, our worship can be in vain. Also, Jesus said in Matthew 15:8, *"This people honors Me with their lips, but their heart is far away from Me."* The condition of our heart is very important to Jesus as a child of God.

In Job 41, speaking of Leviathan in verses 12–24, *"I will not keep silence concerning his limbs, or his mighty strength, or his orderly frame. Who can strip off his outer armor? Who can come within his double mail? Who can open the doors of his face? Around his teeth there is terror. His strong scales are his pride, shut up as with a tight seal. One is so near to another that no air can come between them. They are joined one to another; they clasp each other and cannot be separated. His sneezes flash forth light, and his eyes are like the eyelids of the morning. Out of his mouth go burning torches; sparks of fire leap forth. Out of his nostrils smoke goes forth as from a boiling pot and burning rushes. His breath kindles coals, and a flame goes forth from his mouth. In his neck lodges strength, and dismay leaps before him. The folds of his flesh are joined together, firm on him and immovable. His heart is as hard as a stone, Even as hard as a lower millstone,"* this speaks of false praise and worship, boastings, self-will ruling one's heart, being agitated, unyielding, with a critical, stony heart. Tongue problems and corrupt communication are rooted in a leviathan stronghold.

Pride steals the blessing of the Lord of prosperity. Psalms 37:11 says, *"But the humble will inherit the land and will delight themselves in abundant prosperity."* It works with mammon and believes the value of a man's life is in his possessions. It will look down on those less fortunate and not lift a hand to help them. It is behind robbing God of tithes and offerings, taking ownership of its goods and finances. Serving is out of the question in any capacity for pride; instead, it serves only self. The heart of this death structure will be hard and stony, unable to show compassion and love. Job 41 in verses 3–4 says, *"Will he make many supplications to you, or will he speak to you soft words? Will he make a covenant with you? Will you take him for a servant forever?"* This death structure will have no compassion for others, nor will it serve or keep covenant with you.

Philippians 2:3–8 warns and admonishes God's people, saying, *"Do nothing from selfishness or empty conceit, but with humility of mind regard one another as more important than yourselves; do not merely look out for your own personal interests, but also for the interests of others. Have this attitude in yourselves which was also in Christ Jesus, who, although He existed in the form of God, did not regard equality with God a thing to be grasped, but emptied Himself, taking the form of a bond-servant, and being made in the likeness of men. Being found in appearance as a man, He humbled himself by becoming obedient to the point of death, even death on a cross."* When getting cleansed from this stronghold, one must discipline themselves, walk in the opposite spirit, taking on the nature of Jesus as a servant to avoid reentry.

In Proverbs 16:18, it says, *"Pride goes before destruction, And a haughty spirit before stumbling."* Pride is an enemy of your soul and will always deceive, bringing delusion through rebellion and disobedience to God's righteousness. It desires to rule on the throne in the hearts of men and operating in it gives it your worship. Pride is the outward manifestation of someone who has a spirit of rejection within. Somewhere there is a soul wound that needs to be healed, and walls of false protection have been erected to keep out the love of Jesus. These must come down for healing to flow. Pride is a blinding spirit; one cannot see clearly nor can they hear the voice of God accurately. Stephen rebuked the Sanhedrin in Acts 7:51, saying, *"You men who are stiff-necked and uncircumcised in heart and ears are always resisting the Holy Spirit; you are doing just as your fathers did."* It will be seen in controlling and manipulating practices in relationships. It is a participator of witchcraft and lying divination, works with a religious spirit and is behind false doctrines. It is at the root of covenant breaking in relationships, carrying a spirit of offense, and it is the power behind church splits.

Leviathan, being a twisted water serpent, is usually found twisted around the torso of a body, within the spine and neck. It can be behind neck and back pain, bone diseases and arthritis. Proverbs 14:30 says, *"A calm and undisturbed mind and heart are the life and health to the body, but envy, jealousy, and wrath are like rottenness of the bones"* (AMPC). It will open the door to infirmities within organs. It is very effective during cleansing to dry up the waters of Leviathan and call it out of the waters of its victim. It is unfortunate that it is a generational iniquity that most will justify and be disillusioned by its in their own heart. Only uprooting it and lining up one's life with the humility of Jesus and His teaching, forgiveness, and operating with a servant's heart can break its back. It will be a lifelong journey to keep him out, for it is the fallen nature of humanity to desire to rule their own life.

Iniquity of the tongue

This twisted serpent Leviathan is behind tongue problems. It will bring division, strife, offenses, gossip and slander, twisting communication within the church. Provers 20:19 says *"He who goes about as a slanderer reveals secrets, therefore do not associate with a gossip."* Ecclesiastes 10:8 says, *"He who digs a pit may fall into it, and a serpent may bite him who breaks through a wall."*

Tongue iniquity opens one up to a spirit of destruction with the workings of Jezebel. It will eventually destroy you if not dealt with. It says in James 3:5–6, *"So also the tongue is a small part of the body, and yet it boasts of great things. See how great a forest is set aflame by such a small fire! And the tongue is a fire, the very world of iniquity; the tongue is set among our members as that which defiles the entire body, and sets on fire the course of our life, and is set on fire by hell."* It goes on to say it is a poison, full of cursing, bitter water, full of conflict and death. It tells us in chapter four of James that the source of quarrels and fights come from within the sensual desires that war in our members, and these come out of our mouths bringing the conflicts! Leviathan uses the tongue to release iniquity (perversity) and destruction to humanity. Psalms 10:7 says, *"His mouth is full of curses and deceit and oppression; under his tongue is mischief and wickedness."* Proverbs 18:21 warns us, *"Death and life are in the power of the tongue, and those who love it will eat its fruit."* James 3:2 says, *"For we all stumble in many ways. If anyone does not stumble in what he says, he is a perfect man, able to bridle the whole body as well."*

Jesus said in John 6:63, *"It is the Spirit who gives life; the flesh profits nothing; the words that I have spoken to you are spirit and are life."* Our life is governed by words, positive or negative. We eat the fruit of them and steer our life on a path of our choosing. As angels move in strength to the voice of the Word (Ps. 103:20), so do demons move as we speak negativity, fear, defeat or death out of our mouths? It is a door for spiritual activity to work in our lives, giving the spiritual realm power to move as we direct.

1 Corinthians 10:10 warns us not to be like the children of Israel in the wilderness, saying, *"Nor grumble, as some of them did, and were destroyed by the destroyer."* Ecclesiastes 10: 20 says, *"Furthermore, in your bedchamber do not curse a king, and in your sleeping rooms do not curse a rich man, for a bird of the heavens will carry the sound and a winged creature will make the matter known."* The birds of the heavens are demonic spirits that spread poison and bring accusations against us, even within the bloodline, causing us to be snared by the words of our mouth.

Jesus speaking in Matthew 12:36–37 says, *"But I tell you that every careless word that people speak, they shall give an accounting for it in the day of judgment. For by your words you will be justified, and by your words you will be condemned."* We are accountable for what comes out of our mouth and our words are recorded by angels. Malachi 3:16 says, *"Then those who feared the Lord spoke to one another, and the Lord gave attention and heard it, and a book of remembrance was written before Him for those who fear the Lord and who esteem His name."* So as one can see, our words do matter, and speaking curses over others will bring judgment back on you. Jesus said in Luke 6:37, *"Do not judge, and you will not be judged; and do not condemn, and you will not be condemned; pardon, and you will be pardoned."*

Spirit word curses/judgments/vows

Word curses, bitter root judgments, and inner vows work much the same way to keep one in bondage. Hosea 10:4 says, *"They speak mere words, with worthless oaths they make covenants; and judgment sprouts like poisonous weeds in the furrows of the field."* These evil inner vows and judgments can get planted within the soil of our hearts and can grow into strongholds and cause curses. What a man thinks in his heart, he will become. It invites demonic bondage because when one believes a lie, eventually one will act it out. People will also become what they hate because of the evil judgment one has made of others. These things will block cleansing and deliverance due to the unforgiveness towards oneself. Word curses, bitter judgments spoken against us, or negative things we have spoken against ourselves can open doors to the curse of accidents or other mishap. If one finds themselves having continual accidents, evaluate what has been coming out of your mouth. Also, check your heart for any offense or unforgiveness; this will keep the enemy from having a landing strip in one's life. Again, in Matthew 7:1–2, Jesus says, *"Do not judge so that you will not be judged. For in the way you judge, you will be judged; and by your standard of measure, it will be measured to you."* We use this scripture to mean only those around our lives or who are in our circles. But it goes much deeper than this. I have found that how one judges themselves, others will judge you the same. As a child of God, one must get healed and have a right judgment of themselves in Christ through His redeeming blood.

Do a self-check:

- Do you find yourself living in fear of punishment?
- Do you find yourself feeling guilty or condemned?
- Do you find yourself having unloving, hateful thoughts about yourself?
- Do you feel like a failure?
- Do you have dread about your life?
- Do you have regrets?
- Do you constantly look in the past?
- Do you have unforgiveness towards yourself, or vowed you can never forgive yourself?

These are but a few areas of wrong thinking of personal judgments that will keep one in continued cycles of bondage. These things create snares, hindrances, blockades and traps in the spirit. They will paralyze one from walking in the freedom of peace and spirit-led living! These things will also hinder your God-ordained relationships. So a man thinks in his heart, so is he.

Years of wrong thinking will set up as a death structure that must be torn down with truth and many times cleansing and deliverance. When the demonic has a breeding ground of darkness within one's mind, it will have continued opportunities and resources to grow and multiply! A negative self-image cannot produce a positive, prosperous life.

Be renewed in the spirit of your mind and pay attention to what you are thinking about yourself. Think the God kind of thoughts concerning your life. Learn to speak life! Proverbs 16:24 says, *"Pleasant words are a honeycomb, sweet to the soul and healing to the bones."* Learn to live in and appropriate the blood of Jesus daily and watch God begin to work to bring the needed changes. If you find this is an area that you need freedom in, get it! Don't be prideful but humble yourself and receive all the Lord has for you.

Soul ties will also give word curses more power to land and develop. For instance, in marriage, if a husband continues to tell his wife she is worthless, after a process of time, if she believes the lie, it will begin to manifest in her life in failure and hopelessness. She will internalize the lie and dwell on the curse spoken, and the demons who hear the words against her will work to create failure situations within her life, enforcing the lie, bringing her into bondage. This scheme of darkness will work with authority figures such as parents, bosses and unrighteous spiritual leaders. Different levels of authority give the words more power against you. If you are submitted to or soul-tied, it's much easier for curses to land. If one has offenses or unforgiveness, it will give them a place to land. If one has unrepentance, witchcraft iniquity already working within the bloodline, curses also have a place to land and produce what they were sent to do. We see this a lot in ethnic groups with generational witchcraft practices that have been unrepented. We must break soul ties with family members, especially in the area of witchcraft.

Bitter defilement

In Hebrews 12:14–15, it states, *"Continually pursue peace with everyone, and the sanctification without which no one will (ever) see the Lord. See to it that no one falls short of God's grace; that no root of resentment* (bitterness) *springs up and causes trouble, and by it many be defiled"* (AMP). I have found that the strongman of bitterness is the number one blocker of freedom and even healing to our body and souls. It says that we can come short of the grace of God; meaning, personal unforgiveness in relationships will hinder the grace of God from flowing through our life in the areas needed. This hindrance is one's own making, not God's. Bitterness always has its strength in offenses, unforgiveness and it is always preceded by resentment, retaliation, anger, hatred, and gets stronger with violence and murder. It is usually always two-fold working within self-bitterness. Each spirit operates and thrives in offenses which is connected to oneself or others sin that was committed against one causing wounds in our soul. When we have not practiced a lifestyle of forgiveness, it opens a door for this evil root to begin to sprout and poison us. It is a most defiling poison that will contaminate physically. It is found to be the source of much sickness and disease, such as arthritis and cancer. It can and will often transfer to the children through generational bloodline of sickness.

There are many unloving and unbonding spirits in families. I find many disconnected and disgruntled families due to this divisive evil force. It is rooted in pride and will justify its behavior. We live in a selfish society that only looks out for number one! We not only hold ourselves in bondage, but we chain up others with our bitterness, unable to pray for our enemies as Christ commanded.

Bitterness is an unseen plague that is running rampant in the church. It is a root cause of infirmities, sickness, disease, hatred and destruction spreading throughout humanity. Jesus gave us instruction concerning how to live a lifestyle of forgiveness and how to receive forgiveness. Matthew 6:14–15 says, *"For if you forgive others their transgressions, your heavenly Father also will forgive you. But if you do not forgive others, your Father will not forgive your transgressions."* In Matthew 18:21–22, Peter asked Jesus, *"Lord, how often shall my brother sin against me and I forgive him? Up to seven times?"* Jesus said to him, *"I do not say to you, up to seven times, but up to seventy times seven."* He was telling Peter to always forgive others, and as we forgive others, the Father will forgive us. One must forgive from the heart, being an act of one's will, and in obedience to the Word of God. The Lord will deal with one's emotions so long as one is obedient to repent and release the offense. I have witnessed countless freedom from this stronghold and watched them be healed and set free from years of pain, sickness, and disease. It is amazing, the love and willingness of Jesus to heal the human soul inside and out! The love of forgiveness is supernatural and will release supernatural results if we respond in obedience.

Bitterness is like a spiritual virus that will spread through the whole person. It brings contamination not only to the person who won't forgive, but it will spread through the natural family and the spiritual family if left to mutate. People tend to pick up other people's offenses quite easily. People desire to find someone to agree with them so one can feel vindicated for the wrong done to them. A natural virus is a biological agent that reproduces inside the cells of living hosts. When infected by a virus, a host cell is forced to produce many thousands of identical copies of the original virus at an extraordinary rate. This is a spiritual picture of bitterness. It must be eradicated out of the body or damage will come in sickness and disease. One's health will always be affected spiritually and naturally with a spirit of bitterness.

Spirit of offense

The word offense in the Greek word *skandalizo,* meaning to entrap, trip up, or entice to sin, make stumble; it is where we get the English word scandalize. In Matthew 18:7, Jesus said, *"Woe to the world because of its stumbling blocks! For it is inevitable that stumbling blocks come; but woe to that man through whom the stumbling block comes!"* The English word "offend" means to be irritated, annoyed, resentful, or angry. The enemy is behind the spirit of offense to trap us into the snare of it, opening us up to a bitter stronghold. Offended people refuse to give up the right to be offended. They are being rebellious, prideful, self-reliant instead of God-reliant. They desire to take matters into their own hands, when the word clearly says vengeance is mine, says the Lord, and I will repay. Offended people feel entitled. They feel they are owed something. They demand exemption when Jesus teaches us to serve and to be humble. They can play the victim and feel a sense of unfairness, picking up other offenses easily and spread the cancer throughout the body. Offended people will often operate in a spirit of control, and if they can't have their way in a church, they will usually leave. They could have received healing and began to mature where the Lord planted them, if they would have dealt with their selfish behaviors and woundedness. This spirit will deny human imperfections and will snare you in past sin cycles and patterns. Offense is a defiling, restricting spirit, choking the life out of you. Don't take the bait of Satan and be snared and blocked up. One must forgive and release others quickly, learning to be a good communicator.

Disagreement should be dealt with quickly by application of the Word of God. In Matthew 18:15–17, it says, *"If your brother sins, go and show him his fault in private; if he listens to you, you have won your brother. But if he does not listen to you, take one or two more with you, so that by the mouth of two or three witnesses every fact may be confirmed. If he refuses to listen to them, tell it to the church; and if he refuses to listen even to the church, let him be to you as a Gentile and a tax collector."* Notice Jesus said to go first to the person. Most do not do this because of fear. Instead, one will call friends or family and tell the sin to them, trying to find alliances. That is how this spirit spreads, poisoning the body. Doing things according to scripture keeps things in divine order.

There are times when people will not receive your forgiveness. In this case you must continue to pray for your enemies and bless those who persecute you to be set free from their personal bondage of offense. To tell the offense to the church is speaking of the governing officials, the mature ones, not the entire body of the church. Praying for your enemies will keep one from taking on offenses, plus it causes us to become more like Jesus.

Then Jesus continues and says, *"Truly I say to you, whatever you bind on earth shall have been bound in heaven; and whatever you loose on earth shall have been loosed in heaven."* So, we have power to bind and loose as a child of God. When we do not forgive, we are binding up ourselves in curses and can also bind the other person up spiritually. I find in terms of covenant relationship, we can bind our spouse and continue to snare them in the very sin behavior we are offended about. Because we are an open door to one another, having a legal contract of oneness, demons will traffic if allowed. Likewise, parents are a spiritual door to their children; the evil they tolerate can visit their children with curses, including offense.

Offense is an evil seed operating in direct disobedience to the Lord who taught us to forgive quickly and love our enemies. The Lord also told us to agree with our adversary quickly along the way before you go to the judge! (Matt. 5:25) It takes humility to give up the right to be offended or in some cases giving up the right to be right. Many times, these seeds of bitter roots get planted when we are young through abuse or trauma. Bloodline offenses can get passed down generation to generation causing breaches in family dynamics. Through soul ties, we can pick up other offenses and become a person with evil thoughts. We often develop learned behavior from our parents or family, and even mentors who may have planted the wrong way of thinking. We can unknowingly take on their belief systems of walking contrary to Christ. Some may have even been taught how to fight and get even, instead of how to love and forgive. These behaviors only produce evil seeds that can defile and produce wrong behaviors that become a snare. The longer one lives believing the lies, the more difficult it is to give up your right to be offended and judge others.

A good example of defiling others is when you have been wronged or mistreated by someone such as a former boss or possibly a pastor. Unless you have really released, forgiven and chosen to love them from the heart, a bitter root of resentment will follow you and contaminate your relationship with your next boss or pastor. You will harbor distrust with authority figures, be guarded and unable to give them your best due to the soul wound. You may even start expecting the new relationship to treat you the same as the former relationships treated you. It will hinder and block the blessings that the Lord intended to flow to you, failing the grace of the Lord in your life. His grace empowers one to walk in power and blessings, also to fulfill one's purpose. Because of the offense inside of you, your attitude and behavior will cause the cycles to be repeated. The cycles will in turn affirm the wrong thinking and lies that are set up within, building a stronger fortress of bitterness. This can be a root to a victim mentality and you can offend people easily sometimes because you carry that spirit of offense in you.

We must learn to respect and honor one another. Ephesians 6:2–3 tells us to, *"Honor your father and mother, which is the first commandment with a promise, so that it may be well with you, and that you may live long on the earth."* Childhood is where we should begin to learn how to walk in obedience, but many parents are dysfunctional themselves and have not learned these principles for godly blessings, nor taught them to their children. Even parents that are deceased can affect us through the ungodly, bitter soul ties we have with them. That is how we end up being like the parents we have resented. We will repeat the same cycles and patterns, treating others the same way we were treated, because we still our parents in judgment and unforgiveness. Religion has taught us to wear a mask and hide what's really inside our hearts. That is deception and that is not walking in truth. Our fight as a believer is not against the person but the spirit that has been controlling them and hurting us. Until we see past the sinful acts and look to the spirit behind things, we will never war a good warfare and see breakthrough in our lives from this enemy.

Self-examination of relationships past and present is a great place to begin cleansing. Ask for forgiveness of bitter root judgments you have made in your heart and the ones you have spoken out of your mouth. Start with your parents and then allow Holy Spirit to show you others you have held bitter root judgements against. Allow Him to heal as you forgive them and yourself. Maybe you also need to release the Lord because you had believed He was responsible for past hurts and circumstances of your life. There is power and freedom in forgiveness. It is the first step to walking in wholeness and releasing the blessings the Lord has for you. He will and does always release His empowering grace to us to walk out His obedience when we ask Him to!

It takes maturity to forgive others quickly and give up the right to be offended. It is truly an act of our will and in obedience to His Word to do so. Paul said in 1 Corinthians 13:11, *"When I was a child, I spoke as a child, I understood as a child, I thought as a child; but when I became a man, I put away childish things"* (NKJV). Offenses and unforgiveness can keep one locked in arrested development of childhood or adolescent behavior. This place of unhealed woundedness can cause the delay in spiritual development and places of psyche development, causing many to act out childish behavior.

The roots of bitterness list (the same for self-bitterness):

> *But if you do not forgive others, then your Father*
> *will not forgive your transgressions. Matthew 6:15*

- Offense—The Greek word for offense is *skandalon,* meaning a snare or stumbling block. To become offended means to be snared by irritation, or anger. It means to become annoyed, hurt or have pain from someone or something.
- Unforgiveness—refusing to forgive or show mercy, unrelenting. Not allowing for mistakes, carelessness, or weakness.
- Resentment—a feeling of indignation or displeasure at some act, remark, person, etc., regarded as causing injury or insult. This can be because of a real or imagined offense.
- Retaliation is the act of retaliating, to return like for like, especially to return evil for evil. To desire revenge from a wrong done.
- Anger—a strong feeling of extreme displeasure, hostility, indignation, or exasperation toward someone or something, rage, wrath. It is a strong, heated and negative emotion manifested, stewing.

"Holding anger against someone is like drinking poison and expecting the other person to die."—unknown

- Hatred—the feeling of one who hates; intense dislike or animosity, abhorrence.
- Violence—an unjust or unwarranted exertion of force or power, as against rights or laws. It can be physical force exerted for violating, damaging, or abusing.
- Murder—the unlawful killing of one human being by another, especially with malice aforethought. It is the final fruit or root of bitterness that enters in as a physical or verbal murder, even character assassination.
- Bitter soul ties that need to be broken.
- Envy and jealousy attached to bitterness.

All negative feelings must be confessed to be free of bitterness. Each root is to be used also concerning self-bitterness. One must accept the responsibility for the negative, hateful feelings inside of them. One is responsible for the reactionary sin he does because of the personal pain. We are accountable for what we allow in our hearts. Inner healing must take place first in the areas that are wounded; only then can deliverance come. When there is confession and repentance, as we choose to forgive as an act of our will, and in obedience to the Word of God, legal rights of the demonic are broken. The emotions are not as important as the obedience to forgive. The Lord will heal the emotions as we yield to His obedience (1 John 2:9–11, 3:15; Matt. 5:22–24, 18:1–9; Eph. 4:31–32; James 1:19–20; 1 Pet. 3:8–9).

CHAPTER 11

BREAKING FREE OF MAMMON

O NE OF THE GREATEST ENEMIES WE MUST overcome as a follower of Jesus Christ is mammon. Mammon is a spirit, but it is a ruling prince in the earth that works with Leviathan. It has a voice and speaks very loud within the heart of man. It has a most powerful pull and desires to rule. The Father gave us instructions and strategy on how to deal with and defeat it so we could overcome it. The word mammon is a word meaning riches, wealth, or anything you put your confidence or trust in. It's the word we use for money. Mammon came from Babylon as the Syrian god of riches. The word Babylon speaks of confusion, being the place where the Lord confused the language of the people because they built their own system to get to heaven. This system was built on pride, arrogance, greed, self-confidence and independence without the Lord God.

The Lord spoke about stewardship, finances and possessions in 16 of His parables. One must note that it was an important topic to Him, understanding the heart of a man. Mammon will cause the atmosphere to shift every time money is mentioned or discussed in a church service. This is because mammon is fighting for position in the hearts of God's people. It knows that men cannot serve it and the Lord at the same time. It knows it has the power to destroy the soul. If you get uncomfortable or agitated when money is discussed, or when sermons on tithing and giving are taught, it could very well be you need cleansed from this bloodline iniquity that desires to stay hidden to keep one bound in generational poverty, lack and divided loyalty to God.

In Matthew, chapter six, Jesus talks of mammon, starting in verses 19–24, *"Do not store up for yourselves treasures on earth, where moth and rust destroy, and where thieves break in and steal. But store up for yourselves treasures in heaven, where neither moth nor rust destroys, and where thieves do not break in or steal; for where your treasure is, there your heart will be also. The eye is a lamp of the body; so then if your eye is clear, your whole body will be full of light. But if your eye is bad, your whole body is filled with darkness. If then the light that is in you is darkness, how great is the darkness! No one can serve two masters; for either he will hate the one and love the other, or he will be devoted to one and despise the other. You cannot serve both God and wealth (mammon)."* We note that Jesus speaks of the earthly treasures one stores up and holds so dear to the desire in a man's soul and the condition of it. When one serves mammon, it can cause our soul to be darkened and be earthly-minded instead of eternity focused. One must really desire to come out of mammon's control and beat its power structure in our life as a child of God. We first must realize how it works in us to become free of its influence. 1 John 2:15–16 warns, *"Do not love the world nor the things in the world. If anyone loves the world, the love of the Father is not in him. For all that is in the world, the lust of the flesh and the lust of the eyes and the boastful pride of life, is not from the Father, but is from the world."* These things come out of a mammon mindset and will work to steal your affections.

Characteristics of mammon in operation:
- impulse buying instead of Spirit-led purchasing
- the oppression of fear and anxiety concerning finances
- feeling you are unable to give anything
- fear or grudging giving tithe and offerings
- being discontented and full of ingratitude of what one does have
- always wanting more and feeling you never have enough
- workaholic spirit in operation

- a selfishness and greedy spirit, only caring about oneself
- a poverty mindset that thinks and says, "I can't afford anything"
- having cycles of excessive debt and lack, being unable to pay creditors
- a mindset that money has power and will give one happiness, security or success
- a vagabond job history
- laziness and unable to prosper with the work of your own hands
- entitlement spirit operating, thinking everyone owes you
- being satisfied living off the welfare system

Many hear these thoughts or are tempted by them concerning money and finances. Mammon is an idol god that is out to steal our loyalty, trust and worship in the True and Living God. It can deceive us into putting our hope in its lying promises that it cannot deliver. The Lord, He is God and He is our provider, peace, joy, security and safety, not mammon. Money is simply a medium of exchange, a tool in the earth realm. In Ecclesiastes 10:18–19, it says, *"Through indolence (slothfulness) the rafters sag, and through slackness the house leaks. Men prepare a meal for enjoyment, and wine makes men merry, and money is the answer to everything."* All money has an assignment and is used to meet earthly needs while we are on this earth; it is not to be viewed as our supernatural power, but we are to rule over it. We must keep it where it belongs and that is subjected to the Spirit of God within us!

In Philippians 4:11–13, Paul speaks, saying, *"Not that I speak from want, for I have learned to be content in whatever circumstances I am. I know how to get along with humble means, and I also know how to live in prosperity; in any and every circumstance I have learned the secret of being filled and going hungry, both of having abundance and suffering need. I can do all things through Christ who strengthens me."* As a child of God, we can be tested with seasons of both lack and prosperity. Many allow mammon to control one's emotional state and one's attitude concerning their identity. The point Paul was making was Jesus was his source of strength and affection in whatever situation he had to endure in life. No situation changed his trust in God or his mental position as a child of God. The secret was the contentment and assurance of Christ in him, the hope of glory. He was never in want.

Mammon, working through the spirit of poverty is a mindset of defeat, a mindset of never enough, or one that causes one to believes they will always be poor. In Ephesians 3:20, it says, *"Now to Him who is able to do far more abundantly beyond all that we ask or think, according to the power that works within us."* It is God's power within us, not our own ability, that releases the supernatural into our natural circumstances. Apply that promise in faith to your finances and see what God can do! We must learn to work the Word in our stewardship and we will see increase.

Mammon is in the system of our government, keeping many under its bondage, enslaved to it. This is a poverty mentality and can be a bloodline iniquity. This structure will keep people on a certain level of income and dependent on it. This level is never enough but deceives them into believing that they can't survive without it. This thinking comes as spiritual slavery, answering to Pharaoh's system. It is a blinding deceiving spirit attached to a false peace. When one gets accustomed to bondage, one will get comfortable with the shackles and it will become a "normal way of life." The welfare system many times continues in the bloodline in the form of poverty curses. This idolatry must be broken by the blood of Jesus and a revelation of the prosperity we have as sons of God is revealed and then activated by a new forward motion of obedience to truth with good work ethics.

When the Lord brought the children of Israel out of bondage after 400 years, they came out with the ark of His presence and a strategy to enable their victory. But they continued to look back to Pharaoh's provision of leeks, onions and garlic. This generation that came out still had poverty within operating with a slavery mindset. They forgot about the price they paid, harsh beatings and forced labor to Pharaoh for simple staples. They resisted the war that was necessary for them to establish the abundance of God's provision in their promised land. Fear caused their perspective of God's purposes to be clouded with confusion. They lost courage to advance and have success. They lost focus because of the size of their enemy. Many today feel they can never prosper due to the years of struggle, disappointment and lack they have endured. Just like the children of Israel, the enemy is afraid of God's people getting the revelation of their inheritance that is available. Riches were waiting for the covenant people of God but their release was postponed for another generation—one that would develop a dominion mentality. In Deuteronomy 8:18, it says, *"And you shall remember the Lord your God, for it is He who gives you power to get wealth, that He may establish His covenant which He swore to your fathers, as it is this day"* (NKJV). If one lives in a slavery mentality of poverty, one will be unable to function in the power that God has put within them; the power to prosper and establish the covenant of the kingdom of God in the earth. For this purpose, He sent us to this earth to have dominion in all areas of life, including financial.

The power the Father has put in us could be called an idea, skill, talent or gift that was supposed to bring wealth to us and be a source of provision to establish His covenant here and now. Proverbs 22:6–7 says, *"Train up a child in the way he should go, even when he is old he will not depart from it. The rich rules over the poor, and the borrower becomes the lender's slave."* In Hebrew thought, parents were to recognize the talent within their child and invest in them, releasing encouragement, resources and training so they could excel in that craft, bringing prosperity to their life. They were never to become the borrower but always to be the lender; then God will get the glory from what He has put within them, bringing increase and blessing into earth.

As a child of God, you were created to be a life-giver to others. That is not just in a kind word but also in actions. 1 John 3:16–19 explains this quite well, saying, *"We know love by this, that He laid down His life for us; and we ought to lay down our lives for the brethren. But whoever has the world's goods, and sees his brother in need and closes his heart against him, how does the love of God abide in him? Little children, let us not love with word or with tongue, but in deed and truth. We will know by this that we are of the truth, and will assure our heart before Him."* It takes a kingdom mentality of Jesus to acquire abundant supply and then it requires an obedient heart of good stewardship to maintain and distribute it in love. Jesus is the greatest multiplier; He demonstrated it time and time again by feeding the multitudes.

Mammon will cause one to have an attitude of favoritism and unrighteous judgments. In James 2:1–4, it reads, *"My brethren, do not hold your faith in our glorious Lord Jesus Christ with an attitude of personal favoritism. For if a man comes into your assembly with a gold ring and dressed in fine clothes, and there also comes in a poor man in dirty clothes, and you pay special attention to the one who is wearing the fine clothes, and say, 'You sit here in a good place,' and you say to the poor man, 'You stand over there, or sit down by my footstool,' have you not made distinctions among yourselves, and become judges with evil motives?"* We are not to allow the way the worldviews social status to get within us concerning the value of others. Jesus warned us in Luke 12:15, *"Beware, and be on your guard against every form of greed; for not even when one has an abundance does his life consist of his possessions."* In the parable of the rich man and Lazarus, both were transitioned to eternal life after death; the poor man was received into Abraham's bosom for restoration and comfort while the selfish rich man was in torment in hell. It is very serious to the Lord on how we view money and how we treat others (Luke 12:19–31).

In Luke 16, Jesus commended the thinking of an unrighteous steward on how he handled money. He lightened the load of his master's debtors and Jesus says we should be wiser as sons of light than him. In verses 8–12, it reads, *"And his master praised the unrighteous manager because he had acted shrewdly; for the sons of this age are more shrewd in relation to their own kind than the sons of light. And I say to you, make friends for yourselves by means of the wealth of unrighteousness, so that when it fails, they will receive you into the eternal dwellings. He who is faithful in a very little thing is faithful also in much; and he who is unrighteous in a very little thing is unrighteous also in much. Therefore, if you have not been faithful in the use of unrighteous wealth, who will entrust the true riches to you? And if you have not been faithful in the use of that which is another's, who will give you that which is your own?"* The shrewd manager here did good deeds by lightening the load, the debts of his tenants. Jesus lightened our debt by taking it all upon himself. As you are wise in love and generosity as God's sons, when you transition to eternity, the nations will welcome you into heaven. Your good deed of charity will be recorded in eternity. If everything we own belongs to the Lord, then it should be His to do with as He desires through us. In this parable, Jesus teaches us to redeem the unrighteous mammon by bringing souls in.

Matthew 6:20, Jesus speaking, *"But store up for yourself treasures in heaven, where neither moth nor rust destroys, and where thieves do not break in or steal; for where your treasure is, there your heart will be also."* Everyone should have a vision for their life and wealth. It should be an eternal one connected to kingdom purpose. In the church, many have forgotten that our wealth has an assignment. They have lost sight of establishing His kingdom. We have thought this parable of true riches was about acquiring "stuff." The Father's thoughts of true riches are not gold and silver, but the souls of humanity. Our money should not just bless us personally, but it should free souls from Satan's grip. One should have and use resources to further the kingdom here on earth.

Our stewardship and giving is a supernatural weapon and it affects our bloodline in the generations. In Hebrews 7:1–10, it tells us that Abraham paid a tenth of his best spoil to the priest Melchizedek, who the Bible says has no record of father or mother, remaining a priest forever. The writer also said Levi paid his tithe while in his Father's loins. I believe our giving goes into heaven's treasury record book, not an earthly building. The earthly buildings and ministries should be a tool and a resource the Lord uses to establish His kingdom purpose as we give to keep them running. When one sows, it is going to the altar of alms at the throne of God, into the hands of Melchizedek, who causes it to multiply and release blessing to us in the earth. God will reward the sower for all that ministry accomplished because one was obedient to release the seed. Supernatural blessings flow through that obedience to our generational seed that is even yet unborn. When I do not rob God of what he requires, even my children's children receive an inheritance. The Father sees one's generations connected and one's obedience releases blessing to them.

Look at Cornelius' example in Acts 10:3–4. It says, *"About the ninth hour of the day he clearly saw in a vision an angel of God who had just come in and said to him, 'Cornelius!' And fixing his gaze on him and being much alarmed, he said, 'What is it, Lord?' And he said to him, 'Your prayers and alms have ascended as a memorial before God.'"* Cornelius had an angel sent to him with a message of hope because the Lord said his prayers *and* offerings went up as a memorial unto the throne of God, meaning they had gotten God's attention. Our giving makes a difference in the spirit realm and it can bring breakthrough. Cornelius' giving was built around a covenant relationship with his God, which was his altar of worship. Our giving should be a part of our worship to the Lord, not a ritual, legalistic routine on Sunday morning. It should be holy to us. Romans 11:16 says, *"For if the firstfruit is holy, the lump is also holy; and if the root is holy, so are the branches"* (NKJV). Allow the Spirit of God to transform your thoughts about money and sowing, renewing your mind and having God's thoughts.

I wonder what things were held up over the rich young ruler as he walked away from the invitation to be Christ's disciple because he could not part with stuff? (Matt. 19:16–22) It wasn't the fact that he was wealthy that was his problem; it was that wealth had his affection. It was his idol before the Lord. His wealth brought false security to his imagination of great protection. In Proverbs 18:11, it says, *"A rich man's wealth is his strong city, and like a high wall in his own imagination."*

It is not about the amount of our giving, but it is about the obedience to do so. Jesus said in Matthew 10:42, *"And whoever in the name of a disciple gives to one of these little ones even a cup of water to drink, truly I say to you, he shall not lose his reward."* One's obedience will break off the spirit of mammon's influence in one's life, taking its power away to control our hearts. Become generous and see the blessings that will flow. Give your best and give mammon a black eye! If you are faithful, the Lord will give you more if He can trust your heart to sow. Jesus said in Luke 6:38, *"Give, and it will be given to you. They will pour into your lap a good measure-pressed down, shaken together, and running over. For by your standard of measure it will be measured to you in return."*

The attitude in which one sows plays an important part in the return one will receive. Jesus said when you have an offense, to leave your gift and go make things right and then go present it (Matt. 5:23). We are to give in faith, not offended, under compulsion or in fear, which will steal the harvest that you are sowing for. Without faith it is impossible to please God, so be sure to check the heart before sowing these spiritual seeds. Our money has our testimony attached to it as it is released to the throne of God. What is it speaking to God? Is it a testimony as Cornelius' with prayer and thanksgiving, or is it speaking, "I'm afraid I won't have my needs met" or "I feel condemned about the amount," or maybe it's this, "I feel pressure to please man in my giving?" These are wrong confessions that give mammon worship and power to rule one's heart.

Another area to consider is also the altar of our giving. Deuteronomy 22:9 says, *"You shall not sow your vineyard with two kinds of seed, or all the produce of the seed which you have sown and the increase of the vineyard will become defiled."* We need the blood applied to our altar of giving, especially if we have spent God's money on iniquitous, destructive or sinful activity. Some examples might be purchasing pornography books or videos, witchcraft articles, illegal drug use or distribution, paying for an abortion or even a psychic reading; all of which are forms of idolatry. That would be sowing in one's vineyard, the garden of your personal life, two kinds of seed. It's wise to repent for unrighteous spending habits and ask the Lord to break curses off and purify one's financial altar, washing your history concerning one's money in the blood of Jesus!

Do a Holy Spirit self-evaluation in the areas of your past financial history, such as broken contracts connected to unpaid loans, broken verbal vows or promises, past bankruptcy, and repent and apply the blood of Jesus. If one was a renter of property and not a good steward of it, be reminded that Jesus taught us one must take care of another's property to receive their own. We must learn to be spirit led with money and be faithful in obedience to sow accordingly. We need the blood of Jesus to wash over our earthly financial records that could be a snare or hindrance to us in the spirit realm of our bloodline.

To break the power of lack and poverty and to get out of mammon's grip, kingdom principles must be applied and continued as one shifts out of its bondage. Malachi 3:8–11 says, *"Will a man rob God? Yet you are robbing Me! But you say, 'How have we robbed You?' In tithes and offerings. You are cursed with a curse, for you are robbing Me, the whole nation of you! Bring the whole tithe into the storehouse, so that there may be food in My house, and test Me now in this,' says the Lord of hosts, 'if I will not open for you the windows of heaven and pour out for you a blessing until it overflows."* God says man can test Him in our giving! One needs to become disciplined in the tithe and sowing offerings. The tithe will indeed break the power of the spirit of Mammon off your money and God replaces it with a blessing. One must make giving a lifestyle no matter what state you are in. A prayer for breaking the power of Mammon is in Chapter sixteen. Below are some godly principles of sowing your seed into the kingdom that will position one for greater fruitfulness and harvest.

Faith principles of sowing seed:
- One must give in faith with expectation (Heb. 11:6)
- One must give cheerfully (2 Cor. 9:7)
- One must give without offense or unforgiveness, on a clean altar of sacrifice (Matt. 5:23)
- One must be obedient to the firstfruits principle (Mal. 3:10)
- One must release the seed with a right testimony; a prayer and declaration (Acts 10:4)
- One must give in obedience, being Spirit led (2 Cor. 9:7)
- One must see their giving as an act of worship, not a ritual exercise (Heb. 7:4, Gen. 14:20)

CHAPTER 12

EXERCISING AUTHORITY IN DELIVERANCE

*"Behold, I have given you authority to tread on ser-
pents and scorpions, and over all the power of the
enemy, and nothing will injure you."* Luke 10:19

I N LUKE, CHAPTER TEN, THE COMMISSIONING
of the seventy reveals the will of the Lord for His sent ones.
Those Jesus chooses will be empowered to do His work whatever the calling is. The key to one's success is the sending of the
Lord. The ultimate authority is in the person of Jesus Christ, but
the immediate authority lies in the deliverance minister as we see
in this text. In this text, the seventy returned with great joy and said
to Jesus that even the demons were subject to them in His name. In
general, what they were saying was, "Jesus, we are doing what you
gave us authority to do, and the demons recognized our authority
to exercise your authority against them." The result was that they
were forced to obey them. Jesus rejoiced and was ecstatic at the
report. He thanked the Father that He revealed these things to His
disciples who had childlike faith of simplicity and humility. They
felt their dependence on the Lord and accepted it without prideful
arrogance or intellect, everything that the Lord had revealed to

them. They had a different spirit than that of the Pharisees and Sadducees of His day.

Jesus then looks up in verses 18 and 19 of chapter ten and says, *"I was watching Satan fall from heaven like lightning. Behold, I have given you authority to tread on serpents and scorpions, and over all the power of the enemy, and nothing will injure you."* He was sharing a vision of Satan falling from heaven when the disciples reported their victory over demons. This was the place of Satan's rule and authority before the intervention of the kingdom of God through Jesus. Satan ruled over a vast kingdom of evil, operating in the lives of humanity in the earth without any disturbance. By sharing this vision, Jesus is connecting the fall of Satan from his rule and authority to the deliverance ministry of the seventy. When deliverance is exercised against the powers of darkness, the enemy suffers a notable defeat! They were dethroning principalities and powers of darkness at the word of their command by exercising authority in the name of the Lord Jesus. It is still the same today for the believers of Jesus who obey Him in spiritual warfare.

Using the name of Jesus is not a guarantee for victory, but the victory comes in knowing the Person of the name. When one stands in His character, nature and authority delegated by Him, that brings the power to enforce the Name. Jesus delegated power to His disciples, and to become a disciple means one becomes like their mentor in thought, word and deed. As a disciple of Jesus, one must become a learner of Christ, taking on the mind of Christ so one can then speak His words, and then the fruit or signs of Christ should begin to follow one's life. The Christ-like nature, character and power in operation comes by the Spirit of Christ working within one through salvation.

Faith can operate only when one's belief system is in operation. Faith grows by the revelation of the promises that one has through a relationship with Jesus. *So faith comes by hearing, and hearing by the word of Christ* (Rom. 10:17). In Mark 16:17–18, Jesus said, *"These signs will accompany those who have **believed:** in My name they will cast out demons, they will speak with new tongues; they will pick up serpents, and if they drink any deadly poison, it will not hurt them; they will lay hands on the sick, and they will recover."*

In one's relationship with Jesus, one receives bountiful benefits, of which one is the delegated authority over the enemy as a child of God. This authority will grow as one matures and develops one's relationship with the Master.

In Acts 19, the sons of Sceva were trying to cast out demons by saying to them, *"I adjure you by Jesus whom Paul preaches."* And the evil spirit's response was quite sobering! It said in verse 15, *"And the evil spirit answered and said to them, "I recognize Jesus, and I know about Paul, but who are you?'"* Then the man who had the evil spirit then overpowers them, leaving them naked and beaten. This brought a great move of God with the reverential fear of God, in the name of Jesus. One must know the Man behind the name to use His authority, having a personal relationship with Him.

The victory of the seventy caused Jesus to be overcome with joy and satisfaction. Notice how Jesus balances them out and brings them back to earth (Luke 10:20). He reminded them that the response of their joy should not be only in the victory of demons being subject to them, but that of the grace of God, being His chosen elect, having their names written in the book of life. This principle will keep one's focus on the Giver of Gifts, the power source of all victories we experience here in the earth, giving Him the glory for every breakthrough.

In Hebrews 1:2–3, it tells us, *"in these last days God has spoken to us in His Son, whom He appointed heir of all things, through whom also He made the world, And he is the radiance of His glory and the exact representation of His nature, and upholds all things by the word of His power."* All authority has been given to Him and He has delegated it to us. When Jesus said in Luke 10:19, *"I have given you authority to tread on serpents and scorpions, and over all the power of the enemy, and nothing will injure you,"* the "I have given you" means it is now, not in the future, but it is completed. The word authority is *exousia,* meaning authority, power, right to govern or control, dominion, the area or sphere of jurisdiction. The word power here is *Dunamis,* meaning might and ability, while *exousia* is the right to act. The enemy has might and ability, but the believer has delegated authority over him through Jesus Christ, the Supreme Authority.

Satan is a conquered enemy, and when the authority of Christ is delegated in the name of Jesus, victory is assured. This is for all His disciples to receive who are called upon to face the forces of darkness both in individuals and in territorial expansions of the kingdom of God. Jesus gave His disciples authority to cast out demons. The Greek word cast is *ekballo*, meaning, "to throw out forcibly." We are still operating under the same commission Jesus gave His disciples. To operate in authority, one must understand it and know how and when to exercise it. Jesus only did what He saw His Father do; He and His Father are one. We need to cast out demons by the finger of God, meaning by the instruction of Holy Spirit's leading. Jesus is still saying we are to continue His redemptive ministry, and when the enemy brings opposition, we have been given full authority over all his power that comes against us. Our enemy is defeated, but he is not dead, and is still actively the god of this world (2 Cor. 4:4). He is at war against us and will fight until he is forced to withdraw. He will regroup for a later opportune time, prowling around looking for channels to return! For it warns us in 1 Peter 5:8–9: *"Be of sober spirit, be on the alert. Your adversary, the devil, prowls around like a roaring lion, seeking someone to devour. But resist him, firm in your faith, knowing that the same experiences of suffering are being accomplished by your brethren who are in the world."*

Our opposition Jesus mentioned were called "serpents, scorpions and all the power of the enemy." These are all just extensions of Satan's defeated evil power. He is not omnipresent, omniscient nor omnipotent. He needs his fallen angels, demons and evil spirits, who all have his nature, to carry out his plans against us. It explains this in Ephesians 6:10–12, as listed in a previous chapter. Note that these serpents and scorpions are things that crawl or roam about in the earth. In Colossians 2:15, it says of Jesus, *"When He had disarmed the rulers and authorities, He made a public display of them, having triumphed over them through Him."* The structures and strongholds in regions and territories come down and lose power when the gospel of the kingdom is preached and demonstrated. Our focus should be just as Christ's, in dealing with the souls of humanity, bringing freedom, healing and restoration to lives, taking back territories for the kingdom. Jesus has disarmed the enemy at every level of power for us!

Deliverance was the only miracle that did not take place in the Old Testament because Jesus had not yet come, bringing and releasing the kingdom rule into the earth. It is a miracle ministry of the Spirit of Might in operation. Isaiah 11:2 teaches us that Jesus walked in the 7-fold Holy Spirit, *"The Spirit of the Lord shall rest upon Him, The Spirit of wisdom and understanding, The Spirit of counsel and **might**, The Spirit of knowledge and the fear of the Lord"* (NKJV). In Christ, we have the ability to operate in these dimensions of spiritual power and authority.

In Matthew 12:22–29, it reads, *"Then a demon-possessed man who was blind and mute was brought to Jesus, and He healed him, so that the mute man spoke and saw. All the crowds were amazed, and were saying, This man cannot be the Son of David, can he?' But when the Pharisees heard this, they said, 'This man casts out demons only by Beelzebul the ruler of the demons. And knowing their thoughts Jesus said to them, 'Any kingdom divided against itself is laid waste; and any city or house divided against itself will not stand. If Satan casts out Satan, he is divided against himself; how then will his kingdom stand? If I by Beelzebul cast out demons, by whom do your sons cast them out? For this reason they will be your judges. But if I cast out demons by the Spirit of God, then the kingdom of God has come upon you. Or how can anyone enter the strong man's house and carry off his property, unless he first binds the strong man? And then he will plunder his house.'"* We are called to plunder the enemy by bringing freedom and restoration through the releasing of the kingdom of God in deliverance ministry to the shackled souls of humanity.

Throughout the ministry of Jesus, He endured great persecution because of exercising His authority over demons. The religious spirit of His day was always opposing Him, questioning His authority and His actions. In Luke 4:35–36, when Jesus did a deliverance in the synagogue, they began to talk about Him. In verse 36, it says, *"And amazement came upon them all, and they began talking with one another saying, 'What is this message? For with authority and power He commands the unclean spirits and they come out.'"* It is no different today for those who carry the kingdom message in demonstration and power. There will always be critics! Jesus' greatest persecution came from the religious ones. Today, it is still the same attack and accusations trying to hinder kingdom advancement. Deliverance brings the most warfare on God's servants due to the direct conflict and confrontation of light and darkness. It brings to light/exposes the hidden things of darkness. It demonstrates the power of Jesus' authority and His victory over Satan publicly. It destroys yokes, cycles, sin bondages and takes back the ground Satan has stolen from the lives of humanity. It breaks the chains of resistance, so people can move forward in maturity as a child of God. One should not back down when personal warfare comes and religious spirits attack and accuse. Just be reminded if they persecuted Christ, and you are in Christ, this spirit will persecute you, too! Jesus speaking to us in John 15:20, *"Remember the word that I said to you, 'A slave is not greater than his master.' If they persecuted Me, they will also persecute you; if they kept My word, they will keep yours also."* Rejoice that you are counted worthy to endure suffering with Jesus! (2 Thess. 1:4–6)

In Matthew 16:19, *Jesus said, "I will give you keys of the kingdom of heaven; and whatever you bind on earth shall have been bound in heaven, whatever you loose on earth shall have been loosed in heaven."* The Greek word bind is *deo*, meaning to tie, imprison, tie in bonds, or knit. The word loose means *lyo,* meaning release, untie, to break, destroy, dissolve, melt and put off. These are effective deliverance terms used as weapons for spiritual warfare against the enemy. There is a caution of pride in spiritual warfare and conflict. The abuse or misuse of power can lead to prideful boastings. Avoid boasting, vainglory, spiritual power trips and looking for battles, which will all bring casualties in war. Jesus only did what He saw His father do, and He never went looking for the enemy, He just dealt with him when he showed up!

One must know their assigned place of delegated authority and one needs to be submitted to righteous authority. Our lives must be fully submitted to Jesus and those in authority we are called to work with. In Matthew 8, the Centurion soldier asked Jesus to just speak a word that His servant would be healed. Then he says in verse 9,

"For I also am a man under authority, with soldiers under me; and I say to this one, 'Go!' and he goes, and to another, 'Come!' and he comes, and to my slave, 'Do this!' and he does it." Jesus marveled at his faith and the paralyzed servant received healing. The Centurion understood how the operation of authority worked. He lived and functioned in respect to authority his whole life. By this obedience, it was delegated to him the power or the right to use it. The Centurion's understanding of this principle, and seeing the abilities of Jesus, gave him great faith to believe that His spoken word would have power to heal his servant. Jesus said to him in verse 13, *"Go; it shall be done for you as you have believed."* This speaks to me that one's own personal reality is rooted in one's feelings, attitudes, and belief system and from this perspective life is done to them as they have believed. The Centurion's belief system moved the hand of God and it was in the faith and understanding of authority that he received the miraculous, even for someone else! The works of Jesus came by the Supreme Authority, His Father, who released it to Jesus. The world saw it demonstrated in the great works of power he displayed. It should be the same for us. Being under authority is to have authority operating in power and demonstrating the works of Jesus Christ.

The anointing

The anointing is the ability to do something and the authority is an operating influence through relationship. When speaking of the authority of a believer, we also must discuss the anointing of Holy Spirit. The authority releases to me power or anointing to do a task. Isaiah 10:27 says, *"so it will be in that day, that his burden will be removed from your shoulders and his yoke from your neck, and the yoke will be broken because of fatness."* This word picture of fatness in the Hebrew mindset implied a bull which grows so fat that the yoke will no longer go around its neck. Fatness is a symbol of God's people waxing strong in Spirit and asserting their freedom in Christ Jesus. It speaks of maturity in the anointing. It is because of the presence and strength of the fatness (the oil) that the opposition in our life is destroyed! 1 John 2:20 says, *"But you have an anointing from the Holy One, and you all know."* As believers, we have the Greater One in us who gives us an anointing to operate in His authority, through relationship. This working together brings victorious living in Christ.

The word anoint means to smear or rub with oil, to ceremonially confer a divine or holy office upon a priest or monarch by smearing with oil. This can come through the impartation of Holy Spirit through revelation, communion and participation. In Acts 10:38, it says of Jesus, *"You know of Jesus of Nazareth, how God anointed Him with the Holy Spirit and with power, and how He went about doing good and healing all who were oppressed by the devil, for God was with Him."* Jesus was anointed with Holy Spirit and power. In Luke 4:18 Jesus reads a prophecy over His life saying, *"the spirit of the Lord is upon Me, because He has anointed Me to preach the gospel to the poor. He has sent Me to proclaim release to the captives, and recovery of sight to the blind, to set free those who are oppressed, to proclaim the favorable year of the Lord."* We as believers carry an anointing of Holy Spirit, but we need the power present upon us to do the works of Jesus! The Spirit of the Lord was upon Jesus to *do* something. If we desire more anointing, we must exercise faith with what we have received!

In Luke 3:22, after Jesus was baptized and the heaven was opened, it reads, *"And the Holy Spirit descended upon Him in bodily form like a dove, and a voice came out of heaven, 'You are My beloved Son, in You I am well-pleased.'"* I believe the anointing of God comes from the Father. It is by the measure of the grace of one's calling, by faith and in the relationship and obedience to Jesus and Holy Spirit. His anointing of power can increase in our lives by the measure of the hunger we have for his presence and His purpose. Jesus is the author and finisher of us all. I believe in Him there are no limits to the anointing except those limitations we have received in our belief systems.

In John 14:20, Jesus said, *"In that day you will know that I am in My father, and you in Me, and I in you."* Jesus was speaking of when the Spirit of truth would come and abide in and upon His disciples. This whole discussion in this chapter is about a relationship with the Father through Jesus and the power of Holy Spirit.

The authentic believer can be identified by a love relationship with Jesus and others, a love for His Word, and a lifestyle of obedience to His instruction. He tells them greater works they will do by the power of the Spirit of God in and upon their lives. One should be filled with Holy Spirit to be effective in spiritual warfare. Holy Spirit is the presence and power of Jesus in operation.

Jesus said in Acts 1:8, *"But you will receive power when the Holy Spirit has come upon you."* As they were waiting in obedience for Him to come, it says in chapter two that He showed up as fire upon each of them and they spoke with other tongues. From that point on, they were equipped to walk as Jesus in demonstration and power to evangelize the world. Speaking in tongues opens the door to the supernatural power of the Spirit. Increasing the amount of time one prays in tongues will bring spiritual increase of faith and the anointing! Jude 1:20 says, *"But you, beloved, building yourselves up on your most holy faith, praying in the Holy Spirit."*

To receive greater anointing:
- walk in the fear of God
- honor the authority God has put in your life
- hunger and thirst for righteousness
- be filled with fresh oil continually
- pray in the Spirit more than you pray in English
- study the Word of God
- walk in obedience to the instruction of Jesus
- fellowship with Holy Spirit
- exercise faith by being a doer of the Word

The importance of teamwork and team etiquette

1 Thessalonians 5:12–13 says, *"But we request of you, brethren, that you appreciate those who diligently labor among you, and have charge over you in the Lord and give you instruction, and that you esteem them very highly in love because of their work. Live in peace with one another."*

Jesus demonstrated His perfect plan for effective and successful ministry in Mark 6:7, *"And He summoned the twelve and began to send them out in pairs, and gave them authority over the unclean spirits,"* then it goes on to say that, *"He instructed them."* The Lord would not want us ignorant to the devil's schemes. It is wisdom to pay attention to the instruction of God. Therein is the safety, accountability, strength, and increase of power to do ministry with others. The ministry of deliverance should be one of teamwork under the instruction of the Lord Jesus.

The word team is defined as many persons associated in some joint action; a number of persons forming one of the sides in a game or contest. Whatever you do and how you function as a team should represent Christ, all being on the same side, working together for the common good of the one receiving ministry. How teams function and carry themselves reflects upon the leader of the ministry and more importantly the head of it, which is Jesus Himself.

Paul said in 2 Corinthians 3:2–3, *"You are our letter, written in our hearts, known and read by all men; being manifested that you are a letter of Christ, cared for by us, written not with ink but with the Spirit of the living God, not on tablets of stone but on tablets of human hearts."* Spiritual fruit must be produced in the lives of the team. Bearing fruit that remains is one way the work is tested to see if it is from God. In Matthew 7:18–20, it says, *"A good tree cannot produce bad fruit, nor can a bad tree produce good fruit. Every tree that does not bear good fruit is cut down and thrown into the fire. So then, you will know them by their fruits."*

The call of ministry to team comes from the Lord Jesus. Serving on a ministry team is allowing one's personal anointing to build the church, which means to restore and disciple people. The Lord looks at the condition of the heart, so we must examine ourselves. 2 Corinthians 13:5–6, Paul says, *" Test yourselves to see if you are in the faith; examine yourselves! Or do you not recognize this about yourselves, that Jesus Christ is in you-unless indeed you fail the test?"* A team will be tested personally with the message they carry. There will be backlash if one's personal life is not in God's order and the enemy will try to find areas of entry personally, and with the team itself. Offenses are the number one entry for demonic attacks against team ministry. Each one should be available to receive cleansing personally and have continued spiritual tune-ups. No one is exempt from needing deliverance. If one believes they are exempt, pride is at work. Humility is key to maintaining the anointing! It is wisdom for one who feels called to serve on team to have continued spiritual tune-ups as needed to see lasting spiritual fruit produced in their life. One must continue to grow and mature when on team, and certain things must be in place in their personal life to remain pure in their call.

Personal spiritual questions to consider for growth and maturity when on a team:

- Is one fully submitted to authority and the call of ministry, faithful and obedient?
- Is one a person of prayer?
- Is one a student of the word of God?
- Is one's life in spiritual order and has one been through personal cleansing?
- Is one operating in love?
- Is the character of Christ evident in one's life?
- Is one capable of being a team player?
- Is one teachable?

I start those who desire to work on cleansing teams to work first in the function of an intercessor on the team before they begin to work in cleansing rooms or walk the floor in mass cleansing. Watching and praying is a great tool for developing the strength of will and discernment that is needed. All must be an intercessor and know how to pray to be effective in spiritual warfare ministry. This is a great place to begin one's in personal development. It will test the heart to see if one is really called to work on team, being patient and obedient as the Lord grooms them for the hands-on training. Allowing one to do spiritual warfare ministry before one is equipped can bring spiritual disaster to them and others. Even if one is very gifted, it does not mean one is ready for war. Mature spiritual character development is more valuable in making one ready for warfare than a gift in operation. Many gifted, wounded warriors who were put on the frontlines before any spiritual training are now sitting on the sidelines broken, angry, and more wounded. In James 1:4, it says, *"And let endurance have its perfect result, so that you may be perfect and complete, lacking in nothing."*

To fulfill the call of ministry means meeting the people's spiritual needs wherever they are. Jesus and His disciples did this as they went out and ministered to the lost and dying. To function on team, one must be willing to work in a flexible way with the anointing of Holy Spirit. One must allow Him to flow, learning to listen and then to obey the team leader and respecting other teammates, sharing information and revelation at appropriate times. This will keep the oil of anointing and unity flowing throughout the session of ministry. Each member must recognize the need for one another. In Ephesians 4:16, it says, *"from whom the whole body, being fitted and held together by what every joint supplies, according to the proper working of each individual part, causes the growth of the body for the building up of itself in love."*

John 3:30 says, *"He must increase, but I must decrease."* In biblical qualifications of leadership, the Lord considers their development of godly character, wisdom and humility a priority (John 12:24–25, Luke 9:46–48, 22:24–34, Titus 1:7–9, Phil. 2:3–8). Team must have godly motives when doing cleansing/deliverance ministry. Godly motives will always compel us upward to Christ. Wrong motives will be poison to the work and hinder breakthrough, causing problems in the unity of the team. Team must always examine personal motives for ministry and check their love towards the Lord and His people often.

Deliverance is a power gift that can attract much attention and it brings much personal warfare. Team must also learn to keep their eyes on Jesus and not on the manifestations of demons. Power gifts can cause one to become prideful because of the authority the Lord entrusts the deliverer with. Never do deliverance because of the lust for power or to see manifestations. This is a wrong spirit and will open oneself up to personal demonic oppression. Jesus kept manifestations at a minimal. He was not moved by what the demons did or spoke. He stayed focused on His task at hand and cast them out as quick as possible. He, however, did experience demonic manifestations in people and at times it could not be avoided. On occasion Jesus spoke to them to get its name or revelation concerning its entry into the victim, and then He shut it up and cast it out. Jesus' concern was focused on freeing and healing the soul who was in bondage.

Some things to consider for team concerning ministering to others:

- Does one exercise authority just because they have authority; meaning is the session being Spirit led? Jesus only did what His Father did (John 5:36).
- Is the person receiving cleansing ready to be free and walk holy in that area?
- Is there groundwork that needs to be done before deliverance takes place? (e.g. counseling/mapping to identify possible occult activity or soul ties connected to the spirit manifesting).
- Does the one receiving have unforgiveness or need to renounce some things before ministry?
- Does the individual need inner healing from emotional pain or suppressed anger that the demon is using to stay buried in or attached to?
- Is there enough time to deal with the spiritual bondage one has discerned?
- Are you confident you can handle the battle, or will it require someone more experienced in that area one is ministering?

These are things to keep in mind when taking on spiritual battles of darkness. The one doing the ministry is responsible to cooperate with Holy Spirit for the way it is exercised and its end. It is a serious ministry dealing with the condition of the soul.

We see many people who are terrified of getting delivered due to past experiences going bad, kooky ministry and showboat arenas of deliverance. This draws the wrong attention and can bring a reproach on the deliverance work of Jesus. It is very sad indeed, but those who do damage to God's sheep will answer to the Great Shepherd. It is not a wonder why people will often run away from the ministry of deliverance.

When younger in the Lord, I observed a deliverance attempt that brought more damage than good to the one receiving ministry. A minister was invited in to speak and minister to the people. It was altar time and there was a young teen girl that came up for prayer. The minister said he saw a spirit of suicide and went directly into casting it out. He was very forceful with the girl, being loud and yelling in her face, with hands all over her. The child was understandably terrified and shook to the core. I'm not sure she received anything, but I know she left that altar broken and more damaged. She was crying, asking what happened, and was very confused. The man left her in that state, addressed nothing more with her, and moved on to minister to others. Clearly, in this situation, wisdom would have been to minister to the broken part of the girl in love, getting to the root of the suicide thoughts. She needed inner healing, and if he discerned it accurately, deliverance from the demon, but none of this could happen with this approach. The fruit was not good when it was over. She left, and sadly, I never saw her at church again.

Self-check for team ministry function:

- My personal appearance—One needs to be in the uniform (if applicable) that was requested, and it should be pressed, modest and loosely worn.
- My attitude—One needs at least an hour of personal prayer and ministry time with the Lord before a session or conference. One must check for any offense that will block the flow of Holy Spirit or hinder the team. One should take personal communion.
- My interaction with others—One must be polite, respectful, and loving with people. One must be conscious of facial expressions and mannerisms while interacting and when the cleansing prayers are going on, being careful that one is not too loud when calling out demons, being a distraction in personal or corporate cleansing.
- My interaction with teammates—One must be a team player, not making it about oneself, but be willing to yield to the anointing upon others, no offences present.
- My family—One must be wise concerning backlash, keeping one's family covered properly when one goes out. One must make sure things at home are in order so there will be no distractions out on the field.

- My testimony—if one is called one to share one's testimony, they must always give the glory to the Lord. Testimonies are not about us but about HIM! One must be careful of pride of self when sharing, false humility, and exaggerating the story. The enemy will want to contaminate one's testimony. Also, it is not a time for "you to shine" but for Christ to be glorified in you. It is not a time to share one's spiritual gifts or to boast of one's self. This is a sign of immaturity and others will see through it. This can bring a reproach on the work and steal the power of one's testimony.
- My accountability—One must follow protocol with no "sidewalk prophecies" , no "whisper in the ear" words, being fully submitted to spiritual authority.
- The laying on of hands—One must not be heavy-handed, nor get a "thrill" out of the power gifts or healing anointing that flows through one's hands. One must be mindful of hands placed in the appropriate places while ministering. One must understand that some receiving ministry may have been sexually assaulted or traumatized. One must use the wisdom of the Lord when ministering with the laying on of hands while cleansing prayers are going on.

CHAPTER 13

THE DISCERNING OF SPIRITS

*"But to each one is given the manifestation of the
Spirit for the common good. For to one is given the
word of wisdom through the Spirit, and to another
the word of knowledge according to the same Spirit;
to another faith by the same Spirit, and to another
gifts of healing by the one Spirit, And to another the
effecting of miracles, and to another prophecy, and
to another the **distinguishing of spirits**, to another
various kinds of tongues, and to another the inter-
pretation of tongues. But one and the same Spirit
works all these things, distributing to each one indi-
vidually just as He wills."* 1 Corinthians 12:7–11

THE DISCERNING OR DISTINGUISHING OF
spirits is a gift of revelation of Holy Spirit. It is most helpful
and necessary to understand this function of the Spirit and
to desire it to be operating and sharpened to do spiritual warfare
ministry. This function is the ability to recognize and distinguish
the spirit of a thing or a spirit itself. It can function with the seer/
prophetic and healing gifts of the Spirit of God. In 2 Corinthians
10:4, it says, *"for the weapons of our warfare are not of the flesh,
but divinely powerful for the destruction of fortresses."* We must

discern correctly by the Spirit of God what is demonic or angelic, holy or the flesh.

It says in 2 Corinthians 11:3–4, *"But I am afraid that, as the serpent deceived Eve by his craftiness, your minds will be led astray from the simplicity and purity of devotion to Christ. For if one comes and preaches another Jesus whom we have not preached, or you receive a different spirit which you have not received, or a different gospel which you have not accepted, you bear this beautifully."* Discernment can become active as Holy Spirit wills, at any time, being in a vison, impression, conversation, in prayer, or through dream language. It can also work in spiritual warfare battle, being very helpful and necessary in the counseling and deliverance ministry. It helps in identifying demons and strongholds. Discerning the nature of the atmosphere, encounters, prophetic messages, even the source or origin of a thing is revealed through this spirit. It will cause one to have a heightened awareness of the presence of God and the anointing that is operation through Him.

Discernment is needed today more than ever because of deep the deception of the enemy operating in and out of the church. One needs to recognize and utilize this function of the Spirit for effective spiritual warfare and personal spiritual protection. The operation of the spirit of discernment does not always work alone. Almost always it is used with other functions of the Spirit like wisdom. One must be sensitive when Holy Spirit is unveiling something. It will help us to discern when the enemy is working in our lives and the lives of others.

Jesus desires His church to exercise this operation of the Spirit. In Revelation 2:2, He says, *"I know your deeds and your toil and perseverance, and that you cannot tolerate evil men, and you put to the test those who call themselves apostles, and they are not, and you found them to be false."* We are not just to discern the spirit but also the fruit of those who profess Christ. We are warned that Satan himself can transform himself into an angel of light (2 Cor. 11:14). This does not mean we are to be critical and judgmental of others and full of suspicion of their every move. We use discernment and act with Godly wisdom of the Word. Paul said in 1 Thessalonians 5:21, *"But examine everything carefully; hold fast to that which is good."* 1 John 2:4–5 says, *"The one who says, 'I have come to know Him,' and does not keep His commandments, is a liar, and the truth is not in him; but whoever keeps His word, in him the love of God has truly been perfected. By this we know that we are in Him."* We can and should use the Word of God to discern for us. It tells us in Hebrews 4:12–13 that, *"For the word of God is living and active and sharper than any two-edged sword, and piercing as far as the division of soul and spirit, of both joints and marrow, and **able to judge the thoughts and intentions of the heart**. And there is no creature hidden from His sight, but all things are open and laid bare to the eyes of Him with whom we have to do."* The Word of God is a supernatural tool to test our hearts and motives by which we operate and will keep one safe in truth if we line up with its instructions.

Since we are warned that Satan himself can disguise himself as an angel of light, one should be discerning concerning ministries. One can be led away and deceived because of spiritual gifts and abilities in others and believe that something is good when in fact it is not because of a wrong spirit in operation.

In 2 Thessalonians 2:9–10, it says of the working of the anti-christ spirit, *"that is, the one whose coming is in accord with the activity of Satan, with all power and signs and false wonders, and with all the deception of wickedness for those who perish, because they did not receive the love of the truth so as to be saved."* The gifts and calling of God are without repentance (Rom. 11:29). Functioning in the gifts can be the easy part, however, maintaining purity in the gifts is the challenge. One is responsible to maintain a pure heart as we use them; otherwise, one will become hypocrit-ical, bringing judgment.

In Numbers 22–24, Balaam was noted as a seer/prophet and he would go meet with God and hear the word of God and release it. God would show up and speak with him, but his heart was not right. It was full of covetousness and idolatry. It says in Revelation 2:14 that he kept teaching Balak how to put a stumbling block before the sons of Israel, to eat things sacrificed to idols and to commit acts of immorality. In the end, he died as a false prophet by the sword in

Joshua 13:22. He was false because he led the people away from God's righteousness!

Deuteronomy 13:1–5 warns if a prophet or dreamer of dreams arises working in signs or wonders, and it comes true concerning what he spoke, but then he steers one away to worship or follow other gods, do not listen to the prophet or his words. It goes on to say, it is a test to see if one is devoted to the Living God and if one fears Him, serves Him or will cling to Him. Then God says to purge the evil from among the people. The prophet then was to be put to death because he counseled the people in rebellion against the Lord. Thank God for new covenant grace! Isaiah 2:22 says, *"Stop regarding man, whose breath of life is in his nostrils; For why should he be esteemed?"* Don't be led astray by charisma or gifting but be fully devoted to the Lord God!

One can fall into deception if they make a determination that a ministry is of God based solely on the signs, works or wonders that is operating in them. The spirit of discernment, which should always have liberty to operate in one's life, will help safe guard against such deception. Isaiah 11:3, speaking of our Lord says, *"And He will delight in the fear of the Lord, And He will not judge by what His eyes see nor make a decision by what His ears hear."* One needs to know those who labor among them, that is, knowing them intimately by the discerning of the Spirit of God. Many only look at the outward success of a thing. God looks much deeper within its operation. In 1 Samuel 16:7, God was speaking to His Prophet Samuel, *"But the Lord said to Samuel, 'Do not look at his appearance or at the height of his stature, because I have rejected him; for God sees not as man sees, for man looks at the outward appearance, but the Lord looks at the heart.'"* As a believer, we need to discern as the Lord does, inwardly and not outward by the natural appearance of things. Proverbs 20:25 says, *"It is a trap for a man to say rashly, 'It is holy!' And after the vows to make inquiry."*

Don't allow the influence of an anointing, gift or authority of any person seduce you into unrighteousness, turning your heart away from Jesus. We must pray for God's representatives. Many are deceived and continue in a wrong way. They believe the lie that the anointing or a large following can cancel out the need for accountability or holiness. Some have been deceived into believing God must be winking at their unrighteous, sinful behavior, and that lawlessness does not pertain to them because they are under grace. In Acts 5:3–9, the gift of discernment was working when Peter asked Ananias and Sapphira why they lied to Holy Spirit. They both dropped dead and died. That was not the work of a man, but of God.

1 John 4:1–3 says, *"Beloved, do not believe every spirit, but test the spirits to see whether they are from God, because many false prophets have gone out into the world. By this you know the Spirit of God: every spirit that confesses that Jesus Christ has come in the flesh is from God; and every spirit that does not confess Jesus is not from God; this is the spirit of the antichrist, of which you have heard that it is coming, and now it is already in the world."* This testing of the spirit is very helpful when one is doing cleansing and there is heavy demonic oppression. To be sure a spirit is gone and not still in operation or hiding, I have asked the person to confess this scripture, "Jesus Christ is the Son of God who came in the flesh, and He is my Lord and Savior." If a demon is still in operation, it will not allow the person to speak this, because it is still controlling them. This is an example of using the Word to discern for you.

Some biblical examples of this in operation would be when Jesus saw Nathanael in John 1:47–48, *"Jesus saw Nathanael coming to Him, and said of him, 'Behold, an Israelite indeed, in whom there is no deceit!' Nathanael said to Him, 'How do you know me?' Jesus answered and said to him, 'Before Philip called you, when you were under the fig tree, I saw you.'"* Jesus discerned Nathanael's spirit before he spoke to Him. It also says that Jesus heard or knew men's thoughts without them speaking anything (Luke 9:47, Matt. 9:4, 12:25). Many times, while I am teaching I hear thoughts in the room challenging the Word I'm bringing. This is very helpful in *"destroying speculations and every lofty thing raised up against the knowledge of God, and taking every thought captive to the obedience of Christ"* (2 Cor. 10:5). This is a spiritual wrestling conflict within the minds of the people to whom God has called me to bring restoration to. When the Spirit of God discerns, I can bring more revelation of the truth to the argument that is in the spirit realm. The Lord desires His people to be free and He will work through all the functions of operation of the Spirit necessary to do so!

In the book of Acts 16:16–18, a slave girl followed Paul and continued to cry out that they were servants of the Most High, proclaiming the way of salvation. Paul was greatly agitated, annoyed, unsettled within, because he was discerning a demon speaking through the girl. He called out the spirit of divination and the girl was set free. Note that although she was saying the right things, she had a wrong spirit operating within. He discerned the evil spirit within her "right message" which contaminated the words she was speaking. At times I can be around someone and they are saying nice things to me, but I feel agitated and do not desire to converse, or I feel a caution from the Spirit of God about trusting them. **The Spirit of Discernment will protect one from evil intention if one will listen when He speaks.**

In Ezekiel 44:23–24, the Lord speaks of a Levitical priesthood who kept charge of His sanctuary when Israel went astray, saying, *"Moreover, they shall teach My people the difference between the holy and the profane, and cause them to discern between the unclean and the clean. In a dispute they shall take their stand to judge; they shall judge it according to My ordinances."* For our personal discernment to be holy, we must become holy. To judge righteously, we must live by truth ourselves. When one lives in an unholy mixture themselves, one will be in danger of not operating in purity with their gifts or discerning correctly. I have seen this within the lives of people who clearly needed deliverance but still were functioning in position within the church. Unless there is true repentance or revelation comes to them, this operation will prove disastrous in the end.

In Acts, chapter nine, The Lord appeared to Ananias in a vision and says his name, and the disciple said, *"Here I am, Lord."* Later in 27:23, when Paul was on the ship and a violent storm came and the men feared for their life, he tells them not to be afraid, that an angel of God appeared before him, telling him they would be safe. The angel speaks to Paul, but no one else heard the message, nor saw the angel. Both men discerned these visitations and responded to instruction and it brought safety and advancement to the kingdom of God.

I have had numerous personal experiences discerning spirits through the years, some angelic and many demonic due to the deliverance ministry. This gift is most helpful also in counseling. I will share a few for revelation and teaching purposes as best I can. Many of these spirits appear like a 3D or a hologram-like image, but as they are made visible and the veil is lifted to see the unseen, they are real. God exposes them to bring revelation and breakthrough to people's lives. These visits will charge a spiritual atmosphere when discerned that will be felt by the natural senses either of darkness or the fear of the Lord when holy.

Years ago, I had a dream that a man (I believe it was the Angel of the Lord) came and asked me to walk with him. He took me on a walk through an open country meadow surrounded by a forest with a brook running through it. He said he had a gift for me from heaven. As we walked along, it was a most quiet, peaceful walk and so beautiful was the scenery. We were conversing and enjoying our journey. We arrived at the destination and the man reached into his robe pocket and pulled out a pair of odd-looking, antique eyeglasses. He said, "Put them on," and I obeyed. As I put them on, everything changed, and I could see and feel many things and so much activity all around me. As I took them off, we were in the same peaceful meadow, by the forest and the brook. I did this again and again with the same result. He said I could use them anytime I needed; they were mine, a gift. Within the unseen realm, I saw many things: robed angels flying with fire on the end of their robes as they flew out of the bank of the brook, creatures I had never seen before, people of different eras, all dressed accordingly, and families it seemed, of people groups having interaction and conversations, all of which was behind the veil of the unseen, being exposed by the gift that was given to me. This was not just a seer gift but also a discerning of spirits, both working together in revelation by Holy Spirit. They were a gift to me, but I still had the responsibility to steward them as led by the Spirit of God, so that He would be glorified in them.

Discernment is useful when traveling to different regions to minister. One can discern the atmosphere or spiritual climate to know how to pray effectively for the people. Natural storms can be demonic in nature and discernment can tell one if it is spiritually created. In Mark 4:39, Jesus spoke to a violent storm and commanded it to be still, and it obeyed Him. They were headed across the lake where the demoniac lived. I'm quite certain the storm was to keep Jesus from making it to the other side of the lake to free the man from his bondage.

In 2 Corinthians 2:14–15, it reads, *"But thanks be to God, who always leads us into triumph in Christ, and manifests through us the sweet aroma of the knowledge of Him in every place. For we are a fragrance of Christ to God among those who are being saved and among those who are perishing; to the one an aroma to death, to the other an aroma from life to life."* In discussing the spirit of discernment, there are smells in the spirit realm that are not detected by the natural nose. I have experienced smelling a sweet fragrance, like incense during worship services. One can smell smoke and something burning, but no natural fire is present. There are times when one can "smell a demon." Those smells are awful, foul, pungent odors that can come when evicting demons or when one walks in with certain unclean spirits attached. I have found these demonic smells can come from sexual unclean spirits, witchcraft, sickness, or death. But I'm sure all demons smell foul!

I picked up a woman at an airport who was coming in for cleansing. We will call her Pam. Pam was diagnosed with cancer and was very sick. She also had been in the occult, and when she got in the car, a terrible odor of rotting flesh was present. No one smelled it but me. It was vile and the smell even made it difficult to travel. But I could discern the smell of death by Holy Spirit. I believe it was strong due to the nature of her life, deep in the occult. If believers have an aroma, so do demons.

We do a lot of mission work with the First Nations and this gift is very sharp and active with this assignment, because it is needed. It is not uncommon to have spirits visit us and at times speak a message through a dream or open vision. One trip, I recall an ancient spirit power came in the night and it was in the imagery of a full headdress Indian chief who was very angry, and it came to give me a message that I was not wanted, and to go home. Well, of course, the enemy didn't want us there! The Lord sent us to release the kingdom of God, to bring cleansing and healing to His Native American people. When God sends one, He will provide and protect them. Discernment is never to frighten us but to empower us with wisdom to bring breakthrough. Another time, at night, I had a dark cloud come over my bed and the atmosphere darkened as I felt the evil presence, then as I looked, I saw a vision of a Navajo man, head to chest peering in at me. He was a medicine man coming to see or do me harm, but to no avail because the blood of Jesus protects God's servants. Even though the man himself looked harmless, the evil nature of his spirit was exposed, by the discernment of the presence that came in before him.

While doing a tent revival in New Mexico, I was releasing the cleansing prayers with the first nation people. I discerned (heard) rattles and hissing behind me in the dark. I turned, expecting to see a medicine man standing there with some snakes. It was so real and loud to my ears. It was all happening in the spirit realm, and I continued to pray, unmoved, without hesitation, and the power of God filled the tent, and so many were set free and we saw miracles and healed bodies that night. Intercessors later had told me they saw some of the native people wrapped in snakeskin before cleansing prayers. Discerning, as we have already discussed, is not only about "seeing" but also "hearing" in the Spirit. In 1 Kings 3:9, Solomon prayed and asked God, *"So give your servant an understanding heart to judge Your people to discern between good and evil. For who is able to judge this great people of Yours?"* This meant in the Hebrew translation Solomon was asking for a hearing (discerning) heart. It so pleased the Lord that he wanted a discerning heart to hear his voice that he was given the greatest gift of wisdom and wealth than any other man! It would be wise to ask for a discerning heart to hear and see as the Lord does, and expect to receive it if one's motives are pure.

There are times when I can discern demonic manifestations or tongues and others believe it is Holy Spirit. This is very common in churches, people receiving another spirit. Usually these are religious spirits in operation, hiding within the person. Many times I will discern the pain of someone else in my body, but when their freedom or healing comes, it will lift or go away. Hiding infirmities can be discerned like this because Holy Spirit is working with us to restore lives.

A woman we will call Alice was receiving prayer for a stroke that had affected her left side. During the prayer, I had an intense pain hit my right kidney, which almost took me to the floor. I asked her if she had kidney problems; she said no. I listened to Holy Spirit instead and I began to break curses off her kidneys and commanded the spirit of kidney disease to loose her. The hiding spirit manifested and came out of her. Without the discernment gift, she would have gone home with it and eventually it would have made her ill. She was set free from the stroke paralysis with full function of her body and the hiding kidney disease assignment was destroyed. The pain eased up and eventually was gone from my body. Glory be to God for allowing us to use His power!

Another time of discernment working through feeling was when we were in a new region out west and were going to minister to a new tribe of the First Nations. When it occurred, we thought at first it possibly was an attack. I had a pain in my hip and it went down my leg. It was so severe that I could not walk, but with a terrible limp. It happened as I woke. Immediately the team began to pray for me. We were asking the Lord what this could be. I knew we had been covered and were sent in to minister. We sent out a call requesting for our intercessors to pray. I had got a word from the Lord that I had received a new sword and it was very heavy and I was allowed to feel weight of it! I pressed to the meetings, limping, and as I opened my mouth to deliver the word, the pain left me. I do not believe we realize what kind of spiritual arsenal we carry as a warrior of Jesus in the spirit. That was as experience I will never forget. The meetings were powerful as the Lord moved mightily cleansing His people.

When praying for people, I can discern if there is demonic oppression by a certain anointing that comes upon me, then I must be led by Holy Spirit to pursue it or how to pray according to His will, not what Jeannette wants. Just because something is discerned doesn't mean I need to deal with it at that time or anytime. We must only choose the battles the Lord calls us to so we will experience victorious warfare!

I have seen angels in churches and discerned their presence during the service, especially when the worship or healing is flowing. I have seen them in different forms, human and angelic, and they carry the presence of glory with them. When they come, anything is possible. They carry the atmosphere for the miraculous. We must ask the Lord to help us be more discerning of His presence. Many of these experiences seem unreal to the natural senses, and when they lift, one may ask, "Did I really see that?" It says in 1 Corinthians 2:14, *"But a natural man does not accept the things of the Spirit of God, because they are foolishness to him; and he cannot understand them, because they are spiritually appraised."* One may discern things spiritually, but then one will talk themselves out of the vision or impression because the natural man can't understand it.

I recall a time when the Lord released to me a message concerning fasting to this particular church. It was a serious word on repentance for the body. There was a heavy anointing that came into the house and my sister discerned an angel. She was a seer/prophet intercessor and she did not understand what she saw. The angel that came was described as having a burlap type robe on and a red cord around the waist. His feet were black, covered in ashes. She did not believe it was an angel because of the outfit he was wearing. She expected an angel to be full of glory light, glistening. I told her he was sent to confirm the message the Lord gave me and to release the grace for the body to fast! Angels are sent with a message and assignment.

At times I will see spirits that are controlling a church we are sent into. Once in prayer I saw a winged dragon image flying within the sanctuary. There was much pride and idolatry in operation within that church. Whatever spirit is in operation within the region, leaders or people, it can easily be within that church, especially if there are no intercessors or if people are in sin bondage. In heavy areas of witchcraft, it's not uncommon to see (discern) owls, serpents, werewolves, and things of that nature. I have seen them watching us as a watcher spirit. I have seen divination manifest out of the faces of people in the form of snakes. Often demons manifest and project through the faces as I stand and teach the cleansing message. This is unknown to others, but discernment allows me to see within. I have had a wizard astral project in his human form in front of me. All of which is made known or revealed through the discerning of spirits, by the will of Holy Spirit. This is but just a few ways discernment can operate, in hope to help you get understanding that this treasured gift could be in operation.

The gift of discernment can:
- lift the veil off the unseen realm, through dreams and visions
- cause one to see others or a situation as God sees, working within the seer/prophetic
- help one to get to the root issue of spiritual conflict
- keep one from the deception of the enemy
- work with healing gifts, exposing a root cause of sickness or hiding infirmities
- distinguish between the angelic and demonic, holy and flesh
- can operate through the Word of God
- opens one's spiritual ear to hear in the Spirit
- opens one spiritual sense of smell to aromas or odors in the spirit realm

Guarding one's heart from being deceived in these last days takes the working of Holy Spirit and listening to the wisdom of God. 2 Thessalonians 2:8–12 says, *"Then that lawless one will be revealed whom the Lord will slay with the breath of His mouth and bring to an end by the appearance of His coming; that is, the one whose coming is in accord with the activity of Satan, with all power and signs and false wonders, and with all the deception of wickedness for those who perish, because they did not receive the love of the truth so as to be saved. For this reason God will send upon them a deluding influence so that they will believe what is false, in order that they all may be judged who did not believe the truth, but took pleasure in wickedness."*

This spirit of antichrist is already at work in the earth, bringing these signs and deception. One must be a lover of truth to avoid the deluding influence it brings. It tells us that in the last days, people will gather to sit among teachers who are teaching by seducing spirits. These are those who have itching ears and only want to hear things that please their flesh (1 Tim. 4:1–2). A steady spiritual diet of this will bring demonic oppression and delusion. Wherever one eats spiritually, one will take in the spirit of the house. Paul told his spiritual children to imitate him as he imitated Christ (1 Cor. 11:1). We cast out many seducing spirits, apostasy, denominational demons, false gifts, tongues, legalism, formalism, religion, and many other things connected to this antichrist deception. It says at the end of this warning that this delusion comes to those who took pleasure in wickedness. We must not call ourselves a believer in Jesus and join in with wickedness of the world.

As I wrote earlier concerning apostasy, the grace message taught without the cross is a false message that will bring demonic oppression. Jesus told us in Matthew 16:24–25, *"If any man will come after Me, let him deny himself, and take up his cross, and follow Me. For whosoever will save his life shall lose it: and whosoever will lose his life for My sake shall find it"* (KJV). Any other message is an apostate message and will produces a bound, powerless, weak church, without conviction to become like Jesus to those who are deceived by it. Grace doesn't give one a license to sin, but it empowers one to live holy under the blood of Jesus. The children of Israel were told to put the blood over the doorposts, not on the threshold of their house where they would have trampled upon it. It is spiritual danger to believe when one willingly breaks God's law that grace will operate. James 4:17 says, *"Therefore, to one who knows the right thing to do and does not do it, to him it is sin."* James could not have been more simple and plain than this. Be discerning and do not receive another Jesus or a different gospel.

Deception can come in through:

- those only looking to human leaders for answers; not asking the Lord for revelation
- those only accepting supernatural signs as truth without discerning the spirit behind them
- those who only rely on personal feelings within one's soul

- those who are looking for an identity or need personal flattery to function with confidence
- those unwilling to face any persecution or suffering as a believer
- those who are unwilling to submit to righteous authority or seek counsel with personal revelation
- those who have the fear of man or a man-pleasing spirit

Prayer and declaration for activation of discerning of spirits:

Dear Father, I come before You today and I ask You, the God of our Lord Jesus Christ, the Father of glory, to give me the spirit of wisdom and revelation in the knowledge of Jesus Christ. I ask that the eyes of my heart would be enlightened, so that I would know and understand the calling of Christ within me. I ask for an activation of the discerning/distinguishing of spirits, through Holy Spirit within me to be in operation. Allow me, Father, to know and experience the richness of the glory of revelation in the spirit realm! Give me an understanding heart, and teach me, Holy Spirit, the difference between the holy and profane. Teach me to discern between the unclean and the clean with all wisdom and spiritual insight, so that I would not fall into deception. I ask that you keep me humble as my spiritual eyes see and ears hear, that this gift would only be used to bring you glory. I thank You, Father, that I have asked, and I now receive a greater dimension of grace and an activation of this gift of discernment through, seeing, feeling, hearing, smelling, dreams and visions, in Jesus' name. I decree and declare that I will walk in the fear of the Lord and will not judge by what my natural eyes see nor make decisions by what my natural ears hear! With righteous judgment I will operate as the Holy Spirit leads and enables me in the function of the discerning of spirits! In Jesus' name I pray, Amen.

Possible demonic manifestations

The anointing of God can stir up demonic activity and will initiate deliverance. Some manifestations can seem the same as the anointing of Holy Spirit. One must use discernment to recognize the difference. Don't allow manifestations to dictate one's opinion if one got set free or not. This will cause one to rely on the flesh and not the Spirit of God. I have experiences in deliverance sessions of seeing a lot of manifestation and I have experiences of seeing absolutely none, and in both cases people were set free with lasting fruit following. In Romans 6:22, it says, *"But now since you have been set free from sin and have become [willing] slaves to God, you have your benefit, resulting in sanctification [being made holy and set apart for God's purpose], and the outcome [of this] is eternal life"* (AMP). This tells me that when one is set free, the fruit is lasting righteousness in the area.

Demons have a personality, with a personal intellect, and can only express themselves and assignment through human or animal bodies. They are earth-bound wandering spirits, restless and desiring a house to dwell in. Demons have a personal will. Luke11:24–26 says, *"When the unclean spirit goes out of a man, it passes through waterless places seeking rest, and not finding any, it says, 'I will return to my house from which I came.' And when it comes, it finds it swept and put in order. Then it goes and takes along seven other spirits more evil than itself, and they go in and live there; and the last state of that man becomes worse than the first."* Demons have emotions. James says in chapter 2:19, *"You believe that God is one. You do well; the demons also believe, and shudder."* They have knowledge. In Acts 19:15, *"And the evil spirit answered and said to them, 'I recognize Jesus, and I know about Paul, but who are you?'"* As we see, demons can speak, and they have self-awareness. In Mark 5:9, *"And He was asking him, 'What is your name?' And he said to Him, 'My name is Legion; for we are many.'"* Demons study humanity and their knowledge comes from demonic communication or the information they receive while living within bloodlines.

These manifestations can occur while cleansing them out of the lives of people:

- Being cold can manifest when spirits associated with death or serious evil practices. (Oddly enough, I have seen when ministering healing to people they have had a cold sensation while healing is taking place.)

189

- Trembling and shaking can get strong in the body that a demon is attached, demons may gyrate the body as they are coming out or can also take them to the ground. (Always put people face down and contain them so there is no self-harm.)
- Falling to the ground, very common if it is a stronger spirit. The evil spirit is seeking to control the person's body to usually harm them.
- Palpitations can cause a fear or panic in the person. Sometimes this is a direct result of the natural fear of demonic awareness or the consequence of the spirit knowing it must leave. (Demons can mimic heart attacks to avoid getting evicted.)
- Pressure can be felt around the head or shoulders.
- Physical pain can be present because demons are attached to the body or organs; spirits of infirmities, traumas, and accidents will usually cause pain leaving.
- Lumps in the throat because most common exits are in breath or through the throat. It may feel like a lump in the throat as they come out.
- Deep breathing, or rapid breathing, yawning, sneezing, burping or coughing. Spirits of asthma and death usually dwell in the lungs, but most demons exit the mouth.
- Stirring in the stomach is common, as well as feeling sick or faint.
- Sudden headaches usually indicate mind control, witchcraft, false religions, religious spirits, or idolatry. A tight band can be felt as if the demon is trying to put pressure on the brain.
- Unnatural movements of body parts moving wildly, sometimes showing where demons entered.
- Contortions of the body, especially as they come off spine, arching and twisting. (Leviathan, pride, serpentines, python.)
- Fetal positions are a manifestation of long-buried pain. The person needs release from a spirit of deep emotional pain or trauma.

- Screaming can indicate a demon leaving, but if it persists a long time, the person usually needs inner healing in emotions.
- Pupils dilating. Where light comes in, which is the lamp of the body, demons may look out. The eyes may be independent from their normal response to light and dark as the demon manifest.
- Squinting and fluttering of the eyes. (Looking in the eyes with authority can be helpful to bring deliverance.)
- Eyes rolling back in the head. This is common with witchcraft spirits.
- Sexual movements or feelings can manifest with sexual demons.
- Demonic tongues usually are very harsh and violent, signs of a religious spirit
- Sudden violent actions when people are heavily demonized.
- Running away. (Never allow someone to leave with a spirit up.)
- Hissing is characteristic of a snake. Witchcraft and serpentine spirits will often manifest this way.
- Profanity indicates that the demon is angry they are leaving.
- Snarling and barking are signs of animalistic spirits of false religions, witchcraft, or Satanism, possibly generational evil.
- Roaring can be associated with higher occult powers.
- Strong pungent odors usually from high powers of occult rituals. Also, they can be sexual unclean spirits.
- Claw-like actions may be tormenting demons, mutilation, self-hatred spirits, or bestiality through occult or ancestral sin curses.
- Slithering across the floor like a snake is a serpentine demon, possibly witchcraft or occult (python, divination).

Take authority quickly over a manifestation by binding it up and loosing it, which cancels its assignment. If there is a struggle and only manifestation without any release, there could be a stronger ruling spirit holding it, a soul tie in place, unforgiveness, repentance or a renouncing that needs to take place for freedom to come. Demons are aware if they have a right to occupy the host. Stop and ask questions, take the time to inquire of Holy Spirit for direction, and then continue as directed by Him. If one hears nothing, use your authority over manifestations and tell it to go back down and be silent, binding it up, and release peace over the person. Give the person instructions for further ministry later, such as prayer and fasting.

Always make sure after a manifestation that the person is back in their right mind, peaceful, coherent and pain-free. Always command a demon to go to dry places; never to return. Jesus said this in Mark 9:25, *"When Jesus saw that a crowd was rapidly gathering, He rebuked the unclean spirit, saying to it, 'You deaf and mute spirit, I command you, come out of Him and do not enter him again.'"* Cover the person in the blood of Jesus, sealing their deliverance, and fill them fresh with Holy Spirit. Call back pieces of their soul that were stolen, pour in the healing oil, binding them back together (Deut. 30:3–4, Isa. 61:1). Give them some weapons before they leave and assure them of their new freedom!

CHAPTER 14

WEAPONS OF VICTORY OVER TEMPTATION

"When an unclean spirit goes out of a man, he goes through dry places, seeking rest, and finds none. Then he says, I will return to my house from which I came. And when he comes, he finds it empty, swept, and put in order. Then he goes and takes with him seven other spirits more wicked than himself, and they enter and dwell there; and the last state of that man is worse than the first. So shall it also be with this wicked generation" (Matt. 12: 43–45) (NKJV).

AFTER CLEANSING THE HOUSE, THE ENEMY will most likely try to return, and some ways in which he attempts is through temptation, accusation and deception. But we need not fear, there are promises to us in the Word that tell us the Lord knows how to rescue the godly from temptation. Below are some weapons to use against Satan's tactics.

Satan's main tactics to snare souls:

- temptation—the act of enticing or alluring one
- accusation—a charge of wrong-doing, imputation of guilt
- deception—to deceive is to mislead one by a false appearance, statement, to delude

In 2 Peter 2:9, it says, *"then the Lord knows how to rescue the godly from temptation."*

In 1 Corinthians 10:13, it says, *"No temptation has overtaken you but such as is common to man; and God is faithful, who will not allow you to be tempted beyond what you are able, but with the temptation will provide the way of escape also, so that you will be able to endure it."* So, no matter what Satan may bring, you can be and are an overcomer!

Revelation 12:10–11 says, *"Then I heard a loud voice from heaven, saying, 'Now the salvation, the power, and the kingdom of our God and the authority of His Christ have come, for the **accuser of our brethren has been thrown down**, he who accuses them before our God day and night.' And **they overcame him because of the blood of the Lamb and because of the word of their testimony**, and they did not love their life even when faced with death."* We are overcomers because of the blood and our confession of faith in Jesus.

Jesus demonstrated power over Satan in Luke chapter four. Each time Satan came to test Him, Jesus spoke the written Word of God against him. Jesus passed every test. James 4:7 says, *"Submit therefore to God. Resist the devil and he will flee from you."* Other scriptures for wisdom to study and stay free: 1 Peter 5:6–10, Genesis 3:1–7, 2 Corinthians 11:1–4, and Luke 4. Jesus told His disciples to watch and pray always that they would not enter temptation. He said their spirit was willing, but their flesh was weak (Matt. 26:41). We have a spiritual arsenal that will build up and strengthen our spirit man. We have all we need as a child of God to live victoriously, if we choose to use them. These weapons are proven victorious for your new lifestyle of freedom and identity in Christ Jesus!

Weapons of warfare to maintain your freedom that was received through Cleansing:

- One must be filled with the Holy Spirit after cleansing (Acts 1:8, Acts 2:4). The power of God will come upon to assist in one's personal warfare with the enemy. As one prays in the Spirit daily, one is building up the inner man (1 Cor. 14:1–4, 14:15).

- One must guard the mind; demons will try to come back with thoughts in one's mind (Matt. 12:43–45). Remember, anything the devil whispers to one's mind is a lie (John 8:44). He will try to make one feel that freedom really didn't happen. The devil is a liar, so refuse to believe him. Be prepared to resist thoughts and suggestions that he speaks (James 4:7, Eph. 4:27). Jesus resisted the devil with the word three times by saying "It is written" (Matt. 4:1–11). One must find scriptures according to the area of bondage that one has found freedom. A good example would be, if freedom came from fornication or sexual immorality, use the scripture 1 Corinthians 6:15–18 or Hebrews 13:4. Speak the Word out of your mouth to resist him and by declaring, "Satan, it is written, flee fornication because adulterers, fornicators, and whoremongers, God will judge!" One will discern when he is trying to come back when he brings old thought patterns.
- Renew the mind, meditate daily with the Word of God, especially in the areas demonic spirits had one in bondage (Rom. 12:2–3, John 15:3, 2 Cor. 10:3–5, Eph. 4:22–24, Josh. 1:8). Satan will try to regain entry through a lax, undisciplined life. Get into a Word church, looking for a church that believes in the infilling of Holy Spirit, gifts of Holy Spirit, the preaching and teaching of the kingdom of God, prayer, praise and worship of the Living God (Heb. 10:24–25).
- Realize that sometimes full and complete deliverance can be little by little (Exod. 23:30, Deut. 7:22). Take each day as you apply these steps and continue to grow in grace and strength and take back more ground from Satan. Remind him he is a defeated foe! One should expect continuous and increasing freedom where Satan had previously had one bound (Phil. 3:13–14).
- Apply the blood of Jesus each day. One overcomes Satan by the blood of the Lamb and by the Word of our testimony (Rev. 12:11). Keep all that belongs to one covered in the blood of Jesus.

- Don't hesitate to use also the Name of Jesus. The blood protects you and the name of Jesus causes demons to tremble and flee (Exod. 12:13, Eph. 1:7, Heb. 10:23, Phil. 2:9–11).
- Avoid deliberate sin at all cost. *"We know that whoever is born of God does not sin; but he who has been born of God keeps himself, and the wicked one does not touch him"* (1 John 5:18) (NKJV). When one repents of sin, it immediately is forgiven and cleansed (1 John 1:9). One should make this a lifestyle and it will stop Satan from oppressing one with guilt and condemnation (Rom. 8:1; Heb. 10:22).
- Rely on Holy Spirit to control one's life (emotions, desires, imaginations, will) by deliberately giving Christ lordship over them each day (Rom. 12:1–2, Eph. 5:18).
- One must put on the armor of God for spiritual warfare every day. Put on each piece thoughtfully and prayerfully, which brings protection. Don't forget the seventh piece, which is prayer (Eph. 6:10–18).
- One must avoid old waste places and break off wrong association. Be wise and do not connect back with old soul ties that have been broken. Stay out of old death places that have no life to give, and choose positive, clean living friends who put Jesus first and bring life to one (James 4:4, 1 Cor. 15:33).
- One must develop a life of praise and thanksgiving, putting on the garment of praise for the spirit of heaviness and it will not come upon one (Isa. 61:3, Deut. 30:19).
- One must use one's authority to bind the devil every time it is needed when he tries to attack (Matt. 12:28–29). Ask the Father to release the angels of the Lord to battle demons (Heb. 1:13–14, Ps. 34:7, Psa. 91:11).
- One must avoid offense and unforgiveness. The Spirit of unforgiveness opens the door to the enemy to afflict one's life. Always forgive quickly and walk in the fruit of Holy Spirit. The Lord will give one grace if one asks Him (Matt. 18:33–35, Heb. 12:15).
- Use the anointing oil on oneself and your whole house as often as led by Holy Spirit (Mark 6:13).

- One needs to humble oneself and realize one cannot stay free all by themselves. Stay connected to godly relationships that bring accountability (John 15:5).
- One must build their personal intimacy with their Lord Jesus by personal worship, prayer and even fasting when He directs.

The taking of Communion must become a lifestyle practice daily, not a ritual exercise monthly at a church or yearly in a holiday setting (Luke 22:15–20, 1 Cor. 11:23–26). It is a supernatural weapon and used in faith with revelation will bring great blessing to the believer. Jesus said to do this as often as we think of Him, in remembrance of Him. Taking communion, which is a representation of the body and blood of Jesus, is a great reminder of our new covenant inheritance of Jesus Christ and all that is available to us! We must get a deeper revelation of this weapon against darkness.

What communion does for us:
- gives us deeper intimacy with Jesus
- opens us to deeper revelation of Jesus
- gives us favor and protection
- brings healing to our bodies and forgiveness from sin
- gives us inner peace, hope and assurance

Communion is our marriage connection to Jesus of:
- eternal life
- deeper working of Holy Spirit
- financial provision
- authority over the enemy
- the promise of God to the Jews

Communion should serve as a powerful reminder that we are married to the King of Kings. When Jesus took the Passover with His disciples, He became betrothed to the church. He said He would never eat it again until it is fulfilled in the kingdom of God and until the kingdom of God comes. Someday, He is coming back for us to finalize our marriage and we are preparing for His return in righteousness, and we will eat and drink with Jesus at our marriage supper. Until then, we should daily take this as a reminder that we are His bride and we wait eagerly for His return. In Hebrew culture, the bridegroom took care of his bride's personal needs. He protected her, he showered her with the best gifts and he went away to prepare a place for her! Doesn't this sound familiar? My prayer is that we get a deeper revelation of the communion blessing and by faith access all that it entails for us as we wait for our Beloved.

CHAPTER 15

SPIRITUAL MAPPING GUIDELINES AND QUESTIONNAIRE

"Therefore, confess your sins to one another, and pray for one another so that you may be healed. The effective prayer of a righteous man can accomplish much." James 5:16

Getting started in spiritual cleansing mapping

SPIRITUAL MAPPING WORKS WITH COUNseling and personal inquiry together. One could use a mature prayer partner for counsel. This process is designed for at least 4–6 sessions, usually an hour each week. One gathers information, receiving revelation by Holy Spirit until the scheduled prayer session is made. It is wisdom to keep the weekly time consistent as much as possible to stay on track to finish. These sessions can be in the office or by phone if counselee lives far away. Consent forms need to be signed if one is in a ministry and sent back before beginning the first counsel session. (A copy of a form is in the glossary in the back of the book.) It is to be kept locked away in a safe place.

Qualities to look for in a Christian counselor or prayer partner/mapper:

- One who is born again and spirit-filled with evidence
- One whom one has a trusted friendship and godly relationship
- One who manifests the fruit of the Spirit in their personal life
- One who is versed and solid in scripture
- One who is faithful to a local church
- One who understands inner healing/deliverance
- One who walks in personal forgiveness
- One who is willing to fast and pray with you
- One who demonstrates a walk of love, not being judgmental/critical
- One who has a servant's heart
- One who can keep confidence
- One who has the anointing of God upon their life
- One who can hear the voice of the Lord

To the counselor

Counseling must be ministered with professional boundaries. A prayer partner/mapper must know how to hold information and release it to the Lord as you finish each session. One must open in prayer before and after each session, always making sure spiritual doors are shut and the counselee has peace when you finish the hour. Those receiving ministry must be active in their homework assignments and faithful with their appointment times. One must be sure one is giving them the Word of God on the situations, not your opinion. One is accountable to handle the word of God correctly. One is responsible to keep things confidential, only discussing it with appropriate leadership. One will be tested in this area of pride. Be responsible to keep your life clean and remain faithful to the work of the ministry. Always keep this Truth in your heart and in the forefront of you mind when counseling; all souls belong to the Lord Jesus and He values them and desires them to be free and healed. It is why we do what we do with all diligence to the Lord.

In the first two weeks we are laying a foundation and gathering information. The mapping history sheets must be filled out. Father, mother and personal doors should be covered. Try to keep the counselee on track and let them know you're laying a foundation to build upon in the weeks ahead. The homework is to journal places of rejection, trauma or suffering in childhood, teen or adult life. These things will become open to you in the discussions each week.

By week three, counselee needs to be working on a "70 x 7 forgiveness exercise" coming out of Matthew 18:21–22. When Peter came to Jesus and asked, *"Lord, how often shall my brother sin against me and I forgive him? Up to seven times"* Jesus answered him, *"I do not say to you, up to seven times, but up to seventy times seven."* We use this principle concerning forgiving oneself. One must understand, to be set free, one must release themselves into the freedom of forgiveness. The concept is, each day, for seven days, write a list of things they need to forgive themselves for as Holy Spirit reveals. Head the list with "Lord, I forgive myself for:" and then begin your list. One doesn't have to think long or hard on this; Holy Spirit knows what one is holding against themselves and others. Each day, as one makes the new list, one cannot repeat anything from the previous list, because it has been released and thrown into the sea of forgetfulness! (Micah 7:19) This is a 7-day exercise to clean out the lies of the enemy concerning unforgiveness and resentment toward oneself. These can also be discussed in a session or with a mature prayer partner.

By week 4, one needs to work on release letters of forgiveness. These are letters to family members, spouses, children, siblings, perpetrators, spiritual leaders, old friends, self or any past broken relationships of pain or betrayal. One may have a spirit of grief from a deceased loved one and needs to release them to the Lord. This works well if one has had an abortion and feels they need to repent to the child, letting go of the regrets. Some will need to write a release letter to God if they feel angry towards Him. One must understand the letters need to be written honestly and possibly from the year of their pain, how one really feels, expressing deep feelings. If one was hurt or abused as a child, one can give the child a voice. The Lord already sees what is within the heart; it is no surprise to Him. He desires it to be healed and released, and these letters are a great healing tool for their session. In special cases, some can speak their thoughts out loud instead, as if they were in front of them.

By now, depending if one is ready for their session, the counselor/prayer partner/mapper should be planning a time of personal prayer session, scheduling it with the prayer team of two other intercessors and make sure they know it will take approximately two hours.

The spiritual cleansing prayers are in the back of this book and in the Spiritual Cleansing Handbook, which are very effective and must be done before the expelling of demons. These will break any legal rights or resistance in deliverance. The usual order is information and revelation, listing and identification of strongholds through personal journaling, the forgiveness exercises and letters of release. Letters are to be read before the cleansing prayers, then freedom will flow as one's authority in Christ is exercised over the work of the enemy.

Spiritual mapping generational information
(this is laid out in the Spiritual Cleansing Handbook):
- father's and mother's name: (Step-parents if applicable)
- characteristics, bondages, or personality traits
- ethnic, heritage or cultural background
- fornication, adultery, or divorce
- incest, molestation, or rapes
- homosexuality
- soul ties
- sickness or diseases
- abortions, murders, suicide
- drugs or alcohol
- mental illness
- witchcraft, occult, or divination
- Freemasonry
- were parents married when children were conceived?
- religious heritage or any false religions
- jail or prison
- poverty

On a separate sheet, map out the grandparents on both sides of the family and any significant family members such as aunts, uncles, cousins that have any of these open doors using the same mapping questions.

- Personal mapping information
- Name:
- Characteristics, bondages, and or personality traits-
- Ethnic, heritage or culture-
- Fornication, adultery, divorce-
- Soul ties-
- How old were you and what was the age of your first sexual experience?
- Have you ever been molested, or raped?
- If yes, what was your age?
- Have you ever participated in homosexuality?
- Even kissed the same sex?
- Are there mind battles?
- If yes, what age?
- Have you ever had any traumatic experiences?
- Any accidents?
- If yes, please explain:
- Have you had any abortions?
- Have you attempted suicide?
- If yes, what age?
- Have you ever done or sold drugs?
- Have you abused alcohol?
- If yes, what age and what kind?
- Have you been diagnosed with any sickness or diseases?
- If yes, what kind and when?
- Have you ever been diagnosed with any mental illnesses?
- If yes, what kind, and are you on medication?
- Have you been in jail and/or prison? If yes, explain.
- Have you participated in any witchcraft, occult, or divination?
- If yes, how old were you, and what type of witchcraft?
- Is there any family history of Freemasonry?
- What is your religious background?

- Have you been involved in any false religions?
- Have you experienced poverty or filed bankruptcy?
- Explain briefly your salvation experience-
- Was your life really changed?
- Were you baptized as a child?
- Were you baptized as a convert?
- In one word, who is Jesus Christ to you?
- What does the blood of Calvary mean to you?
- Is repentance part of your Christian life?
- What is your prayer life like?
- Have you ever been filled with Holy Spirit with evidence of speaking in tongues?
- Were your parents married when you were conceived?
- Were you a planned child?
- Were you the sex they wanted?
- Were you adopted?

Whether the counselee is married or divorced, spouses need to be mapped, because they are or were in covenant relationship and have soul ties. Use the same questions.

Also, any children of the counselee need to be mapped, too, using the same questions.

Any significant extended family members that Holy Spirit highlights may need to be discussed and mapped. For example, there could be a relative who is in the occult, severe sexual bondage or maybe they did prison time, or committed suicide. These could be evidence of hidden bloodline curses.

CHAPTER 16

SPIRITUAL CLEANSING PRAYERS

"And all things you ask for in prayer, believing, you will receive." Matthew 21:22

Salvation and consecration prayer

FATHER, I CONFESS THAT I HAVE SINNED and acknowledge my need of a savior. I today receive Jesus Christ fresh and anew as my Savior. I thank you for sending Him to die on the cross for me. I believe that He is God's Son, that He died on a cross for me and He rose again. I repent of sin and ask you to forgive me. I invite Jesus to be Lord over every area of my life. I ask You, Jesus, to be Lord of my mind, my will, all my feelings and reactions, and all of my decisions. I invite Jesus to be Lord of my entire life and all my relationships. I thank You, Father, that the blood of Jesus was shed that I might be set free of my past and all the evil things that have hindered my life in any way. In Jesus' name I pray, Amen.

Sexual bondage and soul tie cleansing prayer

Father, I confess that at various times I have been powerless against the continual attacks of the enemy on my sexuality. I have chosen to sin in various ways and ask You to forgive me for all fornication, adultery or any sexual immorality. I ask You to cleanse my memories, heal my hurts and forgive me, washing my mind of any images or spiritual residue of any illegal covenants. I ask You, Father, as You have forgiven me, to break any ungodly and/or unnatural spirit, soul and body ties of fornication, adultery, abandonment, rejection, grief or any other person, place or evil attachment to my life. I ask that my spirit be loosed from them and from the uttermost parts of heaven. I tell my spirit to forget the unions. I tell my mind to release responsibility for them. I tell my emotions to let go and forget that union. I tell the fragmented pieces of my soul to come back together in Jesus' name. I declare my body is an instrument of righteousness, a living sacrifice, holy and acceptable to You. I reserve the sexual use of my body only for marriage. In Jesus' name I pray, Amen.

Forgiveness cleansing prayer

Father, I thank You for sending Jesus to die that I would be forgiven of my sins. Today, I choose, as an act of my will, in obedience to Your Word, and as the desire of my heart, to forgive all those who have hurt me. I confess that, because of an offense, I have become bitter and have held anger, resentment and evil in my heart against: (name all). You have said unless we forgive, You will not forgive us. So, I acknowledge this as sin, and I now turn from this behavior. I release each one of these people into the freedom of my forgiveness. I ask You to cleanse me and break any bitter soul ties that I may have in my life. I now also choose to forgive myself for all the things You have already forgiven me of. I release myself into the freedom of forgiveness. In Jesus' name I pray, Amen.

Generational repentance cleansing prayer

I forgive and repent of my forefathers, for all the things they did that have affected me and my life. I specifically renounce the consequences of their bloodline iniquities and their sins. I confess that Jesus Christ is my Lord and Savior. I believe He died on a cross for me, becoming a curse for me, for it is written "cursed is anyone who hangs on a tree." It is through the power of Jesus' death and resurrection that I am free from the curse and able to receive the blessing of Abraham. In Hebrews 4:12–13, it says, that the Word of God is living and active and sharper than any two-edged sword and piercing as far as the division of soul and spirit, of both joints and marrow, and able to judge the thoughts and intentions of the heart. It says there is no creature hidden from His sight, but all things are open and laid bare to the eyes of Jesus! I ask that He go into my marrow, my DNA and expose the hidden demonic spirits, contracts, ordinances or structures against me and my generations and that I would be set free by the power of the blood of Jesus! I renounce the devil and all his works. I renounce all hidden things of evil, all activity of demonic strongmen, and all other spirits underneath them, that have cursed me in any way. I command them to obey the belief of my heart and the confession of my mouth. I renounce all iniquities and every curse off me and my ancestors, all the way back to Adam. I ask for forgiveness of every sin committed by me or my ancestors, all the way back to Adam. I renounce (name all) and every vow, every oath, every ritual, every ceremony, every tie and blood covenant and every curse attached to them. I renounce all sorcery, witchcraft, divination, and every abomination, in the name of Jesus. I renounce Freemasonry, false religions, occults, false gods and goddesses, false belief systems, every doctrine of demons, all false worship, all death, and I acknowledge these as the worship of Satan. I choose now to place Jesus on the throne of my life. I renounce all suicide, abortion, infirmity, disease, every sickness and suffering, every despair, every mental ailment, every physical and emotional illness, and activity that opened my ancestors or myself to demonic curses. Now I decree that every curse brought upon me by myself or ancestors is now broken. I ask you to purge and cleanse me, and I claim my freedom. There is no more legal right for the enemy to curse me or my descendants. I decree all curses null and void. They can no longer affect me or my descendants. I am now free from every curse, all iniquity, every evil strongman, and every demonic spirit that was assigned to carry out those curses. In Jesus' name I pray, Amen.

Suicide, self-hatred and death cleansing prayer

Father, I ask You to forgive me for not accepting myself, for hating myself. Forgive me for not accepting Your love for me. By hating myself and wanting to die, I'm declaring that you made a mistake when You created me in my mother's womb and gave me life and salvation. I have come into agreement with the devil and I have opened the door for the spirit of death and suicide to torment me. I now, from my heart, repent and come out of agreement with every lie of the enemy. I now come into agreement and embrace my salvation and all that You have for me! I now choose to love myself and to accept who You created me to be. I open my heart to receive the love of You, my Father. I decree and declare I shall live and not die to declare the glory of God in my generation (Ps. 118:9).

Shedding innocent blood cleansing prayer

I repent for anyone in my generations who has shed innocent blood through human sacrifice, murder, abortion or suicide, anyone, including myself, who has participating in financing abortion, or voting for any authority who advocates abortion. I come out of agreement with all the evil alignments. I repent of any blood-letting or blood oaths or illegal blood covenants, and I ask You to forgive me and wash me with the blood of Jesus. I confess myself and my generations were not proper guardians and keepers of the life You entrusted us to in any areas mentioned. I renounce all child sacrifices or blood-letting that were made to Satan on the altar of Molech. I renounce all selfishness, murder, violence and death. I thank You that the blood of Jesus washes me and my generations clean of any guilt. I now, because of Your forgiveness, can forgive myself for any participation. I recognize that the innocent children are in Your caring hands throughout all eternity. In Jesus' name I pray, Amen.

Mammon cleansing prayer

Father, I repent and come out of agreement with the worship of the spirit of mammon and all the Baal structure that it operates in. I go all the way back to Adam and ask for forgiveness for myself and for all my ancestors for the worship of mammon. I ask that You forgive me for all the iniquity in my bloodline connected to mammon, pride, idolatry, robbery, fraud, theft, greed, covetousness, swindling, cheating, unjust weights and measures, laziness, poverty, or lack. I repent for all my ancestors who denied justice to the poor, judged the rich, and for all those who held onto unforgiveness. I repent for shutting my ears to the poor and any exploitation of the poor, being evil in my judgments concerning money. I repent for fear and anxiety concerning money, robbing God of tithe and offerings. I repent for giving on an impure altar and mixing seed in my vineyard. Forgive me for sowing in unbelief, doubt, offense, anger, worry or under compulsion. I repent for broken covenants, broken vows and promises, the misuse of others' materials and unwise stewardship of what I have received in the past. I repent for not operating in faith with any invention, idea or investment concerning finances that you gave me in the past. I repent for not having a vision for my life and finances. I ask that you forgive and cleanse me, washing my financial history, all impure altars, or any ties, vows, contracts or binding agreements to Baal or Mammon within me or my bloodline with the blood of Jesus. I choose today to place Jesus on the throne of my heart concerning my money, possessions and all that you have made me a steward of. I choose to take on the mind of Christ in finances. I will be obedient with tithing and to the giving of offerings as you speak to me. I will give in faith, generously and cheerfully in love to establish your kingdom in the earth as I am led by Holy Spirit. In Jesus' name I pray, Amen.

Declaration of commitment prayer

Father, I now choose to turn from my sin behavior. I thank You that all my past is forgiven. I ask that you give me the discernment to recognize temptation when it comes and the strength to resist it. Thank You that Jesus' blood was shed that I would be cleansed. I ask You now to deliver me, purging me of all evil. I speak out to Satan and all his demonic kingdom that was assigned to me, that I renounce you and all your works in my life! I, by an act of my will, and in the strength that Jesus Christ gives me, close the doors of my life to all entry points you have previously gained through my sins. I speak out, in the name of Jesus, who defeated you at Calvary, that you no longer have the right to trouble me on these specific issues which have now been confessed, repented of and forgiven!

Father God, I now choose to walk in holiness with my Lord Jesus Christ in every area of my life! I choose to become an active disciple of Jesus Christ, in thought, word and in deed. I commit to develop a deeper and more intimate relationship with my Lord and Savior, through prayer, fellowship with Holy Spirit, and by reading and studying the Word of God! In Jesus' name, I make a new commitment today. Amen.

Practicing self-deliverance

In John 8:32, it says, *"and you will know the truth, and the truth will make you free."* Cleansing is possible by the personal power of Holy Spirit within and the revelation revealed through self-discovery and discernment of the Spirit. If one has never experienced deliverance, one really should seek a prayer partner for safety and the power of agreement. If one is knowledgeable in this field of ministry, self-deliverance is a very good practice. Online mass cleansing/deliverance spiritual cleansing prayers are available and are very effective at home. You can find access to them on our Spiritual Cleansing web site and/or YouTube. We use these often even as a team for personal spiritual tune-ups!

When you are beginning this journey, you should have prayed and fasted before the personal session. Have the copies of the spiritual cleansing prayers available to read (they are in this chapter). The list of identified strongholds should be noted and ready to use. You may do the inner healing exercises of the forgiveness list and letters, speaking them out loud. You must allow Holy Spirit time to minister to you and bring inner healing in these areas. Romans 10:10 says, *"for with the heart a person believes, resulting in righteousness, and with the mouth he confesses, resulting in salvation."*

Preparing for self-cleansing:
- with prayer/fasting
- do your homework by investigating open doors of oppression
- make a stronghold list
- write forgiveness letters
- set aside enough time with no distractions
- have cleansing prayers ready
- speak the self-deliverance declaration out loud before you begin

Pre-self-cleansing declaration:

I decree and declare the Lordship of Jesus Christ in my life and agree that Jesus defeated every evil strongman in my life! I renounce all the work of the enemy and any demons attached to my life. It is written that Jesus said in Luke 10:19, *"Behold I have given you authority to tread on serpents and scorpions, and over all the power of the enemy, and nothing will injure you."* Jesus also said in Mark 16:17, *"These signs will accompany those who have believed: in My name they will cast out demons."* The Greater one lives in me and He has overcome all! Philippians 2:10–11 says, *"so that at the name of Jesus every knee will bow, of those who are in heaven and on earth and under the earth, and that every tongue will confess that Jesus Christ is Lord, to the glory of the Father!"* In Jesus name, you will obey my command and leave my generational bloodline, mind, will, emotions and body today!

With the preparation completed, now you can begin. You must charge your spirit by praying in your prayer language. This will build you up in faith and release the anointing. Spiritual cleansing prayers should be done out loud before one begins to cast out the demons. One should take authority over each spirit discerned and bind it up and command it to go! This must be done under the anointing and authority of the Lord Jesus. Relax after each command as the demons release their hold. One may feel manifestations listed in this book if they are present. Relax your mouth, as most demons exit through the mouth with yawning, belching and coughing. Do not pray during this time, only command and wait. This will take time but be patient and have faith! It may take more than one command to get it to go. The enemy will at times challenge your authority but be strong in the Lord and the Power of His might! After each command, relax as they come out. Continue until you feel a release from Holy Spirit that the session is over.

In Closing out personal cleansing
- ask Holy Spirit to fill you up fresh, praying in the Spirit, thanking and praising Him for freedom.
- read the closing the gate prayer (found below)
- spend the day in worship and allow the peace of God to rule your heart
- share your testimony with others who need freedom
- study the weapons of victory over temptation (Chapter 14)

Closing the gates prayer

Father, I (We) thank you for all the forgiveness, freedom, healing and cleansing I (we) have received today! I (we) ask right now that You release the angels to go and bring back every piece of my (our) soul that has been stolen through sin. According to the promise in Deuteronomy 30:1–4, I (we) believe and receive it. I (We) thank You that even now there is a restoration of wholeness to my (our) soul! I (we) command every spirit that was cast out to go to dry places, never to return to this house again! I (we) thank You for the healing oil that is being released right now to me (us) in Jesus' name. I (we) ask for a fresh infilling of Holy Spirit to fill my (our) vessel now! I (we) command every gate or door that was opened for cleansing of my (our) past to be shut and sealed, by the power of Holy Spirit, in Jesus' name! I (we) thank you for a new season of restoration and healing that will continue in my (our) life. In Jesus' name, Amen.

Spiritual Cleansing

Pre-deliverance prayer for corporate cleansing from bloodline curses

Dear heavenly Father, in the name of the Lord Jesus Christ, I, your servant come before your throne boldly, through the blood of Jesus, on behalf of your people. You have taken them out of the kingdom of darkness and have placed them in the kingdom of your dear Son. You are not angry with us. You were in Christ reconciling us unto yourself because of your love for us. The blood of Jesus, your Son, who is our Savior was the propitiation for our sin and guilty verdict. It satisfied all the demands of your justice and your holiness. Your word says that there is no more condemnation to those who are in Christ Jesus, and we are not condemned because of His shed blood that we have received today!

We thank you Jesus that you forgive all our iniquities and you heal all our diseases! The Word says that all authority has been given to you! The Word declares that everything bows at Your name in heaven, in earth and under the earth. We declare You alone are LORD! With our mouth, we confess your Lordship! Your Father, has established you as Head over all things pertaining to your church, and we belong to your church. We honor You right as Lord of our lives!

Your Spirit within us cries out, Abba Father! Your Spirit within all my brothers and sisters here, in your presence right now, is crying out to you on their behalf. He is making intercession with groanings that we cannot even utter. We bless you, Father, that you know the mind of the Spirit; thus, you answer His cries because He prays according to your will through us, and we thank you for that!

We honor You, Lord Jesus and we thank You that we are called by Your name. Now, by faith, with the eyes of our Spirit, we see you enthroned at the right hand of God interceding for us. We also see all the demons, all evil principalities and powers placed in subjection to you! According to Colossians 2:15, You disarmed

213

rulers and authorities, making a public display of them in triumphant victory through the cross and resurrection! Lord Jesus, you have defeated and bound Satan, You dethroned the enemy of our lives! You took upon yourself human flesh that through death you might render him powerless who had power over death, that is, the devil, in order that you might free us who were in bondage to him. We thank you that you have already rendered Satan powerless against us!

We thank you, Father, that when you placed our sin upon your Son, you nailed the death/debt decree which warred against us to the cross. The whole kingdom of evil supernaturalism has been humiliated and defeated by you. Lord Jesus, you made a public display of our defeated enemies. Your angels and all creation joyfully witnessed the defeat of these fallen angelic beings that had rebelled against your Father. You tell us in your Word, since we are born of God, that evil cannot touch us. You have given us authority over scorpions and serpents and over all the work of the enemy. You said nothing shall by any means hurt us! You have given us authority over the kingdom of Satan in your name, and we thank you for that!

Father, you said in your Word that you send your angels as ministering spirits to minister to us, your heirs of salvation. You say that the angel of the Lord encamps around those who fear him and delivers them. We ask you right now that your angels will encamp around this room and seal us off from all activity of any external evil spirits. They have nothing to do with what's going on here! Father, may your angels expel every demonic power that has been sent against us by evil persons. We thank you and know you are doing that even now! They are being sent back in anger and defeat to the ones who sent them against us!

We seal off this entire building by the authority we have in Jesus Christ, the Lord. We cover it entirely in the blood of Jesus. We command every external spirit that has nothing to do with the lives of these people to go from this room and not come back! Every demonic power which has been assigned against us to disturb or distract this meeting, I command you to go! You have no place here. Go now! God's angels are now removing you from our presence!

Every demonic power, every enemy of Jesus Christ attached to the lives of God's people gathered here, I command you in the name of Jesus to be silent! Any evil spirits hiding within the lives of God's people I command you to be bound within the pit of their stomach! You will not whisper to their minds, touch their bodies, disturb their emotions or influence their will! You cannot do anything to harm them; the blood of Jesus covers them. You are bound, and you are to be silent, and when you are commanded to go, you will go to dry places, never to return to them again! We declare that you are evicted today! You cannot call upon Satan or any other demonic powers to assist you!

Father, we are confessing as representatives of our family lines the ancestral and generational iniquities, sins and trespasses we are guilty of as a rebellious lineage. We are confessing and releasing sinful choices we have made and sinful activities that have opened the door to the demonic oppression in our lives. By confession and renouncing the works of darkness today, I declare that all demonic rights to afflict our lives are now broken! All curses are broken! Any legal grounds for demonic attachment are over today! We also want you, Father, to cleanse and heal us from the sin that was done to us as children. We ask that You restore our foundations!

We want to forgive all those who have hurt us and forgive ourselves for the things you have already forgiven us for. You have told us to forgive so we can be forgiven. I thank you that you are faithful and just to hear us and forgive and cleanse us today! I declare there is no more arrested development and we are free to become mature Sons of God!

(Do corporate cleansing prayers together, then continue with cleansing from corporate curses below, which can also be used with personal cleansing prayer)

Father, in Hebrews 4:12–13, it says that the Word of God is living and active and sharper than any two-edged sword and piercing as far as the division of soul and spirit, of both joints and marrow, and able to judge the thoughts and intentions of the heart. It says there is no creature hidden from His sight, but all things are open and laid bare to the eyes of Jesus! I ask that He go into the marrow, (my DNA) the DNA of Your people, and expose the hidden demonic spirits, contracts, ordinances or structures against (me) them and (my) their generations and that (I) they would be set me free by the power of the blood of Jesus! Father, your Word declares Jesus hung and died on a tree, becoming a curse for (me) them! So, in the name of Jesus, I stand as a representative of (this) these, my brothers and sisters. I take my position (in this) with these, my brethren, as reigning with Jesus Christ. I speak, as we now speak to every enemy of Jesus and every demonic power that has been assigned and attached to (my life) God's people, and declare you are loosed from (my life) their lives. I go all the way back to Adam and I go forward 10 generations and I break the curse of bloodline iniquities in (my) their bloodline: the curse of whoredom, addictions, idolatry, illegitimacy, vagabond, poverty, mammon, reprobate, apostasy curses be broken! I break all witchcraft, Freemasonry, sorcery, divination, occult, and any spiritual contracts, in Jesus' name! I break curses of incest, rape and molestation curses, and all curses from trauma or bonds, be broken! I break all curses of sickness and disease, every mental illness stronghold, all abortion curses, murder, suicide and death curses, in the name of JESUS CHRIST, be broken! I break curses of abandonment, rejection, soul ties, in the name of Jesus, I speak to the evil spirit world in behalf of (my life) these your people who are here right now before the Father. I send you cursing evil spirits out of this room, away from (my life) our lives and back to the one who sent you!

(Now one needs to go down each stronghold and call out the spirits oppressing the people, going in and out of inner healing, breaking soul ties and loosing demons as led by Holy Spirit)

One should begin with the abandonment and rejection groupings from generational bloodlines, childhood soul ties, and trauma. The foundation must be dealt with first. Then as led, release the pain of childhood and childhood abuse. Underneath this is the spirits of rejection, self-rejection and the fear of rejection, with abandonment and the fear of abandonment attached. An arrested developed inner child is in there. I find if you get to the root up front, being patient as Holy Spirit brings it up, the rest of the cleansing and strongholds come out easily. But, as always, be led by the finger of God! This will take some time as the Lord deals with His people.

When one is finished with cleansing, read the closing the gates prayer. Have the people pray in the Spirit, thanking and praising Him for freedom! Tell them as they leave to spend the day in worship and allow the peace of God to rule their heart. At some time, they need to share their testimony with others who need freedom to walk in holiness in those areas.

CHAPTER 17
GLORY STORIES

"For I am not ashamed of the gospel, for it is the power of God for salvation to everyone who believes, to the Jew first and to the Greek." Romans 1:16

I N THIS CHAPTER ARE GLORY STORIES OR testimonies of how the Lord changed people's lives through Cleansing. Some names have been kept or changed for confidentiality, but these are but a few of the many testimonies, written in truth by those who received the freedom.

GLORY STORY #1

A couple other organizers and I hosted Apostle Jeannette and her team early in 2017. We had no real understanding of deliverance or cleansing, and she did a weekender teaching and a mass deliverance at the end. It was definitely a pivotal time for me in my spiritual life. I could feel "things" coming off of me and felt so light when we were finished. It was so powerful against Freemasonry, I literally could not remember the word "mason" for over a week. I was physically healed of arthritis pain and psoriasis that has been in effect for over nine months now. Things I thought were "normal" battles that we all "had" to face left me instantly like lust, addiction, bitterness and controlling thoughts. It was the beginning of true sonship for me. Father had her give me some prophecies that helped launch me as a minister in my city. Since that time, we've helped many hundreds to get free. Jeannette gave me copies of the mass cleansing she did, which I listen to every few weeks. Coupled with undergoing multiple sessions of personal deliverance, this has helped me keep most of the freedom I felt in the mass cleansing and grow in revelation and Jesus's authority over the enemy. I am pursuing deeper and deeper healing to complete the full work in my life. Cleansing has been so sweet to me. Not only I, but also my wife and children have enjoyed this cleansing now. It is truly the children's bread as the Bible teaches in Matthew 15. Freedom is a sweet thing like the taste of bread to a starving person that realizes he is starving. The interesting thing is that if you study starvation, a starving person really only experiences hunger once they eat a little food. This is what happened to me with cleansing. As soon as I experienced the taste of God's goodness through cleansing, I knew that it was Him and that it was good. Now what I have been freely given through cleansing I freely give to others, which has been one of the greatest joys in knowing Father in my life. I'm grateful God is restoring the full work of cleansing to His Church. Go for it!

GLORY STORY #2

I'm going to talk about where I come from as a reformed person who is now unified with Christ. My mom and dad divorced when I was six or seven. I don't remember my exact age, but I remember that they always fought, and things weren't good. After the divorce, my mom was in and out of the psychiatric hospital for many nervous breakdowns. She blamed me for so much that it was almost impossible to get help from my mom. I had been sexually abused and raped and became very sexually active and promiscuous. I had been in numerous polyamorous relationships. This went on for the next few years, regularly. At fifteen, I ran from home and ended up in foster care. The foster home I ended up in didn't seem to help me and the abuse was always in my mind and heart. Well, I ran from the foster system and hid out at a friend's house because the family services people were going to put me into an all-girls facility that was kind of like juvey . . . not where I belonged. I started drinking regularly and smoking weed along with doing ecstasy at this point. I had been placed back into my mom's house. The stuff I was dealing with continued. I only had to make it until seventeen. My mom told me if I didn't like it there to leave and so, I did. I moved in with some friends and hopped from house to house and started using opium on top of weed and alcohol, smoking cigarettes. I was still working and managed to stay in school although it was a struggle. After graduation, I decided to go to the Marines, but I could not manage to stay in and was discharged with a general under honorable conditions discharge due to a " personality disorder," which I am sure came from the disaster of a child hood. I then started to party it up. Coke was added to list and I was living a life of sex, drugs and rock and roll. I thought I was a Rockstar. I met my first son's dad and we were together for a couple of months when I got pregnant, I ended up terminating the pregnancy and we continued to go on. After about nine months we conceived again, and I was not going to terminate this time. And my son was born that year. His dad was not my savior. We were at a constant battle with each other and split up. Now came the meth. I wanted to lose the baby weight and party again. I was working and bounced around to a couple of friends' houses and I met a new guy who was also into meth. I didn't know at that point how big this was. My son slipped into his dad's world more frequently and I slipped further away from reality. I moved in with some new guy and my son stayed with his dad. I quickly found out that the guy I was with was not good. He was nice at first and then after a few weeks of living with him I realized that I was in trouble. I was being beat on and getting high more. I slipped into the strip club scene and was working on the floor and found drugs easily accessible. I was now doing coke, meth, smoking cigarettes and smoking weed, drinking and one night finally started using heroin with my then boyfriend. For seven months I was snorting the heroin, then finally used a needle and shot up. My past was gone and so was reality. For another seven months I was shooting up. I went from 140lbs (about) to 92 lbs. in a year's time. By this time everyone in my family knew something was wrong but didn't know just how bad I was. With the idea of it being meth, they urged me to get out, but I wasn't ready.

One day, I overdosed, and my boyfriend left me at home. I cried out and I know there was an angel there that day. I survived. Barely. I called and told my family what was going on. They finally stepped in with some good friends and got me out. I wasn't done yet, I was just done with heroin and that guy. For about six more months I got high on meth and got off the heroin. Still looking for a way out completely and again tired of the lifestyle I was living, I cried out again. This time God could do something. I finally folded.

I knew someone who was friends with some people from the spiritual cleansing team. I had never met anyone like these people. Unconditional love. I wanted to be free once and for all. I fought my way up there to get free (more of a mental battle) I managed to get homed with a woman from the church and started my journey into freedom and cleansing. I was set free from the bloodline curses of whoredoms, addictions, all the trauma and abuse of my past! Since February of 2012 I have been set free from the drugs and partying. I now have so much to be thankful for. A home, a car, a great job, awesome friends and an amazing husband, a new baby on the way and freedom from guilt and condemnation that I dealt with for so long. I am finally able to prosper the way God planned all along. I am free indeed!

GLORY STORY #3

I went to a mass cleansing and when Apostle began to call out molestation, pornography, incubus, lesbianism and anger and unforgiveness, I was set free! I went home and threw out everything I had in my home—liquor, magazines, sex toys—and then Sunday morning I was baptized in the Holy Ghost and began to speak in tongues!

To God be all of the Glory!

GLORY STORY #4

As my husband and I came to a mass cleansing, I received so much from the Lord. This is our testimonies. As you called out isolation, rejection, abandonment, lust and Jezebel, I felt a release in my spirit. I was very hurt and abandoned by my first pastor, and throughout the years betrayed and rejected by many in the church, so I also had a trust issue, but not anymore! I give God the Glory I am free!

On the Saturday night my husband began to cry from deep within and you began to speak on Santeria which is the religion that my husband and his family practiced. My husband has accepted the Lord and he prays for His family. My husband was being delivered from un-forgiveness, lust and addictions. He was a heroin user and dealer for over twenty-five years until eight years ago and he became cleansed from all of it! Also, Apostle spoke about not just cleaning yourself but that your house needed to be cleansed and not store things in your garage to sell them later, that spoke directly to him and he said to me, "I have a lot of cleaning to do" Praise the lord! God is so good!

GLORY STORY #5

In 4/21/2000 went to Arthur Center -for Mental Health and was diagnosed with Major Chronic depression—recurrent episodes—very severe. In 9/11/2001 I was tested and diagnosed with Adult Attention Disorder with an undiagnosed childhood history of ADD and possibly it was residue of post traumatic disorder, from childhood physical, abuse by my father. I was on Medications from 2000 to 2013

- Adderall XR for Adult Deficit Disorder
- Depakote for Bi Polar—Chronic Severe Depression
- Losartan for High Blood Pressure
- Zoloft then Paxil for anxiety, panic attacks, and suicidal thoughts
- Hydrochlorothiazide for fluid retention
- Allegra for Allergies

- Asthma-inhalers and nebulizer treatments
- Omeprazole for stomach ulcers
- Sonata to help sleep
- Naproxen for pain

I met up with Jeannette in 2010 through a mutual friend, to get rid of all the stuff that was on me. She started counseling me, and by faith in God, He set me free by many spiritual cleansing sessions.

Holy Spirit took me off the drugs, some gradual and some by longer-term weaning. I was set free through Spiritual cleansing of spirits of rejection, fear, bitterness, abandonment, suicide, trauma, victim, double -mindedness, pride, witchcraft, infirmity, rebellion, whoredom, idolatry, bondage, religion, shame, blame and regrets, torment, insecurity-inferiority, lovelessness, unforgiveness, terror, abuse and word curses. I am so thankful for the freeing blood of Jesus and for Apostle Jeannette Connell letting God use her as a vessel to set Father God's people free!

GLORY STORY#6

I went to Spiritual Cleansing last fall and what I experienced was life changing for me. I've experienced the loss of many loved ones in my lifetime; parents, a son and his best friend, a son-in-law, two brothers, a niece and a grandson. The lasting emotions from these has been almost crushing at times. During Spiritual Cleansing, God took away the fear and guilt that I had carried for so very long. and also one of the strongholds that plagued me often was images. I will always remember Apostle's words: "Those images have to go." I am praising my precious Lord forever because He took the images away! The arthritis in my back is gone! Hallelujah and praise to God! I'm ever so grateful for what God has done in my life through "Spiritual Cleansing."

GLORY STORY #7

I began this journey with Apostles George and Jeannette Connell in August 2010. I've been born again and filled with the

Holy Spirit since August of 1994. In those sixteen years I've experienced much in the Lord but continued to consistently fall into a back-slider state and would never grow past a certain point. I spent my entire life in suicidal depression, drug addiction, cycling over and over, destroyed by the condemnation of it all. And before it was all said and done, I was in and out of psyche wards and on many different medications. Extremely bitter and hated everyone. I'm sure I can say that my arrogance and pride were unspeakable, however I knew God's voice, I did LOVE JESUS, so when they started talking about deliverance, in my heart I knew this was a divine appointment but truly had no clue what to expect. Even though in no small or polite way I told her she was nuts. But after three years and much, much, much, mercy and patience (of which I surely tested) from apostle, I know the power and presence of God like *never* before, His precious voice is oh so much sweeter, his love so much more meaningful, and his song in me . . . pure. Vision is more vivid so much deeper in a much softer, pliable heart. Knowing apostle as my truly and deeply dear spiritual mother has been an inexpressible honor. I am thankful to be a part of a body of believers who steps into those greater works, to God be all the Glory!

The Bible tells us in James 5:16 to confess your faults to one another and you will be healed. The effectual fervent prayer of a righteous man availed much. As Christian, we are often afraid to tell another believer what we are going through and the areas we are struggling with because we are afraid we will be judged etc. so we often suffer alone and in secrecy. This is especially true of those in ministry. I found out about this ministry through a friend (she has also testified in here) who was miraculously healed of several different conditions as well as she got freedom in several areas of her life. The whole time I had known her she had always been in pain and very sickly. I also knew there were areas we both struggled with that were common because of the times we confided in one another. When I saw what God had done in her life, I decided I was desperate to get help for some areas in my life that I have struggled with for years as a believer. I was tired of feeling I was constantly in a fight to not give into the thoughts that were going through my head. I would get victory from time to time through prayer and fasting, but the struggles would always come back. I realize now that a lot of what I was going through was because of abuse and other things that I had gone through as a child that I never got complete healing from. Many things I had never even shared with anyone. Because of the things I had went through, I had a very low self-esteem even to the point that I struggled with self-hate even though I didn't realize the extent until I went through counseling and it all came pouring out. I had a lot of anger towards God that I had never dealt with. After all, a good Christian should not be angry at God. Because of everything I had went through I had a hard time really understanding how much God loved me. I knew it at a certain level but not deep inside to the core of my being. In spiritual cleansing, you can share completely about your life, what you have gone through and the areas you struggle with as a Christian in a safe environment. I received a lot of healing by just sharing everything with someone. The devil loses power in your life just by you sharing things with someone else and getting everything out of hiding. He tries to tell you that if someone knew everything about you that they would not love you or want to be around you which is a lie. We all have things in our past or things we have struggled with that we are not proud of. Through my counseling sessions with Jeannette, I really experienced the unconditional love of Jesus through her. When she and her team prayed for me, they prayed for God to heal me from everything I had been through. Then they prayed for God to set me free from strongholds etc. in my life. There was nothing "weird" about the experience. Just believers praying for another believer for healing and to be set free from everything that is hindering them from being everything God wants them to be. Since being prayed for, I have seen huge differences in my life. I am no longer tempted and tormented in an area I struggled with off and on for over twenty years. I can experience and accept the love of Christ in a way I never have before. I have a renewed desire to spend long amounts of time praying and reading God's word. I truly love myself. (That's a big one!) I have also found I have a freedom in ministry I haven't had in years. I'm so thankful for the chains that have been broken in my life.

GLORY STORY #8

I have been truly blessed through the ministry of Spiritual Cleansing. I had osteoporosis, fibromyalgia, crippling migraines, insomnia, and a failing liver due to Hepatitis C. I had chronic pain in my body to the point my clothes touching me—or even others touching me—caused me pain, which caused me to shy away from people and isolate myself. I battled with phobias, like fear of spiders, heights, crossing over bridges. I was afraid of the dark and was very paranoid about someone being in my home or out to get me. I went through a lot of abuse as a child, being molested from the age of three till I was fourteen by multiple men, and several times by the same man when I was between the age eleven and twelve. I also was in a physically and emotionally abusive marriage for fifteen years, where times I feared for my life and the life of my children. I became addicted to IV cocaine, crack cocaine, meth, pot, and alcohol for several years.

Though by the time I received ministry through spiritual cleansing I had been off drugs and alcohol for ten years, I still had an addictive personality. I had also developed an addiction to prescription drugs after being on pain meds, muscle relaxers, triple antidepressants, and much more for many years due to illness. When I went into the prayer time for my cleansing I was unable to straighten my fingers due to the arthritis. Through cleansing, the Lord supernatural healed and delivered me of all these things. All pain left my body, my fingers straightened, and I went off all eight prescriptions that day and have never had to go back on them. I had no withdrawals either. I was completely free of all addictions to the medication as well. I was also freed of insomnia. The doctor said my liver was so bad it could not rejuvenate, giving me at most ten years to live. My liver was completely healed, and I am still alive today, almost fourteen years later! I was delivered of my fears of spiders, heights, bridges and the dark. All my life, in my dreams I was always masculine. I also struggled with mind battles of imagery of the same sex. Though I never acted on the mind battles, it was tormenting. I learned my father was bi-sexual and that spirit through the bloodline came in through the womb. Once

226

I received cleansing from it all, the mind battles stopped. Now when I dream I am myself and fully female! The Lord healed me and set me free of all these things and I have walked out other things that I have received cleansing from over the last six years such as multiple personalities, spiritual schizophrenia, bipolar, and many emotional issues. I was also freed of intellectual pride and perfectionism.

In 2008, both my grandparents, who played a huge part in raising me, where promoted to heaven within two months of one another. Then in 2010 my first husband was promoted to heaven, I am very thankful that two years prior, he received the Lord as his personal savior. I had a deep spirit of grief and the Lord completely healed my mind and emotions from all the grief. During my time of addictions, I was homeless twice, once in the inner city of two major cities. I lived in poverty most of my life, yet through the healing and cleansing today I am remarried to a godly man and we are purchasing our own home! I am free of all those things and walking out my destiny and purpose in the Lord. It has been a process overall and I am thankful for the ministry of Spiritual Cleansing in which the Lord used to give me back my life! One thing I do know for sure, through Spiritual Cleansing the Lord saved and restored my life. My passion is to see others not only saved but healed and set free from all that has them bound that they too may walk in the fullness of the Lord and fulfill the purposes and destiny God has for them!

GLORY STORY #9

I was physically abused from age three until sixteen. It wasn't until when I was sixteen years old that my stepfather passed, whom was my abuser, and I was able to start counseling and get some help, but the counseling didn't stop the feelings and the medications only made me numb. I was still a mess mentally and emotionally. I would deliberately fail classes in school if you involve me having to be the center of attention or talking in front of people. I had a great fear of people. Large crowds frightened me and anytime I was around people I always felt less than. I had a great fear of men because the only example I had was my stepfather. I became depressed and extremely suicidal, at one point attempting suicide and failing. At seventeen years old, I found Jeannette Connell and her spiritual cleansing ministry. It was then that God began to reveal to me who he really was. My anger towards him because I viewed him as a man left. My fear of man left. Many mental and emotional curses such as multiple personalities were broken off me. I today am one person in my mind. I work as a prison guard in a women's prison, speaking in front of hundreds of women a day. I work on a transitional housing unit that holds the offenders getting ready to leave prison and go back into society. It has given many opportunities to influence and encourage many people. I never fear when I am there. I don't get anxious and fearful when speaking or working around such a large group of people. I am now married and have a beautiful baby boy. I am still not completed; you never will be until you reach heaven. But God has healed my mind and my emotions and has brought me up from being an outcast in the world and a lost cause to having a purpose in this life. I am a living testimony that God can turn anything bad into something extraordinary. To God be the glory!

GLORY STORY #10

My husband wanted me to come with him to this thing called "spiritual cleansing." I was open, but honestly thought it was a bit weird. I knew that my fourteenth year was very traumatic. Moving to a new town, an embarrassing rape that I told no one about, poor and fat in a world of pretty and cute girls. It was terrible. No one needed to make fun of me because I hated myself, even though everyone told me how beautiful I am. Besides the self-hatred, I was basically a fourteen-year-old living in a thirty-nine-year-old body, with husband and kids and bills and stress. Of course, I had no idea that I was stuck at fourteen. I only knew it after Jeannette called out "arrested development." I might have walked in fourteen-year-old, but I walked out thirty-nine years old. My husband and I went to lunch and he saw it immediately in my eyes and so was pleased. My self-hatred was cut in half that day, and it took a few more sessions to get to the root of it, but can I tell you that instead of hiding under frumpy clothes that I love to dress up and be the feminine girly girl now. I haven't lost a pound or bought new clothes, but there's a love for myself now that simply wasn't there before. Let me state again that this was all instant. I didn't do a Bible study. I didn't "apply" principles to my life. I didn't try real hard or reprogram my thinking with affirmations in the mirror. No. I walked in a mess, and through a series of prayers and confessions that I had no idea you could even pray—I was instantly healed and cleansed! This wasn't neat, or wild, or rare. This was the gospel that was promised when Jesus said that he came to "heal the brokenhearted and set the captive free"—even when one doesn't know that we need it. Thanks, AJC! You set us on a journey to learn to do this for ourselves and now we have helped over seventy-five others and growing, get the same freedom that we were fighting for!

GLORY STORY #11

The earliest memory I have is when I was in kindergarten and wasn't allowed to do activities or stopped from doing them because I was doing it differently. My teacher even then made fun of me for doing something differently. The feeling of not being good enough entered me at a young age. When I entered my first grade year, I started being bullied by my teacher and my classmates. My teacher praised other students for their handwriting, but when I did the same exact thing, she would tell me I did it wrong and gave me bad grades. She singled me out constantly everyday. The kids were mean and wouldn't let me play with them, so most of my days during recess I was alone and played by myself. It got to the point where I would lie to my teacher and tell her I was allergic to things so she wouldn't make me play. The bullying got so bad that I was pulled from public school and was homeschooled. My mom said that for a long time afterwards I would cry whenever it was time for handwriting lessons.

So, from the first through the eighth grade, I was homeschooled. I was lonely due to not having any friends, but I was happy. I enjoyed my childhood and my homeschooling. But, there was this always looming feeling of that I did everything wrong. When it was time for my eighth grade year, I decided that I wanted to try public school again—so I did. From day one, I was picked on for being different, being homeschooled, etc. I hardly had any friends because I was too scared of everyone. I was thirteen and I had developed a crush on the quarterback. Well, some of the girls that picked on me in my classes had figured it out, so they set me up, asking me to come sit with them and him. When I refused, they decided to announce it to him. Well, he asked me to a dance, so of course, I said yes. It turned out to be a trick and he brought someone else. I was crushed. In come the trust issues. I had another boyfriend that same year who I considered my best friend. Well, he wasn't. I was naive and thought this guy genuinely cared, but he didn't. He manipulated me to do sexual things for him that I really didn't understand at the time, sent me nasty texts, etc. When we broke up, from that point on, all the kids in the school referred to me as a 'whore' and other things. I was asked to do things by other guys. I was ashamed. I was only thirteen. At this point in time, I was starting to become unhappy. I was thinking about things no thirteen-year-old should think about. I was depressed and beaten down by my peers, and it only got worse.

In ninth grade, the bullying escalated. My first day of high school I had my fingers slammed and locked into my locker by a girl I had once considered my friend, and had to go home. Before that, she had threatened me with a knife. I was constantly picked on because I had eczema and psoriasis, so I was constantly broke out or my skin was dry. I was constantly asked if it was contagious and I was treated like a disease. From that point, I tried to hide my body, only liked to wear long sleeves and jeans so no one could see. My boyfriend at the time acted disgusted over the fact I had to wear lotion. I felt like an alien to everyone else. I didn't feel pretty and hated myself. I didn't feel smart. I was having severe self-esteem issues. I cut myself because I was so unhappy.

Around this time, one of my guy friends and I decided to be in a relationship. I was so happy at first; everything was good and sweet in the beginning. He was good to me, even met my family. But it didn't take long before he turned on me. He started being possessive of me, tried to tell me how to dress, pitched fits on me for not texting him and would yell at me in school for no reason. Then after making me cry or upset, he would apologize like nothing had happened. This continued for months, and because I cared for him so much, I overlooked all the abusive behavior. He was verbally abusive and tried to sexually assault me. I was too terrified to tell anyone that he had tried to assault me and let him manipulate me into other things. I cut him off not long after that. His best friend then stalked and harassed me. Boys would try to touch me at school or on the bus. From then on, I feared men and being touched. I trusted no one. I decided after that I wanted to be homeschooled again. But, I was plagued with memories of the abuse and bullying. I never felt good enough. I was being tormented by nightmares, anxiety, depression, hallucinations, fear of being alone, and of the dark. The list goes on. I was in deep pain. During this time, I was diagnosed with psoriatic arthritis. I was scared I would never function like a normal person again, would never have kids, get married, or enjoy life. I went through several years of shots that made me sick. This only enhanced my feeling of no longer wanting to exist. From the age of thirteen to eighteen I had suicidal thoughts all the time, constantly wanted to just take a handful of pills and just leave. I was suicidal until I met apostle Jeannette and went through cleansing. Every lie just started peeling off. I am so happy and thankful that I can say that I am still here, and I haven't been suicidal since. I am no longer depressed or ashamed of my body or myself. I don't seek the constant approval of people anymore. I no longer feel pain in my joints. I no longer have to get monthly shots of Enbrel or methotrexate shots for the psoriatic arthritis. I am good enough. I am not afraid anymore. I feel alive. I feel loved by Jesus more than ever and by the people around me. I have never felt more grateful and I give God all the glory for it!

GLORY STORY #12

"By my grace you are made whole, and no one can come against it." Eleven years ago, on January 2007, at 11:00 p.m., I was rushed to the hospital with complications of breathing. I was admitted.

They gave me a breathing treatment and sent me home. After I had awakened the next morning, I was rushed to the hospital again and admitted. After eight days of uncertainty, they sent me home with a nebulizer and an unclear diagnosis. Their claim was that I was having panic attacks and anxiety, but there was something more to it. It wasn't until after many doctors and specialist visits that they had found a root to the anxiety and fear that I was experiencing. In October of the same year, I was diagnosed with Laryngopharyngeal reflux, which caused my vocal cords to swell together and the sensation of not being able to breathe. It wasn't until five years later that I found out that I had Silent Celiac disease, which was the allergy to wheat. I was extremely allergic. I couldn't touch it, I couldn't eat it, and if we ever passed by a wheat field in one of our travels, I would have to use my inhaler. For many years I had felt like a burden to my family. Here they had this child that couldn't eat food like they could, much less touch it. All of our restaurant visits depended on whether or not I could eat there, and if they had a Gluten-Free menu. I felt very excluded, not because anybody made me feel that way, but because I was different. I also wrestled with the trauma and anxiety caused by what I had experienced in the ER. In the ER, I didn't want to go anywhere or do anything without the oxygen mask they had put on me. It made me feel safe. I depended on it because I felt like I could breathe better with it than without it. It wasn't until seven years later that I met Jeannette Connell at a three-day healing conference and began going to her classes. I soon learned that I didn't have to live with my diagnoses forever, and that miracles weren't just a thing of the past. On June 1, 2014, I received a miracle, and a word from God that I was going to be okay. I was at my aunt's church, and that morning the man that was speaking was teaching on Mark 11.

In Mark 11:12–14, "The next day as they were leaving Bethany, Jesus was hungry. Seeing in the distance a fig tree in leaf, he went to find out if it had any fruit. When he reached it, he found nothing but leaves, because it was not the season for figs. Then he said to the tree, "May no one ever eat fruit from you again." That verse resonated very strongly with me. He said to the tree, "May no one ever eat fruit from you again." To me, the celiac disease was a giant dead tree. It had no good fruit; the only fruit it bore was rotten and malicious. So, I had a thought, if Jesus told this barren tree to shrivel up and die, then could he not do the same thing within me? When the man asked if there was anybody that would like prayer, I went up to him and told him that I would like for him to pray with me, that I had allergies. He began to pray, and soon I found myself lying on the floor, listening to no other sounds than the words of The Father saying, "Take bread and eat it. By your faith, you will be made whole." I felt a pressing on my throat, like someone had their hand laying on it.

When I rose, and went back to my aunt, I told her what had happened and what He had spoken to me. Afterwards my aunt, uncle, and my sister and I went to out to eat for lunch. We were seated, and suddenly I realized that I no longer felt like a burden. When the waitress set the dinner rolls on the table, the first thing I did, much to my aunt's surprise, was to take one and eat it. When the Father says something, always know it to be true. After I ate the roll, I felt no swelling. I felt no discomfort, and I had no allergic reaction. I attended two more cleansing conferences after that Sunday, and many of the anxieties and fear of the past were peeled away in layers. I was also released of a spirit of terror that came in through all of it. I thank God that to this day that I have not been forced to eat from a gluten-free menu. I can eat anything with wheat, and I have no fear in doing so. He also healed me of the anxieties and trauma of my life experiences. I thank God that I don't have to bear those burdens because of what Jesus did on the cross for us. Almost every day he reminds me of it in the joy I feel when I spend time with family and friends.

GLORY STORY #13

Saved and delivered, yet bounded and tormented at the same time, that was my story until I met and began the process of spiritual cleansing with apostle Jeanette. I had given my life to Christ and was no longer living a sinful lifestyle. I had been prayed for before and had undergone deliverance ministry, but I was not free from anxiety, fear, anger, rejection, and demonic oppression. I felt stuck, hopeless, and ashamed. I had even been told that since I had been in church so long that I should be free from all of those issues. I was on the brink of giving up because I didn't believe that I could ever be free. Then, I was blessed to connect with apostle Jeanette Connell and her team. They were literally my ram in the bush and God's way for my escape.

She and her team dealt with the root systems in my life that gave the enemy permission to terrorize me. She was sensitive, compassionate, patient, and truthful. She helped me to realize the lies of the enemies that were influencing my thoughts and emotions. I discovered the generational sins in my family line that predisposed me to sin patterns in order keep me and my family bound, as well as how my own sins further entrenched the enemy's hand in my life.

However, to God's glory, it was like light began to pierce a veil of darkness after each counseling session, and I could begin to see clearly and experience the love and light of God. I experienced a freedom I never thought was possible. Where I once could only think about dying, I could finally envision living. Instead of fear, I had power, love, and a well-balanced mind. I learned that God loved me unconditionally, and I was fearfully and wonderfully made. God approved, accepted and chose me, so, I didn't need man's approval. God alone was enough for me. I had finally experienced for myself freedom for the captive. Before then, my life was stuck at a standstill, but after spiritual cleansing, God gave me a vision for my life, and opened the door for me to go back school and fulfill a dream He had given me when I was third grade. Every step of the way, apostle Connell and her team supported and encouraged me. I'm currently two semesters away from graduating school, and my ability to move forward with my life is because of how God equipping apostle Connell with the ministry of spiritual cleansing. I'm here today because of God' s grace and faithfulness to connect me with such a vital ministry. I'm eternally grateful to God and apostle Connell for the change and deep work that was done in my life!

I wanted to let you know that I watched all the way from California the Saturday spiritual cleansing and I have to tell you that it was so powerful that I went through deliverance right in my home as I was watching and saying the prayers with you and then receiving deliverance from rejection, sexual sins, generation curses—you name it. I could not stop throwing up, and at one point there was a demon that was stubborn and spoke out and said no like it didn't want to leave and I said you're coming out and it came out! I want to thank you so much and give glory to God!

GLORY STORY #14

Many people came against Jesus because he cast out demons and healed the sick, saying that he cast out demons by Beelzebub (Matt. 12:22–29). In Luke 10, Jesus sent the disciples out by twos. They returned and reported that even the demons were subject to them in his name. He said he had given them authority to tread on serpents and scorpions and over all the power of the enemy and nothing will hurt us. Nevertheless, do not rejoice in this, that the spirits are subject to you, but rejoice that your names are recorded in heaven.

I've known apostle Jeannette Connell and spiritual cleansing for about four years. While I can't pinpoint one exact moment, the Lord has used her to bring me into new dimensions of freedom. Line upon line, precept upon precept, layer after layer has been and is being cleansed. Years of feeling rejection and self-hatred, of "never asking to be born" were cleansed by the power of Jesus Christ who is the same yesterday, today and forever. At one Spiritual Cleansing conference, she was praying for rejection even from the mother's womb and I saw the Lord grab me by the hand and we came into this earth realm through the birth canal with a joy and a diving in. I was born breech and have often wondered if that's a baby's way of not wanting to enter this earth realm. I had fallen out with a long-time friend. I allowed bitterness, resentment, unforgiveness, and hurt to set up in my heart. I was sick over three months and could not get well. After attending a Spiritual Cleansing conference that was dealt with and I was healed. Today, I am walking in a greater degree of health than I have for many years!

GLORY STORY #15

The earliest memory that I have is being in my baby bed begging my mom to help me because I couldn't breathe. Much of my childhood was spent in doctor's offices, emergency rooms, and as a patient at our local hospital. I had severe respiratory problems and allergies. Breathing treatments, oxygen tents, shots and medicine became a normal part of my life. I was a victim of molestation from the earliest age I can remember being around six or seven to around the age of sixteen. I led a life ruled by fear: fear of dying, fear of being alone, and fear of unwanted touches. Add to this being raised in a legalistic type denomination. I was afraid of God, or maybe I should say afraid of *failing* God, afraid of hell. I became angry, introverted, and very lonely. I spent a lot of time alone because of sickness. I lived in my own little world, so to speak. I was very detached from reality in some ways, fantasizing became an escape from the reality that I lived. I was miserable. This followed me into my teenage years. My dad was an alcoholic and wasn't a big part of my life and I had a very unstable relationship with my mom. We fought often. Escaping was my dream; I hated my life.

As a teen I developed a close relationship with a childhood friend. He had also had an alcoholic father and had suffered abuse as a child. Our demons were much the same, "birds of a feather" they say, "like spirits attract." We loved one another but it wasn't a healthy relationship. We married young and moved 1,000 miles away. Escape came at last was my thought. I was going to be better, have better, and do better than I ever did before. But alas, escape didn't really come because those same demons followed and haunted me even 1,000 miles away. I suffered nightmares and flashbacks of the sexual abuse I went through. All the anger and resentment that I had was still there. Moreover, my marriage was a mess. We were two big kids haunted by our pasts and not mature enough to know what to do about it. We were divorced after three years. Add a broken heart to the list now. I moved back home and began attending church. I had always loved the Lord, even from a child, but I had never really been able to really receive His love, being bound by so much fear. This church seemed so very different, very prophetic in nature. I was received by all and felt a great deal of peace considering the situation I now found myself in. I was still very dysfunctional. I carried so much baggage from childhood. Add to that the loss of the person I had always considered my best friend, my husband. I was a mess.

Never having had a stable relationship with my dad, I developed an attachment to my pastor; I looked to him for guidance and advice. I had made him a father figure; this became an unhealthy soul tie that would last twenty-four years of my life. I met my current husband, love of my life, at church during this period of time. It had always been a heart's desire of mine to have children and I carried a fear that I wouldn't be able to because of my lifelong health issues. We became pregnant that first year, but our son was delivered straight into heaven a few months in. I now carried a heavy grief that I still don't have words for. We were able to have two other children, but I always carried that baby in my heart. Our marriage has had much joy, but it held that grief of loss and we fought through many ghosts of our past. I began having some odd symptoms while pregnant with our second child and became very sick carrying our third child. When she was ten months old, I was diagnosed with Meniere's disease. This is a disease that I have since learned has affected four generations of my family that I am aware of. My health was unpredictable at best, at times being unable to even stand or care for our family. This progressed over the years until I became agoraphobic, afraid to leave home because of what might happen, afraid one of those attacks would come. I became bedridden, unable to stand without aid for some years. Our two children had bad health issues that I wasn't even able to attend to at times. Add guilt to my list. I spent most of forty-four years being tormented and haunted. I met apostle Jeannette at this time. I began attending Spiritual Cleansing classes and the Lord opened my eyes. I knew the Lord healed and I had stood in every prayer line, called every prayer call, did everything I knew but He revealed so much to me. After a personal session with apostle and going through the conferences much healing came to me. The roots of unforgiveness, anxiety, bitterness, anger, torment, fear, delusion, infirmity had been laid bare. The haunted years began to peel away. I was now able to receive the love and healing of our heavenly Father. The timing of the Lord is perfect as on my forty-fifth birthday I received a triple negative breast cancer diagnosis. This type of cancer is aggressive and has a high rate of metastasis and recurrence after treatment. They have no targeted treatment for it. In the past, because of fear, hearing those words, I would have probably crawled into a ball and would have most likely been consumed by it and died.

Instead, I was able to walk through that journey in a peace I can't even explain. What was meant as a death sentence brought life to me in so many ways. God showed Himself faithful as always to His word. He stopped the enemy at the door! The genetic tests done showed that it was not genetic, and my children are safe.

Three years later, I am still here telling of the goodness of my Jesus. I am now able to leave home without fear, I am free from medication that I had been dependent on for ten years or better. The nightmares have stopped, as have the severe anxiety attacks and unhealthy soul ties. I have freedom in Christ! Spiritual Cleansing ministry brings healing through revelation. It sheds light, the Light, exposing the darkness. I am thankful for the equipping I have received from this ministry as well. I now am learning to recognize the enemy and how to battle attacks when they come. I am so thankful the Father brought Jeannette and the team into my life!

GLORY STORY #16

Spiritual cleansing ministry saved my life! I had the opportunity to hear her speak one day and I was with so much passion and power for this type of ministry, it was just awesome! Not many months after hearing her minister, I was served with divorce papers. It seemed as though everything on the inside of me was ripped apart. Been in ministry myself, I knew I couldn't continue to preach, pray and prophesy knowing that on the side there was war going on. There was much healing, repairs and cleansing to be. I refused to be a part of the growing number of leaders that were "dysfunctional" and seeking to be seen, heard and not seeking to be whole. I was praying and looking a place for deliverance, apostle

Jeannette face appeared before me more than once. I located her, even though the devil tried to block our coming together BUT GOD! Every session that I attended, God was there also! There is a thankfulness that's hard to express. The Lord allowed me to be placed in hands of a pure, powerful, dedicated, unconditional loving ministry. I was too able to lay the ax at the roots of pain, rejection, abandonment, accusations, condemnation, disappointments, low self-esteem, crushed confidence, and so much more. I knew I was still saved but I knew too the enemy was trying to shut my spirit man down. It's amazing how we understand in natural about being clean, however in the spiritual, it's about being seen or heard rather than being whole. Everyone should go through cleansing especially leaders. I'm thankful for this ministry! I thank God that He has allowed me to receive so much from this ministry that has saved my life! It has equipped tools need to continue to walk in victory, knowing that this is a daily lifestyle. This ministry has followed up with me and still prays with me until this day!

GLORY STORY #17

I was adopted into a family of a mom, dad and an older brother. My adopted father died when I was three, my mother never came to terms with it. My brother who is four years older than I started playing with Ouija boards and fortune tellers, all the things of that sort and before anyone knew it he was hanging with a satanic cult of people. This was my life for twelve years, being drugged with a paralyzing drug so all the rapes to me and around was evil at its highest. At five, I did have an angel/Jesus encounter, but I did not have anyone to show me or teach me the Jesus way and as I got older I lost sight of who I was. I grew up fighting the internal fight of feeling unworthy, useless, and I have always felt like I was a disappointment to myself and everyone else. I have always felt in whatever I said or did I had to "prove" something. I never was taught or experienced love, never getting a hug or saying you did a good job so I never could give it, nor would I let myself feel it, as I really didn't know how. My mom sadly was not shown love either, so she could not show me, a cycle for sure. I went on to get married and have four beautiful children, but my marriage ended in a disaster, so I raised them alone.

In 2011, I was 54 and was introduced to Jeannette thru a mutual friend. She told me about Spiritual Cleansing and at that time I had no clue what it was, I was set up with a session, had a lot of roots come out and even had the miracle of my left foot growing an inch. Outwardly I was excited, inwardly I was miserable not know how to receive love thru Jeannette caring. All my life I portrayed as "being strong" as I thought that was being a friend. I have read the Bible secretly ever since I can remember and used to quote scripture, but Love was missing so it was empty. I really didn't know how to receive anything in life so the people who genuinely cared scared me, but you would of never known it; I was really good at pretending. Spiritual Cleansing came into my life and for so many the Cleansing comes quickly, but for me it was a process that took till 2017. I am still a work in progress, but I am so much better than I was.

It has been a roller coast ride for me as I went through the Cleansing process I rebelled as no matter what I said or did all I was shown was love, I was petrified and didn't even recognize it at first, so all those deep root issues that I had formed to "protect me" were not working. I didn't know how to deal with this, not to mention authority that I have always resented.

In 2017, I finally submitted everything I could. I let go off the old and let God have me totally. I am so grateful to God for bringing me to spiritual cleansing, so I could let go of my pride that I was so full of, my criticism for me and others, my selfish, my thought of my rules only, and just plain being irresponsible. I now know who I am, I have a purpose and as I am letting love in, I am learning to love others. Glory to God for Spiritual Cleansing!

GLORY STORY #18

My journey started in 1979. I gave my life to Christ he filled me with his Holy Spirit with the evidence of speaking in tongues while praying for my father to go into the ministry. My life was a life of turmoil. I was in and out of the hospital due to many female problems; the doctor said I would never have children. I have one ovary removed. The second ovary was reconstructed twice but the desire of my heart was to conceive a child. I believed that God would give me the desires of my heart if I would earnestly seek after him! I believed and trusted I have a daughter that's now thirty-five years old. There are facts and then there's the truth; God's word is the truth. Along the way I had my mountains and valleys. In the valleys where I was running from God, I had breast cancer, epilepsy, and Hepatitis C for fifteen years. Then I was healed. In my life, I have been addicted to drugs, prostitution, homosexuality, but through it all I found divine agape love through Christ! I'm now free 100 percent healthy with the help of my brothers and sisters in Christ I live a free life grounded in the word of God. We have a living, loving God that cares about us!

GLORY STORY #19

I'm so praising God that I got major deliverance of many demonic spirits and it's been life changing for me. I felt for years that I needed deliverance and studied deliverance ministry on my own and sought people to help me. Finally, in 2013 God connected me with Jeannette Connell and Spiritual cleansing ministries on Facebook. Then apostle Jeannette placed me in personal spiritual counseling with one of the deliverance team ministers.

After some months of counseling by phone, I had my first deliverance on March 10, 2014. It lasted almost four hours. I got delivered from many generational curses and soul ties and from trauma such as rejection fears self-hatred, self-rejection, sexual spirits, pride, bitterness, jealousy, etc. It was personal major spiritual surgery. I said then and still do that on March 10, 2014 was when my life first began. My mindsets changed drastically. I started seeing myself the way God does and began walking into my true identity in Jesus Christ. I want to make sure I tell of all God has done for me since I started deliverance in 2014. Some major miracles are I no longer have panic attacks and no more suicidal thoughts and depression all that I had suffered for years and some things since birth. One big way I changed is I quit being a hoarder. I had been a hoarder for years living with stacks and bags of boxes all over my home and not wanting to give anything away. After this major spiritual surgery, I have been able to get rid of stuff and I finally started living in a nice decent clean home. Many of my family and friends visit me and see this visible change. Another big way I changed right away is I started driving far distances by myself to ministry and more deliverance conferences. For years, I would have much fear, anxiety, and fatigue. that I couldn't drive even an hour by myself. Now I love to get in my car and go, go, go! Such freedom! I've had more confidence in myself and more productive in work for God's kingdom since I've had deliverance.

In December 2015, I took my last allergy shots and now I'm able to mow my yard with no asthma and I have energy to do it. I suffered with allergies since childhood and on allergy shots and asthma. This is a big miracle for no more shots! I can do all things through Christ who gives me strength. I have learned much about deliverance and making it an ongoing process in my life. I attend mass deliverance conferences through apostle Jeannette and Spiritual cleansing ministries and I listen to the cd's and materials they send me and work on growing and being more free, every day. It's all about God and being the person God has designed us to be and able to more effective do the work he's wants us to do for his Kingdom. I give God all the glory for how he has delivered changed and set me free. Total transformation! I so want more, Yea glory! Deliverance is a God thing indeed. Total freedom! Thank you, Jesus.

GLORY STORY #20

I had a stroke at work, went home in a wheelchair, unable to care for myself, paralyzed on my right side. My daughter wheeled me into church during praise and worship, I dropped out of my wheelchair onto the floor, and I cried out to God, This is unacceptable! Apostle Jeannette put her hands on my ankles and an intercessor named Judy put her hand on my back and I felt like my foot and leg are on fire, burning up, burned up my right side and my shoulder down to my hand. God was healing me! After prayer, I jumped up and ran to the front and was able to walk and jump and run. God healed me! I was also diagnosed with high blood pressure; I'm healed and no longer on meds for it yet. Through cleansing God delivered me from many childhood traumas and generational things, schizophrenia, fear, anger and many other things. While sitting through the teachings, I have learned to forgive and let go. After five failed marriages, I'm finally OK being alone. All my children were on drugs and alcohol for twenty years, and by prayer and great grace, they are all saved and serving God. One still in prison, but currently going through pathway to freedom and asking for a Bible! Bless the Lord! As I learn to release and let go, through the biblical teaching of Apostle Jeannette, I've witnessed my prayers being answered one by one. Praise the Lord!

GLORY STORY # 21

I was invited to Jeannette's Spiritual Cleansing classes after I had shared with my old pastor and his wife how long I had been using marijuana. The revelation that impacted me the most was how the enemy speaks to you. I had already been saved, but I was still in so much bondage and my mind and emotions were such a wreck. The part I want to share is when I finally realized the emotions I had didn't have to rule me. Even though I felt rejected or anxiety or anger or whatever it was that I believed was true at the time wasn't even real in most cases. The idea that these thoughts I would have weren't even mine was freeing despite how real they felt. I still remember the class Jeannette was teaching when she said, "bondage always speaks in the first person." I realized—that's not even me thinking—I just listen to this spirit talking to me. It was a struggle, but it was finally possible for me to believe I didn't have to stay a slave to it any longer. I wanted her to lay hands on me and cast that spirit out of me and never desire it again. But because of the state of my heart it was not so. It was so hardened toward myself that God had much work to do but I didn't realize it. She taught me and counseled me and prayed for me and spoke life over me. She taught me that the Bible says, "How can to walk together lest they be agreed. I came out of agreement with it by an act of my will and called her to confess when it was tempting me. It took a lot of prayer and will power and others praying for me to "walk it out." The Bible teaches us to confess to one another and I found that the enemy kept me silent by shaming me and I listened to him for years sitting in church with my desire to always quit but not able. But after I had initially confessed it, He brought me a way out. This is only the beginning of what He has done in my life.

GLORY STORY # 22

Ever since apostle Jeannette and the ladies came to our church in Atlanta, my wife has had a 'peculiar' feeling that they were sent to the church just for us. After an amazing Spiritual Cleansing and guiding the two of us through some moments of strife, or as we like to call it, "intense worship." I tend to lean towards her understanding. That is why we knew driving the nine-hour journey to Missouri would be worth every mile. A brief reprieve from our 50-day fast and a powerful weekend of soul search . . . finding and spiritual cleansing. It is a blessing and a gift to get right to the core, to the root of a generational or environmental curse and purging it from our lives! Apostle also equipped us to maintain the life afterwards and better avoid the snares of temptation and backsliding. The foundation for all of the teachings and processes come straight from the Sword of the Spirit itself, the word of God. My wife and I, separately and collectively, have stood down and faced some inner demons and threw them back into the pit of hell. May the Lord continue to bless apostle and her team as they do his anointed work all around the globe. Shalom!

GLORY STORY # 23

My testimony of my alcoholism began in 1976 at the age of seven. I bought my first beer in a bar when I was seven years old. As I grew older, I would drink only on the weekends with my family until my latter teenage years. Around the age of eighteen to nineteen I would buy beer and go out driving with my friends. During this time, I had started drinking during the week as well, eventually drinking a case of beer a day. I ended up with two DWI'S and 10 Driving while revoked. I was an alcoholic for about twenty-five years. At the age of forty I finally gave my life to the Lord and through "Spiritual Cleansing" I was cleansed of the generational curse of alcoholism. I should have had several felony charges for my driving while revoked, but by God's grace and His purpose over my life, I did not receive any felonies. The Spirit of God is more powerful than our human minds can fathom. You can be free from any addiction or curse through Spiritual Cleansing.

GLOSSARY

Common spiritual roots of disease

Infirmity Spiritual Roots revelation taken from *A More Excellent Way* by Henry W. Wright.

- autoimmune diseases: results of an unloving spirit producing feeling of not being loved or accepted, self-rejection, self-hatred, and self-bitterness, coupled with guilt, can also have; fear, anxiety, and stress attached.
- diabetes: self-hatred, self-rejection, and guilt with fear, anxiety, and stress attached.
- acne, eczema, psoriasis, asthma, allergies, sinus, hay fever, high blood pressure, irritable bowel syndrome, ulcers, acid reflux: fear, anxiety, and stress.
- heart disease, mitral valve prolapse (heart valve disease): fear, anxiety, and stress.
- coronary artery disease: self-rejection, self-bitterness, self-hatred.
- strokes: self-rejection, self-bitterness, self-hatred.
- aneurysms: anger, rage, resentment.
- varicose veins: anger, rage, resentment.
- cancer: roots of resentment and bitterness.

- breast cancer: can be (but not always) caused by sins of conflict and bitterness between her mother, sister(s), or mother-in-law.
- ovarian cancer: caused from a woman's hatred for herself and her sexuality. Self-bitterness and self-loathing concerning sexuality.
- Hodgkin's disease and leukemia: deep-rooted bitterness from unresolved rejection by a father.
- prostate cancer: anger, guilt, self-hatred, and self-bitterness.
- arthritis: bitterness, unforgiveness.
- osteoarthritis: self-bitterness, unforgiveness of self and guilt.
- ADD (attention deficit disorder), epilepsy: both coming out of a deaf and dumb spirit.
- migraines: guilt, then fear.
- fibromyalgia: fear, anxiety, and stress.
- thyroid: fear, anxiety, and stress.
- hypoglycemia: anxiety, fear, self-hatred, self-rejection, and guilt.
- vertigo: free-floating fear, chronic anxiety.
- Alzheimer's: self-hatred and guilt.
- ulcers: fear, anxiety, and stress.

SAMPLE RELEASE OF LIABILITY FORM

I _____ acknowledge that the team members from Troy Freedom Outpost along with the Spiritual Cleansing ministry have voluntarily agreed to council with me in Spiritual Cleansing Classes and prayers for healing and deliverance. I understand that these sessions are not professional counseling and that none of the team are licensed counselors as recognized by the world, but spiritual counselors and ministers of the Gospel as ordained by God. I understand that these team members are, to the best of their ability, under the grace of Jesus Christ, doing what they can to help me achieve more freedom in my life through counseling and deliverance prayers.

I understand that Troy Freedom Outpost/Spiritual Cleansing is a nonprofit Missouri Corporation that makes no charge for its services. I further state that I have voluntarily sought assistance of my own initiative and that I am under no obligation to accept or reject any of the advice or help I might receive from the team members of this ministry.

Troy Freedom Outpost/Spiritual Cleansing team members offer biblical spiritual services to anyone who desires them regardless of ability to pay. Although there is no charge for their services, all efforts to build the ministry and train team members are paid directly from the donations of those receiving these services. Any contribution to this ministry is greatly appreciated because it supports further development of this ministry of transformation.

I understand that if I receive ministry from Troy Freedom Outpost/Spiritual Cleansing, the team is committed to respect the disclosed information, but not to complete confidentiality. The information, as needed, may be shared with other leaders of Troy Freedom Outpost/Spiritual Cleansing to further my total healing process. This may include future meetings with spiritual mentors in the church to set appropriate boundaries for my personal and spiritual growth.

I agree to hold Troy Freedom Outpost and its Spiritual Cleansing team members free from any and all liability, loss or damage of any kind that may arise because of assistance, counsel or cleansing prayers, which I have received or from my involvement with Troy Freedom Outpost/Spiritual Cleansing.

I have read this disclosure and release of liability and understand and agree with it and have executed it as my free and voluntary act.

Sign and date _____

Counselor sign and date_____

CPSIA information can be obtained
at www.ICGtesting.com
Printed in the USA
BVHW040302251022
650201BV00001B/46

9 781545 634639